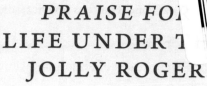

PRAISE FOR
LIFE UNDER THE
JOLLY ROGER

"In addition to history, Gabriel Kuhn's radical piratology brings philosophy, ethnography, and cultural studies to the stark question of the time: which were the criminals—bankers and brokers or sailors and slaves? By so doing he supplies us with another case where the history isn't dead, it's not even past!"
  —Peter Linebaugh, author of *The London Hanged* and coauthor of
    The Many-Headed Hydra

"Kuhn has written a tract pointing the way for tomorrow's revolutionaries."
  —B.R. Burg, author of *Sodomy and the Pirate Tradition*

"Even if you think you'd never be interested in the history of pirates, take a look at this book and you will be."
  —Nora Räthzel, Institute for Migration and Racism Studies,
    Hamburg

"Stripping the veneers of reactionary denigration and revolutionary romanticism alike from the realities of 'golden age' piracy, Gabriel Kuhn reveals the sociopolitical potentials bound up in the pirates' legacy better than anyone who has dealt with the topic to date."
  —Ward Churchill, author of *Acts of Rebellion*

"*Life Under the Jolly Roger* is an absorbing mixture fulfilling both the needs of the theorist and the curiosity of the pirate-story lover. This book will be enjoyed by anyone who sees no contradiction between adventure and scholarly care."

—Katharina Lacina, Department of Philosophy, University of Vienna

"*Life Under the Jolly Roger* is a carefully researched account of golden age piracy that departs from the usual ideological banter. Its fresh perspective on the cultural and political implications of pirates breathes new life into dusty historical accounts, connecting them to contemporary social issues with insight and clarity."

—Emily Gaarder, author of *Women and the Animal Rights Movement*

"I'm astounded by how clearly the book cuts into the mythos of the golden age pirates and immediately shows you what is fucked up and what is interesting."

—Margaret Killjoy, author of *The Lamb Will Slaughter the Lion*

"If you're someone whose knowledge of pirates stops with Errol Flynn and Jack Sparrow but you want to learn more, *Life Under the Jolly Roger* will be just the grog you're thirsting for."

—J.M. Hielkema, *The Tiger Manifesto*

"Win/win, really."

—Deric Shannon, editor of *The End of the World as We Know It?*

Life Under the Jolly Roger:

Reflections on Golden Age Piracy

Second Edition

 Gabriel Kuhn

PM

2020

Contents

Preface to the Second Edition

IT ALWAYS FEELS REWARDING if a book you've authored sees a second edition. With regard to *Life Under the Jolly Roger*, it is also a testimony to the ongoing interest in golden age piracy. Like everything, this goes in waves—anything from a new Hollywood flick to a new wave of modern-day piracy can cause an upsurge—but the overall fascination with pirate life in the Western world is very steady. The so-called golden age receives particular attention since it has given us all of the popular images we are familiar with, from the peg leg to the pirate flag, the Jolly Roger.

While there is always some new material unearthed by scholars, the basic sources that researchers on golden age piracy are working with haven't changed in a couple of hundred years. What has been changing are the interpretations of them. This book was an attempt to contribute to these debates, mainly by trying to find a way out of the stalemate between the demonization of pirates on the one hand and their idolization on the other.

The original text has been corrected, and the notes and the index have been updated and improved. Most significantly, an appendix has been added with a number of interviews I was invited to do after the first edition was released. There was a surge of piracy along the coast of Somalia at the time, and many people were wondering about the relationship between the golden age pirates and contemporary forms of piracy. The questions I was asked also revealed what political readers seemed to be most interested in concerning the golden age pirates themselves: race, social organization, and revolutionary consciousness were recurring themes. The interviews that originally appeared in German were translated for this edition.

Repetitions are inevitable in such a collection of conversations, but each interview includes questions not discussed in others—or, for that matter, in the original book. Some interviews have been slightly abbreviated to avoid redundancy. The conversations can be treated as a supplement, summary, or introduction to the book, depending on the reader's preference. The last conversation stands out, as it is not an interview but rather the documentation of a 2018 email exchange I had with a person who attended the very first launch of *Life Under the Jolly Roger* in Sydney, Australia, 2009.

Gabriel Kuhn, Stockholm, October 2019

Preface to the Japanese Edition

IN APRIL 2010, TEN Somali pirates were arrested by Dutch soldiers after boarding the German-registered freighter *Taipan* near the Somali coast. They were handed over to German authorities, which led to the first piracy trial in Germany in four hundred years. The trial was held at the district court of Hamburg, the country's most famous port, where the legendary pirate Klaus Störtebeker and seventy-two of his men were executed in 1401.

The Somali pirates escaped this fate. In October 2012, they were sentenced to prison terms between two and seven years. During the trial, a support campaign for them was organized, which included public talks and discussions, demonstrations outside the courthouse, legal advice, and a solidarity fund. The campaign was primarily run by political radicals. This was no coincidence.

The piracy witnessed along the coast of Somalia in recent years is, in many ways, very different from the piracy of the so-called golden age, which is the subject of this book. Modern-day pirates use speedboats, machine guns, and satellite navigation systems, not sailing vessels, grappling hooks, and magnetic compasses. Modern-day pirates also have a limited interest in the cargo that merchant ships carry; they are more interested in getting hold of the ship itself, including its crew, in order to demand a ransom. Finally, modern-day pirates don't constitute a society of seaborne outlaws, uprooted, and with its own laws and regulations; instead, they live in coastal towns as regular members of the community and engage in piracy as an illegal profession. Still, their lives and actions, too, contain elements that attract radical activists: they challenge the law and international powers; they interfere with capitalist trade; they risk their lives for riches rather than working underpaid jobs; and they retain elements of the noble robber: they take from the rich to give to the poor, and they defend the waters of their ancestors against overfishing and toxic waste. In short, the myth of the outlaw pirate as a political rebel is alive.

It is this myth that is explored in *Life Under the Jolly Roger*, which looks back at the time in which it was born. In the late seventeenth century, a motley crew of ex-mercenaries, runaway slaves, adventurers, and mutineers decided to set sail from the colonies in the Caribbean to "wage war on the whole world," which meant, primarily, the political authorities of the day by whom these people felt betrayed and oppressed. For about thirty-five years, these people spread fear among the powerful in the Caribbean, the Americas, the Indian Ocean, and along the west coast of Africa, before being hunted down and exterminated. Their exploits became legendary and made the pirate life famous worldwide: colonial rulers and businessmen saw them as their fiercest enemies; in Europe, large audiences were treated to theater plays about the wild life in the autonomous pirate republics of Madagascar; and the moguls of India lost some of their most precious possessions when the pirates advanced all the way into the Red Sea. It is this era, the "golden age" of piracy, that has given us all of the popular pirate images we know: extravagant clothing, earrings, peg legs, cutlasses, and parrots resting on scar-faced men's shoulders. It is also the era that has given us the ultimate pirate symbol of them all: the Jolly Roger, the menacing pirate flag, usually featuring a simple image of skull and bones against a black background. The Jolly Roger conveyed a simple message: "We defy your authority, we stand our ground, and we do so with joy and pride." Few symbols have become so closely attached to an unrepentant commitment to freedom and independence.

The Jolly Roger not only attracts political radicals, but also a huge number of apolitical people, even if most of them prefer the safe world of fiction and fantasy, rather than political activism. Most people dream of freedom and independence, even if—for different reasons—they are not ready or able to fight for it in their daily lives. Tales of pirates are welcomed substitutes. This explains the success of so many pirate-themed stories, not least the highly popular *One Piece* manga series. But it is the political activists who try to turn these dreams into reality.

We don't have to go far to find confirmation of the Jolly Roger's ongoing popularity among political activists. Various projects and organizations have used Jolly Roger–based logos and images, among them the Sea Shepherd

Conservation Society, Earth First!, and the CrimethInc. Ex-Workers Collective. The flag is a regular sight at mass protests: from rallies for file sharing and the free flow of online information to demonstrations against austerity measures and to Occupy camps. Sometimes, the Jolly Roger is even displayed on ships, providing the message with particular strength: in October 2010, union members of the French CGT brought a Jolly Roger aboard a ferry shuttle in Marseille's old port to protest against the French government's pension reforms, and in October 2011 Russian activists hoisted a Jolly Roger on the cruiser *Aurora*, an important symbol of the October Revolution, in order to draw attention to poverty in Russia ahead of the International Day for the Eradication of Poverty.

In the end, the question pursued in this book is simple: is there more to this embrace of the Jolly Roger in activist circles than mere romanticization? Is it a simple gesture of provocation and defiance, or do the pirates of the golden age actually have something to teach us? Did they set examples for a better way of life? Did they develop morals that can serve as guidelines even in contemporary struggles? Some historians deny this categorically. Others affirm it enthusiastically. My own thoughts are contained in this book.

Gabriel Kuhn, Stockholm, August 2013

0. Introduction

In his 2007 essay "Flying the Black Flag: Revolt, Revolution and the Social Organization of Piracy in the 'Golden Age,'" Chris Land suggests that "the pirate is a figure in full sympathy with the Zeitgeist of the early 21st century."[1] Arguably, the figure of the pirate has been in full sympathy with many eras over the past 300 years, achieving "semi-legendary status,"[2] creating its "own mythology,"[3] and leaving "an indelible mark in the psyche of the Western world."[4] However, the current pirate craze is certainly of a particular strength. Even if epitomized in the *Pirates of the Caribbean* series and its charismatic villain Jack Sparrow (or the devilishly handsome Johnny Depp), the attention that pirates have received in recent years is by no means limited to the big screen and the toy sections of department stores. There have also been significant scholarly contributions. This does not make it easy to find a place for yet another pirate book. After all, one does not want to reiterate but to contribute. This book attempts to find its place in linking the historical data collected on piracy's "golden age," originating in the Caribbean and spanning from roughly 1690 to 1725, to a number of theoretical notions and concepts that might allow us to view the cultural and political significance of golden age piracy in a new light.

An important aspect of this venture is the desire to go beyond a certain antagonism that seems to have developed over the last decade with respect to the political interpretation of golden age piracy. On the one hand, there are scholars who insist that "the real world of the pirates was harsh, tough and cruel"[5] and that the pirates "acquired a romantic aura ... which they certainly never deserved";[6] on the other hand, there are those who maintain that "these outlaws led audacious, rebellious lives, and [that] we should remember them as long as there are powerful people and oppressive circumstances to be resisted."[7] The ideological assumptions behind these two perspectives are as clear as their respective consequences. While for the adherents of the former, "pirates tend to get a better press than they deserve, often being admired for their laid-back life-style and praised as proto-revolutionaries or democrats rather than condemned as the murderers and thieves that most of them were,"[8] the adherents of the latter embrace Marcus Rediker's perception that pirates were "rebels" who "challenged, in one way or another, the conventions of class, race, gender, and nation," "expressed high ideals," and "abolished the wage, established a different discipline, practiced their own kind of democracy and equality, and provided an alternative model for running the deep-sea ship."[9]

In the end, both sides accuse the other of substituting fiction for fact. While skeptics of an alleged pirate romanticism find it important "to present the difference between myth and reality for those who want to peer behind the romantic legacy of piracy,"[10] their radical opponents accuse them of maintaining a reactionary law and order philosophy. In short, self-declared reason and alleged conservatism oppose self-declared radicalism and alleged romance.

Although this book is written from a radical perspective, it will try to avoid this debate for several reasons:

1. *It cannot be decided:* The lack of reliable material on the everyday lives and exploits of the golden age pirates is notorious. Philip Gosse's conclusion that "of the life on board buccaneer and pirate ships a somewhat hazy and incomplete picture reaches us" is a very generous way of phrasing it.[11] While there exist a few precious—and probably authentic—accounts of the life on buccaneer ships (most notably those of Exquemelin, Dampier, Ringrose, de Lussan and Reyning[12]), our images of life on pirate ships still rest to an overwhelming degree on Captain Johnson's *A General History of the Robberies and Murders of the Most Notorious Pirates.*[13]

The first volume of the *General History* appeared in London in 1724, containing almost two dozen stories about pirate captains, from Henry Every and Blackbeard to Bartholomew Roberts and Edward Low. Literary liberties were certainly taken in transcribing these stories—for example, the frequent inclusion of on-ship dialogue provokes indeed the comment that "it would be hard to imagine who had been able to record it"[14]—yet subsequent research has confirmed many details and the volume is generally considered to be a reliable historical source. In 1726, Johnson added a second volume, expanding the number of stories to over thirty. Confirmation for many of these remains scarce. The most famous—about Captain Misson and his utopian community Libertalia—is almost certainly fabricated. Some pirate scholars have taken this as reason enough not to cite or reference the *General History*'s second volume at all.[15] This book follows the decision of most others and includes the parts that appear plausible according to later historical research. As far as the story of Captain Misson is concerned, it will be discussed as an important story for radical pirate lore rather than as a historical event.

The main reason for the continuing significance of Johnson's classic for pirate historiography is, quite simply, a lack of better sources. Reliable firsthand accounts of life on pirate ships and in pirate communities during the golden age are missing, and even the outstanding work conducted in recent decades by historians like David Cordingly, Peter Earle, and Marcus Rediker, who have unearthed many valuable secondary sources, cannot make these accounts magically appear. The evaluation of golden age pirate life—and hence its politics—continues to rest on guesswork and speculation.

2. Given the lack of historical sources, the danger of romanticization is indeed imminent: Romanticization is a double-edged sword. Under certain circumstances, it can be a useful tactical weapon to provoke and inspire. In the mid-90s, the members of Minneapolis's anarcho-punk collective Profane Existence offered the following interpretation:

> The idea of objective truth is bullshit. The belief that you can describe
> or interpret history exactly as it happened is a lie. Those who are
> in power are also those who usually get to define what is 'true.' By
> romanticizing events we not only offer an alternative interpretation
> to the 'truth,' we also challenge the ruling class and the mass media's
> claim to a monopoly on truth. We say our interpretation of politics
> and history is as good as theirs and that if you're going to believe one
> pack of lies you might as well believe ours![16]

On a political plane, this sounds convincing. However, what sometimes works as a tactical weapon does not necessarily work for levelheaded discussion—which can be as inspiring (and provocative) as no-qualms romanticism.

In fact, it can be more so. After all, romanticizing is an inherent part of the bourgeois tradition as well. This also applies to piracy:

> The pirate tale ... is the product of the bourgeois imagination. One of its most important functions is to provide a safety valve against the pressures put on the individual by the demands of bourgeois morality. ... The key fantasies are those of unrestrained liberty and power—compensations for what the prudent bourgeois can never achieve, however successful he is materially.[17]

In these lines, we might find the answer as to why the "Zeitgeist factor" of piracy has always transcended radical circles. Maurice Besson asserts that already in the 17th century, the buccaneers "offered Europe, at a moment when the formalism of the classic revival seemed to be banishing adventure, a dream world founded upon fabulous stories, astounding fortunes, heroic deeds, and orgies of the camp."[18] And even non-radical historians concede that "pirates are a recognizable and emotive image that represents a freedom of action that is denied to most law-abiding modern citizens."[19]

According to these observations, the bourgeois creates imaginary alter egos that help him accept the libidinal restrictions of his everyday existence. In this context, the alleged freedom and might of the pirates serve the same purpose as Hollywood action heroes or the Marlboro Man—not exactly characters suitable as radical role models. In the end, romanticized notions about golden age piracy might often play more into the hands of economic exploitation than into those of radical activists.

3. *It is questionable whether evaluating golden age piracy politically is at all relevant for contemporary radical politics:* Contemporary radical politics are not about pirates from a past long gone, they are about people right here and now. The question is whether and how they can relate to golden age piracy in ways that inform and inspire their radical aspirations, no matter the pirates' faults or shortcomings—particularly if Hans Turley is right in stating that "I am not sure that the 'reality' of the pirates, their day-to-day social existence, is something readers want to know."[20] Politically, the question of how contemporary activists can relate to golden age pirates seems much more crucial than the inevitably contested truth about golden age piracy. In other words, the political *interpretation* of golden age piracy matters less than its contemporary political *adaptation.*

In light of this, the intentions of the book can be summarized as follows:

One, adding guesses and speculations about golden age pirate life to those that already exist, and thereby engaging in a dialogue with others studying the subject.

Two, trying to explore the pirate myth rather than trying to disclose an alleged pirate truth, following the verdict that here, "the legend and the reality are woven into a fabric impossible to unravel. However, the *way* this fabric is woven can be examined."[21]

Three, rendering the radical fascination with piracy politically valuable in the contemporary context, and suggesting ways in which the Jolly Roger can fly from balconies and at rallies without this being mere symbolic ritualism. In this vein, it becomes one of the book's main intentions to disprove the conclusion that "the ... pirates left us with no legacy except an aura that they never deserved."[22]

While I sincerely hope that this book can arouse the interest of a broad spectrum of readers—a spectrum that goes beyond the narrow confines of political self-labeling—it would make little sense to deny that it was written from what has been called a radical perspective. By this I mean a perspective that envisions social change running deeper than a series of reforms within the prevailing social, cultural, economic, and political order: social change that affects the very fundamentals of our society and makes way for non-authoritarian and egalitarian communities.

Unsurprisingly, the volume builds on the exceptional work done by several radical pirate scholars such as Christopher Hill, Marcus Rediker,[23] Peter Lamborn Wilson, Stephen Snelders, and Chris Land. Any criticism that might be voiced with respect to some of their conclusions must be understood as a criticism of solidarity that aims at advancing the political discussions on golden age piracy. Without these scholars' work, and the inspiration drawn from it, this book could not have been written. The same is true of course for the equally exceptional work conducted by non-radical scholars like Robert C. Ritchie, David Cordingly, Angus Konstam, or Peter Earle.[24]

The volume is laid out as follows:

Chapter One will provide a brief historical sketch of golden age piracy and the preceding era of the buccaneers. It mainly intends to build an adequate empirical frame of reference for the discussions that follow. Extensive histories of golden age piracy have been written by authors much more capable of the task than I am. Please see the "Notes on Pirate Literature" at the end of the book for more details.

Chapters Two and Three approach the culture of golden age piracy from two angles. Chapter Two focuses on the interpretation of golden age piracy as "an alternative world governed by different kinds of norms."[25] It will attempt to provide an ethnography of golden age piracy. Chapter Three focuses on golden age piracy as an "alternative" or "subversive" part of Euro-American cultural history.

Chapter Four will address the concrete political implications and possibilities of golden age piracy: its politico-historical significance, its social and organizational structures, its economy, and its ethics. Comparisons to different political theories and movements as well as reflections on the readings of commentators on pirate politics are of particular importance.

The concluding essay, "The Golden Age Pirates' Political Legacy," will summarize the book's main arguments, tie them to contemporary politics, and attempt to make them valuable in a radical context.

The bibliography contains some introductory commentary to orient readers within the ever-growing body of English pirate literature.

For didactic purposes, capitalization, punctuation, and, very rarely, the spelling in quoted passages have been adjusted for consistency with the main text, except when misapprehensions seemed possible. I take full responsibility for these decisions.

On a final note: some of the themes developed in this book build on a short German essay I wrote in 1993. The essay experienced a somewhat curious publishing history and an English translation, entitled "Life Under the Death's Head," appeared as part of the Black Rose book *Women Pirates and the Politics of the Jolly Roger*—a volume that one critic described as "agitprop … by three German anarchists … clearly designed as a situationist challenge."[26] Apart from the petty (or not so petty) details that I am not German and that I have my doubts whether Ulrike Klausmann and Marion Meinzerin—who wrote most of the book—would identify as anarchists, I take this to be a rather flattering description.[27]

1. Background

1.1. Privateers, Buccaneers, Pirates: Matters of Terminology

"ONE GREAT DIFFICULTY WHICH the author of this work is met with is to decide who was, and who was not, a pirate,"[1] wrote Philip Gosse in 1924, as part of the introduction to *The Pirates' Who's Who*. The same difficulty is still faced by anyone writing about pirates today. In general, a wide definition of piracy competes with a narrow one.

The former builds on the suggestion that a pirate, in the words of David Cordingly, simply "was, and is, someone who robs and plunders on the sea."[2] In a similar vein, German author Reiner Treinen writes that "generally, we can understand sea robbery and piracy as analogies to common robbery and the activities of common robber gangs."[3] Obviously, the problem with this definition is that it depends on our understanding of "robbery"—a notion that has been highly contested throughout history, usually based on conflicting political interests. While, for example, in the eyes of the Spanish all ships preying on Spanish commerce in the Caribbean were "sea robbers" and hence "pirates," many were licensed raiders ("buccaneers" acting as "privateers") in the eyes of the English, French, or Dutch. As Hans Turley suggests, "the buccaneer differs from the pirate because he was an outlaw-made-national-hero."[4] It will not surprise us then that some observers have also coined the term "patriotic piracy"[5] for the activities of the buccaneers.

The narrow definition of piracy attempts to escape this conundrum, as it considers pirates only those sea robbers who carry no license by any legal authority, who target all ships, regardless of the national colors they fly, and who are "unwilling to be registered or corrupted by either money or office."[6] These are the *"hostes humani generis,"* the "enemies of mankind,"[7] the "villains of all nations."[8] Their activities have been coined by some as "autonomous piracy"[9]—in the eyes of the authorities, "a Kind of Piracy which disgraces our Civilisation."[10] In order to distinguish them from licensed sea robbers, these pirates have been called "the pirates proper,"[11] "out-and-out pirates,"[12] "full-blown pirates,"[13] or "pirate[s] in the truest sense."[14] In the English legal dictum of the early 18th century, they were defined with the following words: "A pirate is in a perpetual war with every individual, and every state, Christian or infidel. Pirates properly have no country, but by the nature of their guilt, separate themselves, and renounce on this matter, the benefit of all lawful societies."[15] This definition also accounts for the succinct observation that "piracy was never *merely* robbery"[16]—a fact on which much of its mythology is grounded.

This book will mainly work with the narrow definition of piracy. In fact, the group of pirates on which it focuses not only excludes those being licensed by legal authority, but also those who operated from secure land bases. The reason for this is the particular attention given to the *nomadic* element of golden age piracy—a feature that asks for a special and unique analytical approach. Despite certain structural similarities stemming from their common profession, historical pirate communities like those of the British Channel, the Barbary Coast, or the China Sea constitute fundamentally different social phenomena, as their relations to the land, local communities, and political authorities were much more clearly defined, even if great diversity existed within their respective modes of organization and activities.[17] The same goes for current pirate communities like those operating along the Northeast African coast. Robert C. Ritchie provides a useful distinction when dividing pirates according to two different methods of operation:

> One can be defined as *organized* marauding, the other as *anarchistic* marauding. Many men were involved in both; yet a distinction can be made. Organized pirates remained attached to a port as their base of operation. Anarchistic marauding involved leaving behind the base of operation and wandering for months—even years—at a time.[18]

An explanation of terms that commonly appear in connection with pirate history follows:

A *buccaneer* was originally a hunter on the island of Hispaniola (today divided into the Dominican Republic and Haiti). This was the meaning of the term for the first half of the 17th century. As the buccaneers gradually turned to sea robbery and raiding—often licensed, sometimes not—the term became a synonym for Caribbean pirates. It was used as such until about 1690, when buccaneer culture came to its end and gave way to "proper," or golden age, piracy. Due to the strong cultural ties between the buccaneers and the golden age pirates, the former will feature prominently in this book.

A *privateer* is a sea robber who acts under the license of a legal authority. In the Caribbean of the 17th century, such a license was usually conferred by a *letter of marque*. In a sense, privateers were seaborne mercenary forces who engaged in "piracy with state-sponsorship."[19] Captain Johnson described privateering indecisively as "something like pirating."[20] Privateering served those in power well, since it "was a useful extension of naval warfare which not only created an income for the government issuing the privateering contract, but also helped to harass enemy shipping in times of war, without the issuing authority having to do anything."[21] Most buccaneers worked as privateers. According to Jenifer G. Marx, buccaneering became "a peculiar blend of piracy and privateering in which the two elements were often indistinguishable."[22] Despite this, the implications of both activities seen separately remained diametrically opposed. In Janice E. Thomson's words: "Privateering reflected state rulers' efforts to build state power; piracy reflected some people's efforts to resist that project."[23]

Flibustier was the French term for a buccaneer. It has sometimes retrospectively been translated into the English *filibuster*, even though this term only came to be used in the 18th century, partly in connection with illegal American military infiltration into Latin America, and more lastingly as the signifier for a legal procedure.

Corsair was a French term sometimes used synonymously with pirate, but usually reserved for the pirates of the Mediterranean.

Sea dog was often used for the English privateers of the 16th century, the most famous being Francis Drake.

Other synonyms for *pirate* not employed here include *sea rover*, *freebooter*, *marooner*, the picturesque *picaroon*, or *swashbuckler*, which originally served as a 16th-century term for brigands and was was first applied to pirates by 19th-century novelists and 20th-century scriptwriters.[24]

1.2. What "Golden Age"? A Little History

The following pages provide a brief overview of the development of piracy in the Caribbean leading up to the "golden age," during which the operations of originally Caribbean-based pirates extended along the coasts of the Americas, into the Indian Ocean, and, finally, to the west coast of Africa.

Different historians have given the golden age different time frames, depending both on their respective definitions of piracy and the weight given to certain historical events and developments. While most place the end of golden age piracy somewhere between 1722 (the death of Captain Roberts and the mass arrest of his crew) and 1730 (the execution of Olivier La Buse), there is less of an agreement on its beginnings. While some include even the age of the buccaneers and let the golden age begin around 1650, others quote years as late as 1716, when the last major outbreak of non-licensed piracy in the Caribbean took shape.

It seems most useful to follow those scholars who place the beginning of the golden age in the early 1690s. At that time, some Anglo-American privateers and mutineers began to sail their vessels into the Indian Ocean to prey on ships of all nations, those of the English and their allies included. It is told that the New England privateer captain Thomas Tew convinced his crew to go pirating in 1692 by suggesting "that it was better to risk your life for plunder than for government."[1] If there is any truth to this tale, then this moment seems indeed decisive for the pirate phenomenon studied in this volume.

The following timeline intends to shed some light on the genesis and development of the golden age:

1492: Christopher Columbus and his crew arrive at the island of Hispaniola.

1492–c. 1620: Spain establishes a near-exclusive hold on the Caribbean region and punishes "interlopers" indiscriminately. Most famously, a short-lived French Huguenot settlement in Florida is crushed with brutal force in 1565. Throughout the entire period, there is *no peace beyond the line,* meaning that whatever peace treaties are signed in Europe, they do not apply to the areas west of the meridian the Spanish drew in the 1494 Treaty of Tordesillas to demarcate their newly "discovered" American territories.

c. 1520–1550: French privateers start preying on Spain's transatlantic trade. At first, Spanish ships are almost exclusively attacked on their return journeys to Europe. In the 1530s, however, French ships begin to venture into the Caribbean itself, initiating a period that turns the region into "a happy hunting-ground"[2] and "a paradise for an adventurous robber."[3]

c. 1550–1600: English privateers, the *sea dogs*, increasingly penetrate the Caribbean realm to attack Spanish commerce. Francis Drake, called "my pirate" by Queen Elizabeth, is the most legendary. The era of the sea dogs ends with the death of Philip II in 1598.

c. 1600–1635: Dutch privateers cause enormous damage to Spanish commerce in the Caribbean and weaken the Spanish hold over the area to a degree that allows the establishment of non-Spanish settlements which, in the words of one historian, "developed out of the piracy of the preceding century."[4] The Dutch privateers also make it possible for Dutch traders to take control of Caribbean commerce for decades.[5]

During the same period, men who have been described as "a remarkable blend of human flotsam"[6] as well as "a motley crowd"[7] begin to form a "male, maritime and migrant culture"[8] in the western parts of Hispaniola (modern-day Haiti), leading a "half-savage, independent mode of life,"[9] sustained by hunting wild boars and cattle. The animals are remnants of Spanish settlements evacuated by the Spanish authorities in 1603 after its inhabitants had been suspected of trading with rival European nations.[10] This marks the beginning of the buccaneers, "these strange people,"[11] "a ruffiantly, dare-devil lot, who feared neither God, man, nor death,"[12] "tough frontiersmen living beyond the law,"[13] "outlaw hunters"[14] "scarcely less wild than the animals they hunted,"[15] "men who could never live in the bosom of ordered society, men who lived for the moment, swaggerers, lovers of glory, men sometimes cruel, often generous, but cowards, never."[16]

The buccaneers are named after a meat-smoking device apparently called *buccan* in the language of the indigenous Caribs. Some conservative historians have drawn a rather dramatic picture of the buccaneers' existence:

> They were savages in dress and habits. No amount of bathing could eradicate the stink of guts and grease that clung to them. Their rough homespun garments were stiff with the blood of slaughtered animals. They made their round brimless hats, boots, and belts of untanned hides, and smeared their faces with tallow to repel insects. On the coast they lived in shacks covered with palm leaves and slept in sleeping bags next to smoking fires to ward off mosquitoes.[17]

This has led certain authors to the pointed conclusion that "life among the 'Brethren of the Coast' cannot have been pleasant for anyone with a sensitive nose."[18] Others, however, have conceded that "for many it was a good life, impossible to duplicate in Europe: enough to eat, independence, freedom from masters."[19]

"The origins of these men we do not know," writes C.H. Haring,[20] but it has to be assumed that they constituted a blend of "stragglers from all three nations"—meaning France, England, and the Netherlands—"stranded, marooned, or shipwrecked crewmen; deserters; runaway bond servants and slaves; adventurers of all sorts."[21] Maybe they indeed included "all such as disliked organised society."[22] "All, whatever they were originally, seem to have been hearty, care-free men who preferred a life of semi-savagery to the tiresome laws and orders of the civilised world."[23]

c. 1620–1640: Despite fierce Spanish resistance, the English, French, and Dutch all establish holds in the Caribbean, particularly on the islands of the Lesser Antilles. The colonial tables in the Caribbean are about to turn. As one historian has noted, "living cheek by jowl with their enemies, they brought the Spanish crown a century of unrelieved woe."[24]

c. 1630–1650: The number of buccaneers on Hispaniola steadily increases due to displaced settlers, runaway slaves, and fugitive or dismissed indentured laborers. According to Stephen Snelders, "the Brethren of the Coast functioned as a kind of chaotic attractor, serving as a focus for adventurous, rebellious, and outlaw elements,"[25] while Carl and Roberta Bridenbaugh suggest that "buccaneering syphoned off the most adventurous, pugnacious, and greedy of the landless males of the crowded English islands."[26]

Worried about the expansion of the multinational buccaneering community in the heart of their empire, the Spanish conduct ill-conceived attempts at chasing the buccaneers from the island in the 1630s by killing off the herds of boars and cattle. The attempt backfires. The buccaneers stay but have to turn to new means of livelihood. One is sea robbery. By the 1630s, buccaneer gangs in dugout canoes or flyboats embark on nightly attacks against Spanish galleons. By the 1650s, the term *buccaneer* "was exclusively used to refer to maritime raiders."[27]

During the same time, the island of Tortuga (across a small strait off Hispaniola's northwestern tip) turns into a buccaneer center and remains highly contested for decades. With the well-protected island as a safe haven, the buccaneers slowly develop into a community that will have "a tremendous impact on the life of the West Indies"[28] and prove much more disastrous to the Spanish than the presence of some "savage hunters" in the remote areas of Hispaniola could have ever been.

1655–1697: The English expedition sent to the Caribbean by Oliver Cromwell takes Jamaica in 1655. Subsequently, many English buccaneers from Hispaniola and Tortuga flock to the island—enough that by the 1660s, buccaneering has turned into "the island's principal source of revenue."[29] This constitutes a split in the buccaneer community along national lines. While the English buccaneers establish themselves in Jamaica, their French "brethren" remain on Tortuga and Hispaniola.

Meanwhile, "buccaneering evolved from small-scale operations in the West Indies to massive land raids."[30] "A practice that started as a few men in a canoe waiting to catch an unwary coastal freighter, gradually grew to large ships with over a hundred in the crew, and finally to whole fleets."[31] The buccaneers turn into a military force, engaging in ambitious amphibious raids under legendary leaders like Henry Morgan (most renowned for the sack of Panama in 1671). According to Franklin W. Knight, they "achieved international fame,"[32] all this to the delight of the colonial English and French authorities. As Peter Earle explains:

> The governors of Jamaica and Tortuga for their part believed that
> privateering had many advantages, providing as it did employment
> for some very rough men, profits from fitting out and victualling the
> privateers' ships, a stream of prizes to be sold cheaply in their markets
> and an effective and costless naval defence against counter-attack by
> the Spaniards. As for the governments at home in London and Paris,
> they were normally happy to condone or even actively encourage
> the issue of commissions in the West Indies. They believed that this
> continued pressure was the best method of encouraging Spain to
> recognise their de facto colonies in the Indies and ideally allow their
> traders to break into the lucrative Spanish colonial markets which
> were maintained as a monopoly for Spaniards. They were also aware
> that the capture of Spanish shipping was an effective means of removing the competition and so providing an encouragement for English
> and French merchant shipping to break into the trade of the region.[33]

Apart from Tortuga/Hispaniola and Jamaica, buccaneer havens include New Providence in the Bahamas, St. Croix, Curaçao, and Danish St. Thomas. Many buccaneers also find temporary homes in the Bay of Campeche and the Bay of Honduras, where they work as logwood cutters from around 1670.

Eventually, however, the importance of the buccaneers for the colonial struggle in the Caribbean wanes. Christopher Hill succinctly sums up the situation in the late 17th century: "In the short run buccaneering may have been a convenient investment for big planters. But in the long run the buccaneers were a nuisance, expendable once the Caribbean was policed."[34]

The Dutch are the first to officially abandon privateering with the Treaty of The Hague in 1673. The English follow suite with the Treaty of Windsor in 1680, and—after a last ill-fated employment of buccaneer forces in the attack on Cartagena in 1697—the French finally complete the official withdrawal from privateering with the Treaty of Ryswick. As the 18th century begins, the buccaneers are gone. Their legacy, however, remains. As J.H. Parry and P.M. Sherlock contend: "At no other time in Western history can a few thousand desperadoes have created a reign of terror over so vast an area, or have exercised so great and so continuous an influence upon the policy of civilised states."[35]

c. 1690–1700: As the buccaneers disappear, the "pirates proper" arise. Many former buccaneers have little interest in a settled existence and intend to further secure their economic survival by raiding. Since official licenses are increasingly harder to come by, they turn to illegal raids—often on all ships, regardless which flags they fly. Stephen Snelders describes the transition thus: "In the struggle for dominance in the seventeenth century, the Brotherhood had played its role in the grey border zone between sanctioned privateering and outright piracy. In the golden age its successors were relegated to a black zone, outlawed by all nations."[36]

In the mid-1690s, the successful pirate voyages into the Indian Ocean by Henry Every and Thomas Tew, both of whom get away rich and unharmed (at least initially—Tew dies during his second voyage), help provide "a new role model for the whole fraternity of seagoing mercenaries"[37] and incite a pirate boom in those longitudes that also prompts the famed pirate settlements in Madagascar. They also give birth to a distinct, "transnational," pirate culture. As a result, "soon after the return of peace in 1697, there was an explosion of piracy on a scale never seen before."[38]

In 1700, after an English navy vessel gives chase to a ship under the command of Captain Emanuel Wynn, there are first reports of pirates flying the Jolly Roger—the infamous black flag adorned by allegories of death (skull and crossbones, hour glasses, bleeding hearts, etc.). It soon comes to signify an affirmative pirate identity, indicating that "unlike the generations of pirates before them, who called themselves privateers—in truth, anything *but* pirate for fear of the death penalty that soon came with the name—the freebooters of the early eighteenth century said yes, we are criminals, we are pirates, we are that name."[39]

Accordingly, a *war against the pirates* is waged by the authorities: "The problem was tackled in a number of ways: by the introduction of legislation; by issuing pardons to pirates in the hope that they would abandon their lives of crime; by stepping up naval patrols in the worst affected areas; by promising rewards for the capture of pirates; and by the trial and execution of captured pirates."[40] The most significant legal innovation is the 1700 *Act for the More Effectual Suppression of Piracy*, making it possible for a seven-person court of officials or naval officers to try pirates wherever such a court is able to assemble, thus making transfers back to England unnecessary.

1701–1714: The War of the Spanish Succession brings a relief from unlicensed piracy as it produces a new need for privateers. With the big buccaneer communities dissolved, many pirates return to raiding under national flags. As Peter Earle puts it: "The pirates became patriots again."[41]

1713–1722: With the end of the war, piracy reemerges. Hundreds of demobilized soldiers fill the pirates' ranks. While the navy enlisted more than 53,000 men in 1703, the number dwindles to 13,430 in 1715.[42] A year later, Caribbean piracy reaches previously unknown heights with New Providence, Bahamas, as its headquarters. The island loses its prominent role in 1718, however, with the arrival of British governor Woodes Rogers. The arrival of Rogers—himself a former privateer—is part of a British government design to curb piracy. The plan also includes the offer of a pardon and the dispatching of three warships—something to "demonstrate to a wise pirate that the days of their 'very pleasant' way of life were numbered."[43]

While some of the New Providence pirates accept the pardon and help Rogers turn New Providence into a stable, "lawful" colony, others debark, vowing not to bow to any government authority and *waging war on the whole world* instead. "From this point onwards the only pirates were those who explicitly rejected the state and its laws and declared themselves in open war against it,"[44] as the anonymous authors of "Pirate Utopias," an article in the British anarchist journal *Do or Die* put it. Paul Galvin describes the situation with the following words:

> True outlaws working the fringe of a closing maritime frontier, these pirates owed allegiance to none but themselves and preyed upon the shipping of any nation, whether Spanish, English, French or Dutch. Consequently, unlike their buccaneer forebears, they enjoyed no cloak of legitimacy from any government (though many a colonial governor colluded in trafficking their spoils) and were therefore doomed to swift eradication.[45]

Once more, the pirates venture into the Indian Ocean, now also raiding along the west coast of Africa, where many new slaving posts have been established. The route between the Caribbean and the Indian Ocean via West Africa and Madagascar soon becomes known as the *Pirate Round*. This marks the strongest period of golden age piracy, "a decade or so of maritime hoodlumism set loose under the japing countenance of the Jolly Roger."[46] It is the time of the best-known pirate captains, Blackbeard, John "Calico Jack" Rackam, and Bartholomew Roberts, and of popular figures like Anne Bonny and Mary Read. According to David Cordingly, pirate activity reaches its peak around 1720 with an estimated 1,500 to 2,000 pirates operating in the Caribbean and North America.[47]

The heyday of piracy's golden age does not last very long, however. Angus Konstam, from the non-radical strain of pirate historians, concludes somewhat complacently: "The worst of these pirate excesses was limited to an eight-year period, from 1714 until 1722, so the true golden age cannot even be called a 'golden decade.'"[48]

In the words of Marcus Rediker, with the killing of the period's most successful pirate captain, Bartholomew Roberts, and the subsequent capture of most of his crew in 1722, the golden age "turned crimson."[49] These events have drawn self-satisfied commentary: "The complete destruction of Bartholomew Roberts and his gang, much the strongest pirate combine at sea, was a devastating blow to the pirate community as a whole. It was rather

humiliating that the two well-gunned, well-manned pirate ships should surrender so pusillanimously without a single royal sailor being killed in either
action."[50]

1722–1726: A last, more desperate generation of golden age pirates tries to
keep the Jolly Roger alive even after "the war against the pirates was virtually
won."[51] The tide, of course, has changed and "the years 1722–26 were a time
when pirates fought less for booty than for their very survival."[52] Peter Earle
draws the following picture:

> Getting on for a thousand pirates had been killed or captured on
> their ships or in attempts to escape ashore. Many hundreds of oth-
> ers had been pardoned or had crept ashore in haunts such as the
> Virgin Islands, the Bay Islands of Honduras, the Mosquito Coast,
> Madagascar or West Africa where many former pirates were said to be
> living among the natives. Many hundreds more must have died of the
> diseases prevalent in West African and West Indian waters, for mor-
> tality was likely to have been higher in the densely packed and very
> unhygienic pirate ships than those of the Royal Navy who lost well
> over a thousand men to disease in this campaign. Such destruction
> and dispersal meant that there were not many pirates left at sea, less
> than two hundred according to one estimate, most of them in gangs
> led either by Lowe or by former consorts or subordinates of his, such
> as Spriggs, Cooper, Lyne, and Shipton. These last remaining pirate
> captains and their men were to be hunted remorselessly by the navy,
> but they were to prove amazingly elusive.[53]

The composition of the pirate crews changes as well. With many former
buccaneers and privateers retired or killed, the majority of pirate crew members now comes from captured merchant vessels, with a fair number of sailors
having been forced to join.[54] This leads both to a disintegration of the "pirate
brotherhood," and to new increasingly violent tactics.

Captain William Fly is the last notable pirate captain hanged in the
Americas. He dies on the gallows in Boston in 1726. Frenchman Olivier
La Buse meets the same fate in the Indian Ocean on the French island of
Bourbon (today Réunion) in 1730. His death effectively ends the golden age
of piracy, its protagonists now "hunted down and, it may be said, extermi-
nated."[55] The most tangible expression of this extermination are numerous

mass hangings of pirates. In 1718, thirty-one members of Stede Bonnet's crew are hanged in Charleston, South Carolina. In May 1722, forty-one members of Mathew Luke's crew are hanged in Jamaica. In the same year, fifty-two members of Bartholomew Roberts's crew are hanged in West Africa. In July 1723, twenty-six members of Captain Charles Harris's crew are hanged at Newport Harbor. All in all, "no fewer than 400, and probably 500–600 Anglo-American pirates were executed between 1716 and 1726."[56]

This contributes significantly to the decline of pirate numbers overall: "From the peak of 2,000 pirates in 1720, the numbers dropped to around 1,000 in 1723 and by 1726 there were no more than 200. The incidence of pirate attacks declined from forty to fifty in 1718 down to half a dozen in 1726."[57] Peter Earle sums up the situation dryly:

> And so at last the golden age of piracy came to an end. The freedom- and drink-loving pirates had their moment of fame, but in the long run the navy, the law, and the self-destructive nature of the pirates themselves ensured that piracy was not an occupation with very long life expectancy. Of the fifty-five pirate captains of this period whose fate has been determined—about two-thirds of the total number— twelve surrendered and lived out their lives in varying degrees of comfort or destitution, one retired in poverty to Madagascar, six were killed in action, four drowned in shipwrecks, four were shot by their own men, one shot himself and one was set adrift by his men in an open boat, and never heard of again. The remaining twenty-six were hanged, often under their own black flags, by the French, Dutch, Portuguese, and Spaniards as well as by the British, in Africa and Antigua, Boston, the Bahamas and Brazil, Carolina, Curaçao and Cuba, London, Martinique, Rhode Island and the island of Bourbon in the Indian Ocean where Olivier La Buse, the last pirate of the golden age to be captured, was hanged on the beach in July 1730 'before a cheering crowd.'[58]

La Buse might have been hanged before a cheering crowd, yet his tombstone receives nightly offerings from secret admirers to this day. While Peter Earle might see this as hopeless romanticism, the practice proves the political complexity of the pirate legacy, a legacy this book attempts to investigate.

Finally, a short overview of those golden age pirate captains who will be referenced in the following chapters more frequently. The list is purely didactic and meant to function as a quick reference guide. It neither claims to be exhaustive nor to list the most notorious of the golden age pirate captains. In fact, some names, such as that of William Kidd will be conspicuously absent. According to the authorities, Kidd was a privateer-turned-pirate; according to Kidd himself, he was loyal to the crown and behaved within the confines of the law. Kidd was hanged in 1701 and his body displayed in chains on the banks of the River Thames for years. His story is crucial for analyzing the arbitrary legal borders between privateering and pirating, yet I do not consider it of particular concern for the questions discussed in this book. For everyone interested in Kidd's history, Robert C. Ritchie's *Captain Kidd and the War against the Pirates* comes highly recommended. Other pirate aficionado household names that will be missing are those of John "Calico Jack" Rackam—who mainly rose to fame as Anne Bonny's lover—and of the unconventional "gentleman pirate" Stede Bonnet. Again, despite the undeniable entertainment value of their biographies, their exploits will not play a significant role in the following chapters.

The focus on pirate captains—i.e. on individual "big men" rather than pirate communities—may appear ironic in a radical context that likes to stress the egalitarian and democratic character of golden age pirate communities. At the same time, the historical sources pay so much attention to pirate captains that it is hard not to employ them as a useful frame of reference. This, however, should not lead to a false impression concerning the primary protagonists: they remain decidedly the common pirate sailors.

Thomas Tew: Embarked on a privateering mission against the French from Rhode Island in 1692. Soon convinced his crew to sail to the Indian Ocean *on their own account* instead. A huge Indian prize was taken there in 1693 and the sailors came back to America as rich men. Tew embarked on another journey a couple of years later, but this time he was met with a grisly fate after attacking a ship belonging to the Great Mogul. In the graphic description of

Captain Johnson, "a shot carried away the rim of Tew's belly, who held his bowels with his hands some small space [before] he dropped."[59]

Henry Every (Avery): After lack of payment, Every led a mutiny among English privateers in the Spanish service in 1694 and sailed for the Indian Ocean. A year later he took an enormous prize in the Red Sea, the merchant ship *Ganj-i-sawai*. The *Ganj-i-sawai* belonged to the Great Mogul, and given the good relations between the Mogul and the English, as well as England's investment in Indian trade, the attack undermined English interests and was hence pivotal for the history of golden age piracy. Every escaped capture and punishment and rose into legend, imagined to be living in luxury on Madagascar. Novels and plays were dedicated to his name. In reality, he died a pauper in England after being cheated by Bristol merchants, which in Philip Gosse's version of the story made him realize "that there were pirates on land as well as at sea."[60]

Emanuel Wynn: French pirate captain who flew the first documented Jolly Roger, the black pirate flag, while chased by an English navy ship off the Cape Verde Islands in 1700.

Captain Misson: An almost certainly fictional French captain who founded a utopian community by the name of Libertalia in Madagascar, soon destroyed by Madagascan natives.

Samuel Bellamy: According to Gosse, a "pirate, socialist, orator."[61] Captain Johnson contributes some of the politically most conscious quotes of all golden age pirate captains to Bellamy in the second volume of *A General History*.

Edward Teach a.k.a. Blackbeard: Possibly the most legendary of the golden age pirate captains. According to Edward Lucie-Smith "full of strange freaks,"[62] and famously described by Johnson:

> [His] beard was black, which he suffered to grow of an extravagant
> length; as to breadth, it came up to his eyes. He was accustomed to twist
> it with ribbons, in small tails ... and turn them about the ears. In time
> of action he wore a sling over his shoulders, with three brace of pistols,
> hanging in holsters, like bandoliers; and stuck lighted matches under
> his hat, which, appearing on each side of his face, his eyes naturally
> looking fierce and wild, made him altogether such a figure that imagina-
> tion cannot form an idea of a fury from hell to look more frightful.[63]

Killed in battle against navy forces along the North Carolina coast in 1718.

Charles Vane: Famous pirate captain during the New Providence heyday. Defiantly left the island one morning after the arrival of the new governor Woodes Rogers by slipping out of the harbor while firing at Rogers's ship. Hanged in Jamaica in 1721.

Bartholomew Roberts: Though not as sensational as Blackbeard, clearly the most successful of the golden age pirates. Elected captain of a pirate crew only a few weeks after he was conscripted from a taken slave ship, Roberts led his crew for four years (an exceptionally long time for a pirate captain during the golden age) and took reputedly over 400 prizes. His death in 1722 and the subsequent defeat and imprisonment of almost all of his crew (fifty-two of whom were executed) is considered a decisive moment in the demise of golden age piracy.

Edward Low: Possibly the best-known captain of the golden age's final phase, gaining a reputation for particular cruelty. Active in the Caribbean, along the North American coast and around the Azores in 1722–1723, he suddenly vanished, his fate remaining unresolved to this day. According to Captain Johnson, "the best information we could receive, would be, that he and all his crew were at the bottom of the sea."[64]

Nathaniel North: Bermuda-born, well-educated, unconventional pirate who sailed to Madagascar around 1720 and spent the last years of his life among a community of Europeans apparently deeply entrenched in local politics. Eventually killed by Madagascan natives in his sleep.

Christopher Condent: English pirate captain whose crew took a huge prize in the Indian Ocean in 1720. Pardoned by the French colonial authorities off the island of Bourbon (Réunion), Condent later became a wealthy merchant in Saint-Malo.

John Taylor: Took one of the biggest prizes in pirate history from the richly laden and storm-damaged Portuguese merchant ship *Nostra Senhora de Cabo* off Bourbon in 1721. Retired into service in the Spanish navy fleet.

Olivier La Buse: Taylor's partner in the coup at Bourbon; remained at large in the Indian Ocean until hanged in 1730.

2. "Enemy of His Own Civilization": An Ethnography of Golden Age Piracy

THERE SEEMS TO BE wide agreement among scholars that the golden age pirate community constituted a special—and possibly unique—cultural phenomenon. Stephen Snelders speaks of "pirate customs,"[1] "a shared pirate culture,"[2] "an alternative society with alternative rules,"[3] and even of "an unbroken social tradition of piracy with clear forms of organization, a repertoire of behavior, and a developed code of ethics."[4] He concludes that "the pirates were clearly very conscious of their traditions, as is shown by their adaptation of common symbolic forms and their regard for elder representatives of their kind."[5] The authors of "Pirate Utopias" identify "a specifically 'pirate consciousness,'" a "'pirate ideology,'" "a world of their own making," and "one community, with a common set of customs shared across the various ships."[6] German scholar Heiner Treinen speaks of the pirates' "own world,"[7] his compatriot Rüdiger Haude of a "common pirate culture,"[8] and Frank Sherry of an "original and lurid style of life"[9] as well as a "separate community in the world."[10]

Some observers stress the distance that the golden age pirates put between themselves and their cultures of origin. Peter Lamborn Wilson even calls "the pirate ... first and foremost the enemy of his own civilization."[11] For Marcus Rediker, too, "everything pirates did reflected their deep alienation from most aspects of European society."[12] As a consequence, "pirates constructed their own social order in defiant contradistinction to the ways of the world they had left behind,"[13] and created—borrowing the title of a Christopher Hill book—a "world turned upside down"[14] with "common symbols and standards of conduct,"[15] set "apart from the dictates of mercantile and imperial authority."[16] The fact that buccaneers allegedly shed their Christian names by joining the buccaneer communities would only confirm this.[17]

If the world and culture of the Caribbean buccaneers and pirates was indeed so distinct, it might be worthwhile to attempt an ethnography of golden age piracy, i.e. trying to recognize patterns of the community's social, political, and economic life. Obviously, such an attempt must remain tentative due to lack of reliable data and because it is uncharted terrain. However, even if little more can be done than to stimulate discussion, such an endeavor promises to aid the study of our political relations to golden age piracy.

The following principles laid out by David Graeber in *Fragments of an Anarchist Anthropology* serve as useful guidelines for this chapter:

> When one carries out an ethnography, one observes what people do, and then tries to tease out the hidden symbolic, moral, or pragmatic logics that underlie their actions; one tries to get at the way people's habits and actions makes sense in ways that they are not themselves completely aware of. One obvious role for a radical intellectual is to do precisely that: to look at those who are creating viable alternatives, try to figure out what might be the larger implications of what they are (already) doing, and then offer those ideas back, not as prescriptions, but as contributions, possibilities—as gifts…. Such a project would actually have to have two aspects, or moments if you like: one ethnographic, one utopian, suspended in a constant dialogue.[18]

2.1. "From the Sea": Maritime Nomads

The association between pirates and nomads appears evident: after all, pirates lack a home, are not settled and take to roaming. In this sense, it seems likely that a comparative study of golden age piracy and nomadism may shed light on the sociocultural circumstances of pirate life. However, we have to be cautious. Many ethnologists would refuse to include marauding seafarers into their definition of nomadism. A.M. Khazanov writes in his seminal *Nomads and The Outside World*:

> In my view … the term 'nomads' is not applicable to other mobile groups, whether ethnic-professional groups such as gypsies, or the

so-called 'maritime nomads' of Southeast Asia, or shifting horticul-
turalists, or certain groups of workers in contemporary industrial
societies (so-called industrial mobility). Consequently, hunters and
gatherers who do not lead a sedentary way of life are best described by
the term 'wandering' ... and mobile extensive pastoralists by the term
'nomadic.'[1]

Khazanov concedes, however, that "some scholars have defined nomads as
all those leading a mobile way of life independent of its economic specificity."[2]
If we apply this latter definition, the golden age pirates—a fluctuating community of marauding bands ranging in number from a few dozen members
to a maximum of about 200 without a secure home base—would definitely
belong to the wider community of nomads. The clearest expression of the fact
that the golden age pirates themselves—who "knew themselves to be homeless and cut off from their countries of origin"[3]—understood their community to be nomadic was the common pirate response to enquiries about where
they came from: *From the Seas*.[4] In fact, the early buccaneers of Hispaniola
already revealed nomadic tendencies. "According to the French missionary
Abbé du Tertre, 'they were without any habitation or fixed abode, but rendez-
voused where the animals were to be found.'"[5] How radically these tendencies expressed themselves during the golden age of piracy is best described
by David Cordingly:

> Apart from the obvious desire to avoid North America in winter, and
> a sensible use of the trade winds when crossing the Atlantic, there
> was no consistency in the planning and execution of most voyages.
> Indeed, there was very little forward planning by any of the pirate
> crews. The democratic nature of the pirate community meant that a
> vote must be taken by the entire crew before the destination of the
> next voyage could be agreed on, and this inevitably led to many deci-
> sions being made on the spur of the moment. A study of the tracks
> of the pirate ships shows many zig-zagging all over the place without
> apparent reason.[6]

One aspect of the golden age pirates' zig-zagging nomadism is the complete
lack of a productive economy. Pastoralists, for example, develop patterns of
movement that guarantee grazing opportunities for their herds, while the

pirates' movements are bound to the availability of "prey." In this respect, the nomadic culture they most closely resemble in terms of economics is that of hunters and gatherers. Raiding merchant ships—and the occasional onshore community or trading post—might be a peculiar way of hunting and gathering, of course, but a structurally similar one. Golden age pirates share with hunters and gatherers a "nomadism required by the foraging economy."[7]

The dependency on prey in the form of European merchant ships reveals another structural similarity between golden age pirates and other nomads, namely their dependency on the outside world. As Khazanov explains: "Nomads could never exist on their own without the outside world and its non-nomadic societies, with their different economic systems. Indeed, a nomadic society could only function while the outside world not only existed but also allowed for those reactions from it ... which ensured that the nomads remained nomads."[8] A historian of the Caribbean realm confirms that this is true for the buccaneers as well, who he calls "essentially stateless persons who lived comfortably by commerce with the settled communities of European colonists."[9]

The structural similarities between golden age pirates and other nomadic societies are not only restricted to economic matters, however. They are also reflected in the sociopolitical realm. As Marcus Rediker points out, "egalitarian forms of social organization and social relations have been commonplace among history's nomadic peoples."[10]

Particularly interesting parallels can be drawn to nomads who inhabit the same natural environment as the golden age pirates, namely the sea, or, more specifically, "an extensive and diversified world of islands."[11] The so-called sea nomads of Southeast Asia are even known to occasionally employ sea robbery as a means of income. As David E. Sopher explains in his study *The Sea Nomads*:

> Three conditions appear to govern the incidence of piracy: first, the existence of productive, but defenceless coast communities or the existence of regular sea trade along regular routes; second, a fluid, if not quite nomadic, way of life, in which tribal warfare, feuds and raiding are accepted institutions—a way of life which would foster piracy; third, superior striking power and speed on the part of the piratical force together with a degree of invulnerability and immunity in its own home.[12]

If by "in its own home" we understand retreats like Hispaniola or Tortuga, or temporary shelters and safe havens, this description applies practically word for word to the Caribbean buccaneers and pirates.

It is not surprising that the *myth of the nomad* (a myth that "may be even older than the myth of the 'noble savage'"[13]) echoes the *myth of the pirate* in a striking fashion. As A.M. Khazanov writes:

> A stereotyped view of nomads has arisen in which their real or imaginary freedom and political independence almost occupy pride of place. Moreover, despite its poverty and other drawbacks, nomadic life is thought by nomads themselves and by many onlookers to have one important advantage, which was defined by A.C. Pigou at the beginning of the century as 'quality of life.'[14]

2.2. "Smooth" vs. "Striated": The Question of Space

If it is true "that the nomads have no history [but only] a geography,"[1] then the question of space deserves particular attention. In the case of Caribbean piracy, this specifically means the sea. Its significance can hardly be overrated. All of Caribbean society has always been intrinsically linked to it:

> The sea led men to the West Indies, and away from them. A unique fact about the Caribbee islands was that all the inhabitants— Caribs, Arawaks, white planters, merchants, and servants, and black slaves—had arrived by sea in very recent times. To these islands, with their motley populations, merchants and factors came and went with some regularity; they brought craftsmen, servants, and slaves to the West Indies. Communication from one island to another by means of small sloops was both facilitated and obstructed by the incessant trade winds; Barbados lay so far eastward of the Leeward Islands that very little exchange took place. All life, everywhere, depended on wooden hulls: in the outward passage they carried food and supplies of all kinds, and wines from Madeira and the Canaries; on the homeward voyage they took back the island staples and a few passengers.[2]

This meant ideal conditions for aspiring pirates: "While petty thuggery and brigandage might be easily subdued close to home, these far-flung new trade routes offered a tempting outlet for an entirely different breed of marauder, a mobile and elusive adventurer who could sail to the far ends of the earth, and seek his fortune amid its most lawless frontiers."[3]

In general, too, the sea has long been a symbol of freedom, a *free space* par excellence. Rüdiger Haude calls it "the unlimited, unpredictable space, the negation of everything 'national.'"[4] Marcus Rediker adds: "'The vast ocean cannot be possessed.' It was a commons, a place to be used by many, including the sailor who dared to turn pirate."[5] This was especially true as long as those who traveled the seas were dependent on the elements: "The source of power that took them from one haven to the next was everywhere and always available, since it was only the wind."[6]

In the terminology of Gilles Deleuze and Félix Guattari, the sea constitutes a *smooth space*, "perhaps the principal among smooth spaces, the hydraulic model par excellence."[7] As they explain: "Smooth space is a field without conduits or channels. A field, a heterogeneous smooth space, is wedded to a very particular type of multiplicity: non-metric, acentered, rhizomatic multiplicities which occupy space without 'counting' it."[8] In simpler words, the smooth space is a space for creating self-determined, creative, "free" forms of life. Here, the nomads reach their full potential as raiders: "With practical skill a nomad band can strike, steal, and disappear beyond hope of pursuit in the great waste, fading away without trace.... "[9]

The supplement to the open space of the sea were the pirates' coastal refuges, the "many small inlets, lagoons and harbours, ... solitary islands and keys."[10] If we stick to the terminology of Deleuze and Guattari, we might call this a *rhizomatic* terrain, since a rhizome is "open and connectable in all of its dimensions ... it always has multiple entryways."[11] All of the favorite operational areas of the pirates are described accordingly: "the Caribbean islands provided innumerable hiding places, secret coves and uncharted islands";[12] "the Gulf of Honduras and the Mosquito Coast [were] dotted with numerous small islands and protecting reefs, ... creeks, lagoons and river-mouths";[13] "the American coast from Boston to Charleston, South Carolina, is a network of river estuaries, bays, inlets, and islands."[14] These coastal labyrinths provided the pirates' natural onshore environment. "'As surely as spiders abound where there are nooks and crannies,' wrote Captain the Hon. Henry Keppel, the great hunter of Oriental pirates in the nineteenth century, 'so have pirates sprung up wherever there is a nest of islands offering creeks and shallows, headlands, rocks and reefs—facilities in short for lurking, for surprise, for attack, for escape.'"[15]

Between the extremes of the wide-open sea and the impenetrable coastal mazes of reefs, inlets, and river-mouths, the pirates were able to escape the wrath of the law for several decades.[16] Eventually, however, the smooth space of the sea—and with it its coastal boundaries—became "striated," i.e. ordered, regulated, and controlled. This contributed significantly to the end of golden age piracy:

> The sea is ... of all smooth spaces, the first one attempts were made
> to striate, to transform into a dependency of the land, with its fixed
> routes, constant directions, relative movements, a whole counter-
> hydraulic of channels and conduits. One of the reasons for the
> hegemony of the West was the power ... of its State apparatuses
> to striate the sea by combining technologies of the North and the
> Mediterranean and by annexing the Atlantic.[17]

The most tangible aspect of this annexation—or the striating process—was an increased navy presence. The number of permanently employed royal ships in the Americas rose from two in the 1670s to twenty-four by 1700,[18] "by 1723, increased surveillance on the sea routes by the Royal Navy was severely limiting [the pirates'] freedom of operations,"[19] and by 1724, "the world was becoming too small for a wanted pirate to be able to find a safe hiding place."[20] This coincided with significant technological innovations. As David F. Marley explains: "Steam, advanced ballistics, telegraphic communications and other technological innovations meant that the advantage swung decisively to the professional services."[21] Edward Lucie-Smith stresses the first in particular: "What put an end, in its classic form, to a crime which had existed since history began, was chiefly the coming of steam. Mechanical propulsion, which meant that the men who traveled the oceans were no longer at the mercy of the winds, also removed much of the danger they had hitherto felt from the man who made the wind his ally, and cast himself upon its mercy as the price of an irregular and ferocious independence."[22]

Robert C. Ritchie concludes:

> Ultimately the buccaneers' success in expanding their geographic
> range aroused the forces of order and brought the pirates into

collision with the demands of empire. The struggle that ensued was lopsided: the resources mobilized by the rising imperial states far exceeded those of the pirates. [This ends a time] when the world was younger, when it was possible for a group of men to seize a ship and sail to the end of the world seeking their fortune, while living in a consensual society free of the constraints that dominated their lives at home.[23]

2.3. Pirate Captains and Indian Chiefs: Remembering Pierre Clastres

The fact that many of the historical accounts and popular images of piracy focus on pirate captains often leads to notions of men with huge power and influence—something they might have never had.

In the 1970s, radical French anthropologist Pierre Clastres described the chief's role in "stateless" Indian societies[1] in his essay "Exchange and Power: Philosophy of the Indian Chieftainship."[2] Clastres reached the controversial conclusion that "the most notable characteristic of the Indian chief consists of his almost complete lack of authority."[3] He stresses in particular the following aspects: 1. The chief is elected and replaceable. 2. His power rests on merit only. 3. His power is controlled by the community. 4. He is a peacemaker. 5. He is generous with his possessions. 6. He is a good orator. 7. He is an able leader in war. This reveals startling parallels to the role of the pirate captain.

The chief is elected and replaceable: There is plenty of evidence that this was true for pirate captains. Even non-radical pirate historians concede that "there was an admirable tradition of democracy that enabled crews to vote their captains in and out of office."[4] Captain Johnson's *A General History of the Pirates* contains several passages that describe the election of new pirate captains, maybe most notably that of Bartholomew Roberts.[5] Philip Gosse claims that "it is on record that one ship had elected thirteen different commanders in a few months."[6]

The election—or dismissal—of captains was already practiced among buccaneer crews. Basil Ringrose provides a credible firsthand account of the way in which Captain Bartholomew Sharp, deemed inept by many of his crew, is replaced by John Watling:

On Thursday, January 6th, our differences being now grown to a great height, the mutineers made a new election of another person to be our chief captain and commander, by virtue whereof they deposed Captain Sharp, whom they protested they would obey no longer. They chose thereof one of our company, whose name was John Watling, to command in chief, he having been an old privateer, and gained the esteem of being a stout seaman. The election being made, all the rest were forced to give their assent to it, and Captain Sharp gave over his command, whereupon they immediately made articles with Watling, and signed them.[7]

His power rests on merit only: Frank Sherry notes that "for the most part pirates chose their captains on the basis of merit. Because of the dangers inherent in their calling, they could not afford to apply any criterion other than ability to the selection of their leaders."[8]

His power is controlled by the community: Stephen Snelders writes that "regardless of how pistol-proof, bold, terrifying, or beloved a pirate captain might be, all hierarchy and authoritarianism were constantly questioned by the Brethren. Their transmitted customs and the fleeting and evanescent character of their lives severely limited, and in the end nullified, any attempt by authority to assert itself."[9] This sounds very much like the "diffuse, collective mechanisms" that—according to Deleuze and Guattari, who included a "Homage to Pierre Clastres" in their book *A Thousand Plateaus*—"prevent a chief from becoming ... a man of State."[10]

He is a peacemaker: Several passages in Captain Johnson's *History of the Pirates* echo this responsibility. In Johnson's account of Captain North, for example, the captain's peacemaking abilities are even extended to the Madagascan natives: "North deciding their disputes not seldom, with that impartiality and strict regard to distributive justice (for he was allowed by all, a man of admirable good natural parts) that he ever sent away even the party who was cast, satisfied with the reason and content with the equity of his decisions."[11] Compare this description to the one by Clastres:

> The chief is responsible for maintaining peace and harmony in the group. He must appease quarrels and settle disputes—not by employ-ing a force he does not possess and which would not be acknowledged

in any case, but by relying solely on the strength of his prestige, his fairness, and his verbal ability. More than a judge who passes sentence, he is an arbiter who seeks to reconcile.[12]

He is generous with his possessions: The pirate captain was often granted a larger part of the booty than ordinary crew members. However, this did not necessarily help him amass greater riches. In fact, due to possessing more, he was also expected to give and share more. Captain Johnson illustrates this in connection with Bartholomew Roberts, arguably one of the pirate captains who exerted a more than average amount of authority over his crew: "They separate for his use the great cabin, and sometimes vote him small parcels of plate and china (for it may be noted that Roberts drank his tea constantly) but then every man, as the humour takes him, seize a part of his victuals and drink, if they like it, without his offering to find fault or contest it."[13] It was the captain's responsibility to store wealth for times of need. Some anthropologists have identified this as an almost universal feature among elected leaders of so-called primitive societies. Marshall Sahlins contends that "big-men and chiefs are compelled to relieve shortages among the people,"[14] and Boris Malinowski goes as far as saying that "the chief, everywhere, acts as a tribal banker, collecting food, storing it, and protecting it, and then using it for the benefit of the whole community."[15] According to Pierre Clastres, "this obligation to give, to which the chief is bound, is experienced by the Indians as a kind of right to subject him to a continuous looting. And if the unfortunate leader tries to check this flight of gifts, he is immediately shorn of all prestige and power."[16]

He is a good orator: Even if the significance of oratory was probably much less pronounced in pirate than in Indian communities (Clastres suggests that Indian chiefs "gratify the people of his group with an edifying discourse ... every day, either at dawn or sunset"[17]—something hardly imaginable for pirate captains), Johnson's *General History* knows many captains who excel in the art of oratory, most notably Saul Bellamy.

He is an able leader in war: In one of the most regularly cited passages of the *General History*, Captain Johnson writes that during military engagements, the pirate captain's power "is absolute and uncontrollable, by their own laws, *viz.*, in fighting, chasing, or being chased."[18] This echoes the following description by Clastres: "During military expeditions the war chief commands a substantial amount of power—at times absolute—over the group of warriors. ... But the conjunction of power and coercion ends as soon as the group returns to its normal internal life."[19]

In light of all this, it is a curious play of words when Heiner Treinen speaks of pirate captains as *"Piratenhäuptlinge"* in a 1981 essay—*Häuptling* being an antiquated German term for Indian chief.[20] While Clastres declares the Indian chief to be "a kind of prisoner in a space which the tribe does not let him leave,"[21] Captain Johnson outlines the relationship between the pirate crews and their captains with the famous words: "They only permit him to be captain on the condition that they may be captain over him."[22] And while Clastres calls the Indian chief "the effective instrument of his society,"[23] Rediker calls the pirate captain "the creature of his crew."[24] Like Clastres in his analysis, pirate historians describe "a chieftainship without authority"[25] in which the chief "has no instituted weapon other than his prestige, no other means of persuasion, no other rule than his sense of the group's desires" and is "more like a leader or a star than a man of power ... always in danger of being disavowed, abandoned by his people."[26]

The parallels reach even further,[27] to the point where the analysis of Indian chiefdom implies social mechanisms against state formation. This is of significant importance for the political investigation of golden age pirate communities. It is worth quoting Clastres once more at length:

> Hence there is no king in the tribe, but a chief who is not a chief of State. What does that imply? Simply that the chief has no authority at his disposal, no power of coercion, no means of giving an order. The chief is not a commander; the people of the tribe are under no obligation to obey. The space of the chieftainship is not the locus of power, and the 'profile' of the primitive chief in no way foreshadows that of a future despot. There is nothing about the chieftainship that suggests the State apparatus derived from it.[28]

The biggest danger in the dependency of the chief's power on his warring abilities lies in his desire for war as a way to consolidate his power. In Clastres's words, "it occasionally happens that a chief tries to *play the chief*:[29]

> Occasionally a chief ... attempts to put his personal interest ahead of the collective interest. Reversing the normal relationship that

determines the leader as a means in the service of a socially defined
end, he tries to make society into the means for achieving a purely
private end: the tribe in the service of the chief and no longer the chief
in the service of the tribe. If it 'worked,' then he would have found the
birthplace of political power, as force and violence; we would have the
first incarnation, the minimal form of the State. But it never works.[30]

There were certainly some pirate captains who tried to "play the chief."
Most famous is the tale of Blackbeard, who justified shooting and crippling a
crew member for no apparent reason with the remark that "if he did not now
and then kill one of them, they would forget who he was."[31] Stephen Snelders
also reckons that "toward the end of his career, [Captain] Davis, and his most
important lieutenants seem to have lost some of their egalitarian character,"[32]
while the reaction of Nathaniel North to being elected captain, as related by
Captain Johnson, does not exactly evoke the praised egalitarian character of
the pirate community either: "The ceremony is ended with an invitation from
the captain to such he thinks fit to have dine with him."[33] The same can be
said for Bartholomew Roberts—according to David Cordingly, a "man with
a natural flair for leadership"[34]—who allegedly accepted his role as captain
by saying that "since he had dipped his hands in muddy water, and must be a
pirate, it was better being a commander than a common man."[35] As in Captain
David's case (Roberts's predecessor on the *Rover*), a group of crew members
under Roberts's command apparently also established a privileged vanguard,
unattractively named the House of Lords.[36]

Whether these pirate captains and their cronies succeeded in "playing the
chief" or not, is hard to tell, as their lives were cut short.

2.4. Potlatches, Zero-Production, and Parasitism: Pirate Economy
The economy of the golden age pirates combines "primitive" and "criminal"
features in a curious blend. Let us consider the former first.

Pirate Economy as "Primitive" Economy
☠ *Work*
Pirate historians across the political spectrum seem to agree that work was
not high on the agenda of Caribbean buccaneers and pirates. Frank Sherry

states that "the crew of a pirate ship worked only as much as was necessary,"[1] while Peter Earle suggests that "less work because of large crews was ... one of the attractions of service on a pirate ship."[2] David Cordingly expands on the latter point:

> The daily routine on a pirate ship was considerably easier than life on a merchantman because the crew were not driven by owners and captains to make the fastest possible passage with the biggest possible cargo, and because the pirates operated with very much larger crews. The typical crew of a merchantman of a hundred tons was around twelve men. A pirate ship of similar size would frequently have a crew of eighty or more.[3]

Contemporaneous accounts seem to confirm the buccaneers' and pirates' lack of enthusiasm for work. Exquemelin wrote about the buccaneers that, "so long as they had cash to spend, it was difficult to persuade them to the sea,"[4] while "Père Labat, a priest who sailed with the flibustiers on their raids into the South Sea ... attributed their preference for the use of barques or sloops, vessels with a simple sail-rig that called for a minimum of seamanship, 'to a dislike of work in the first place.'"[5]

The parallels to so-called primitive societies are obvious. Clastres states candidly that "the Indian devoted very little time to what is called work,"[6] and explains further: "Primitive societies are, as Lizot writes with regard to the Yanomami, societies characterized by the rejection of work: 'The Yanomamis' contempt for work and their disinterest in technological progress per se are beyond question.' The first leisure societies, the first affluent societies, according to M. Sahlins's apt and playful expression."[7] Sahlins himself writes: "Tribal people work less than we do, as well as less regularly. They probably also sleep more in the daytime. ... Working conditions are hardly ideal, and perhaps tribesmen ought to have a union [but] about the hours they needn't complain."[8]

Arguably, a highlight of the pirates' work was taking other ships, especially when we consider Stephen Snelders's description of pirate life as one in which "everything happened at once [after] nothing happened for whole days."[9] This, once again, evokes images of a primitive economy as a "necessary cycle of extreme activity and total idleness."[10] According to Douglas Botting, "pirates suffered prolonged agonies of boredom."[11] In any case, the golden age pirate was certainly a strong competitor to the hunter when it came to "the lowest grades in thermodynamics—less energy/capita/year."[12]

☠ Non-accumulation/Potlatch

The above scenario confirms the buccaneers' and pirates' "penchant for living for the day."[13] In direct relation to so-called primitive societies, "this means that once its needs are fully satisfied nothing could induce primitive society to produce more, that is, to alienate its time by working for no good reason when that time is available for idleness, play, warfare, or festivities."[14] It also indicates "the determination to make productive activity agree with the satisfaction of needs. And nothing more."[15]

The fact that the buccaneers (and later the golden age pirates) displayed a similar attitude used to frustrate those who dedicated themselves to the economic advancement of the Caribbean colonies. Jean-Baptiste Ducasse, governor of the French colony of Saint-Domingue (founded in 1659 and comprising Hispaniola's western part—modern-day Haiti), reportedly despaired in his anxiety about economic development, since this was a matter "which was absolutely indifferent to the Brothers of the Coast."[16]

Contrary to popular belief, most buccaneers or pirates never demonstrated a big interest in accumulating wealth. It is probably going too far to cite them as an example of Marshall Sahlins's original affluent society and its Zen approach of desiring little (some—if distant—dreams of material riches must have haunted most buccaneers and pirates who were, after all, subjects of an early capitalist society), but there certainly existed a common behavioral trait that anthropologists call *prodigality*: "the inclination to consume at once all stocks on hand."[17]

The buccaneers' and pirates' economic wastefulness is indeed legendary. The eyewitness Exquemelin reports how the buccaneers "spend with great liberality, giving themselves freely to all manner of vices and debauchery."[18] He writes that "according to their custom [they] wasted in a few days in taverns all they had gained.... Such of these pirates are found who will spend two or three thousand pieces of eight in one night, not leaving themselves peradventure a good shirt to wear in the morning."[19] Likewise: "They squander in a month all the money which has taken them a year or eighteen months to earn."[20] Sometimes the riches didn't even last until "the crew went ashore and indulged in an orgy of riotous living,"[21] as David Cordingly and

John Falconer report: "After plundering Maracaibo in 1625 L'Ollonais, the French buccaneer, divided the spoils so that each man received one hundred pieces of eight. He and his men returned to Tortuga and 'in three weeks they had scarce any money left them, having spent it all in things of little value or at play of cards and dice.'"[22] Maurice Besson sums up the buccaneers' attitude towards gathering riches convincingly: "In a few hours, the booty was dissipated on gambling, woman and drink. Without a country, with no home, with no care for the future, the flibustiers fought, not to enrich themselves, not so that one day they might rest upon their laurels, with a comfortable fortune; they fought to conquer, to pillage, and to make the best of what the moment offered."[23] The assessments of other pirate researchers ring equally true: Ulrike Klausmann and Marion Meinzerin suggest that "these pirates did not view plundering as a means to becoming wealthy. Their goal instead was to attain booty as quickly as possible, at a minimum expense of labour, so as to squander it just as quickly. ... 'Why save, when tomorrow we could be dead?' That was their motto."[24] Chris Land confirms this: "in this sense 'booty' was incorporated into the way of life the pirates were developing, rather than an end goal to which that life was subordinated."[25] Finally, Stephen Snelders even offers a Marxist analysis of the buccaneers' and pirates' spending habits: "A pirate kept the surplus value of his work for himself and his comrades, to spend on the good things of life."[26]

Once again, the similarities to so-called primitive economies are striking:

> We are accustomed, because of the nature of our own economy, to
> think that human beings have a 'natural propensity to truck and
> barter,' and that economic relations among individuals or groups are
> characterized by 'economizing,' by 'maximizing' the results of effort,
> by 'selling dear and buying cheap.' Primitive peoples do none of these
> things, however; in fact, most of the time it would seem that they do
> the opposite. They 'give things away,' they admire generosity, they
> expect hospitality, they punish thrift as selfishness.[27]

Gustavo Martin-Fragachan tells us that the Taíno, the Indians who mainly populated the island of Hispaniola at the time of Columbus's arrival, celebrated "large festivals ... in part, to consume all the excess that had been produced, in a phenomenon that reminds us of the potlatch so well known to anthropologists and ethnologists."[28] The Taíno culture was reportedly extinct by the mid-1500s, but it does not seem too far-fetched to see a continuation of potlatch-like rituals in the behavior of the region's buccaneers and pirates.

For some radical authors, the golden age pirates "consciously chose a non-accumulative life."[29] If there is any truth to this claim, then Silver, one of the pirate girls in Kathy Acker's *Pussy, King of the Pirates*, might indeed, against all common presumptions, express the true spirit of golden age piracy when rejecting her share in a chest of gold: "I'd rather go a-pirating … If me and my girls take all this treasure, the reign of girl piracy will stop, and I wouldn't have that happen."[30]

☠ No Division or Alienation of Labor

Since the daily work that had to be done by buccaneer and pirate communities (mainly the handling and maintenance of their ships) constituted no separate sphere of their existence, one could argue that labor as an autonomous aspect of life did not exist within the pirate community, and hence none of the alienation processes associated with it existed either. The same would be true for a division of labor since it is hard to divide something that does not exist. Here, too, one finds compelling parallels to "primitive" societies:

> It is difficult at any time to say just what actions of hunters and gatherers are economic or political or religious, or even artistic. This unspecialized characteristic of primitive society results in one especially important contrast to modern civilization. It means that an individual adult participates much more fully in every aspect of the culture than do the people of more complicated societies.[31]

With this in mind, the social experiment of the golden age pirates did indeed throw a monkey wrench into the industrialization process. As Marshall Sahlins writes about societies who do not abide by this process:

> Work is not divorced from life. There is no 'job,' no time and place where one spends most of one's time not being oneself. Nor are work and life related as means to an end (as they often are for us): the former a necessary evil tolerated for the sake of the latter, 'living,' which is something to do after business hours, on your *own* time, if you have the energy. The Industrial Revolution split work from life. The reintegration has not yet been achieved.[32]

♟ Self-Management

Apart from the relative lack of work, the refusal to engage in accumulative practices, and the absence of a distinct labor sector and alienation processes, the golden age pirates' economy distinguished itself in another important way from the capitalist development that surrounded it: namely, the pirates controlled their own means of production. This is one of the aspects of golden age piracy that does indeed mark a break with the tradition of the privateering buccaneers. As Frank Sherry points out, while "privateer crews ... were still only hired hands despite the fact that they received fair shares of their ship's plunder, pirates regarded themselves as self-employed, collective owners of their own ships."[33]

♟ No Exploitation

As there was no contradiction between means and forces of production, there was also no room for exploitation in the economic set-up of the golden age pirate communities either. Again, in contrast to the privateers who still paid a share of their plunder to the ship owner (and often enough to the political authorities), the pirates kept all their own profits. Some of these profits were shared by the crew in a way reminiscent of both Friedrich Engels's simple description of "original communism" ("whatever was produced and used in common was common property"[34]) and the "generalized reciprocity" described by Sahlins and other anthropologists as "a form of exchange based on the assumption that returns will balance out in the long run."[35] Among the buccaneers and pirates, this mainly concerned the part of the booty that was to be used communally until the end of a voyage. ("Pirate Utopias," the article from Do or Die, suggests that "this sort of share system was common in mediaeval shipping, but had been phased out as shipping became a capitalist enterprise and sailors wage labourers."[36]) The rest of the prize was divided according to the specific articles drawn up by each crew, most of the time in a very egalitarian way. Even then, however, exceptions could be made for the common good, as Basil Ringrose reports:

> On that day, therefore, a little Spanish shock-dog, which we had found
> in our last wine-prize, taken under the equinoctial and had kept alive
> till now, was sold at the mast by public cry for forty pieces-of-eight,
> his owner saying that all he could get for him should be spent upon

the company at a public merriment. Our commander, Captain Sharp, bought the dog, with intention to eat him, in case we did not see land very soon. This money, therefore, with one hundred pieces-of-eight more, which our boatswain, carpenter, and quartermaster had refused to take at this last dividend, for some quarrel they had against the shares thereof, was all laid up in store till we came to land, with the intent of spending it ashore, at a common feast or drinking bout.[37]

Possessions were not always shared so smoothly, of course. Peter Earle, in quoting S.C. Hill, relates an anecdote about fourteen pirates who "by consent divided themselves into sevens to fight for what they had (thinking they had not made a voyage sufficient for so many), one of the said sevens being all killed and five of the other, so that the two which survived enjoyed the whole booty."[38]

Pirate Economy as "Criminal" Economy

Since the pirates' means of procuring wealth were illegal, they shared a world with others engaged in illegal, i.e. "criminal," economic acquisition and transaction. If a serious comparative study of the economy of golden age piracy was conducted, the pirates' dependency on smugglers, corrupt officials, and black markets would have to be as much investigated as the structural similarities of their economies to those of wreckers or bandits on land. Pirates were without doubt part of an economic underground—or an underground economy.[39]

☠ Zero-Production/Parasitism

While the economies of "primitive" people have been described as voluntary "underproduction" by Marshall Sahlins,[40] the golden age pirates' economy must be described in terms of "zero-production." Practically all their means for survival came from robbing and raiding. Not a single commodity is known that pirates produced for themselves or economic profit. This again reveals parallels to nomadic societies. Sahlins writes:

As is the lot of pastoral nomads, constant movement also restricted the quantity and character of Plains Indians' wealth. They made no pottery, cloth, or basketry, and developed only early manufactures in wood, stone, and bone; but relied instead on leather products and metal trade goods, and lavished most attention on their beaded, bangled, and befeathered costumes.[41]

This is arguably true for golden age pirates as well.[42]

While the Plains Indians' economy was largely built on hunting, the golden age pirates' economy was almost exclusively built on plunder. (Turtling is the only productive activity that is fairly commonly reported. Just like fishing, it seems to have been mostly the task of Indians, however, who traveled with buccaneer and pirate crews.[43]) Ever since the buccaneers' existence as hunters ended, their supply of "clothes, arms and ships...depended on the loot they acquired."[44] Cordingly and Falconer maintain that the golden age pirate was "essentially an opportunist, and many of the necessities of life were taken from his victims. Medicines, food and ship's stores were all valuable."[45] On another occasion, Cordingly explains that "much of the loot which was stolen consisted of ship's gear and what might be termed 'household goods.' This is a point that does not come across in pirate stories of fiction."[46] Peter Earle concurs:

> What [the pirates] chiefly sought aboard a prize were those things which would enable them to maintain their ships and sustain themselves and their way of life, the life itself being as or more important than the dream of returning home rich. And so, while they always looked for money and other valuables, their main focus was on food and drink, clothes, arms and ammunition, cables and sails and whatever else they might need for themselves or for the ship.[47]

It has even been suggested that "unlike the pirates of fiction, these maritime criminals never expected to plunder cargoes of gold and silver, but preyed on the everyday commerce of the Colonial Americas."[48]

It is hence not surprising when Anne Pérotin-Dumon suggests that pirates were "mere parasites."[49] Stressing the lack of self-sufficiency in more academic terms, A.M. Khazanov speaks of the "non-autarky" or "in many cases...anti-autarky," of nomadic societies.[50] In any case, the "zero-production" related to their illegal modes of acquisition as well as their nomadic existence is a notable aspect separating the golden age pirates from many other pirate communities who were still connected to a certain territory and certain forms of production: fishing, agriculture, even craftsmanship.

☠ Fast Riches

Though seldom a common occurrence or a prime objective of the golden age pirates, it is hard to imagine that the lure of wealth played no role at all in enticing men to sail under the Jolly Roger, even if this role seldom amounted to more than chasing a distant dream. After all, the life of a pirate provided two things that the life of a sailor on a merchantman or a man-of-war did not: the *possibility* of becoming rich very fast (there were pirates such as the crews of Every, Tew, Taylor, or Condent who retired wealthy after one big score, many of them taking their shares and vanishing or bribing their way back into mainstream society), and a generally decent income combined with much less effort and much more freedom. Especially considering that "the life of an ordinary sailor was no less dangerous ... than that of a pirate,"[51] these advantages seem so strong that one can indeed conclude with Charles Grey that "with so many convincing reasons why they should become pirates, it does seem strange that so many mariners, who had the opportunity, refrained from going 'On the Account.'"[52] This echoes the fact that it is not surprising to see many gangsters in economically underprivileged communities—what is surprising is not to see more. The logic that Philip Gosse applies to the buccaneers can be applied to all poor communities: "When a man has for years lived the free life, sailed out from Jamaica a pauper, to return in six weeks or less with, perhaps, a bag of gold worth two, three, or four thousand pounds, which he has prided himself on spending in the taverns and gambling-hells of Port Royal in a week, how can he settle down to humdrum uneventful toil, with its small profits?"[53]

The individual dimension expressed here is mirrored by a collective dimension that once again reminds us of the similarities between the golden age pirates and (other) nomadic societies: due to the usual economic imbalances between sedentary and mobile folk, "raid must often present itself to the nomads a better choice than trade."[54] In short, the pirate economy was an expression of people refusing to accept their lack of privilege, obey orders, and toil for crumbs. Instead, they decided to live off of others—ideally the rich, but probably often enough those who simply sailed into their ambushes.

☠ Redistribution of Wealth

As a "criminal" economy, pirate economy helped to redistribute some of the wealth in the Caribbean. Thanks to the buccaneers and the golden age pirates, significant amounts of the money from international trade found its way into local economies. As Franklin W. Knight explains: "The ill-gotten plunder of the buccaneers, lavishly dispensed in the local towns, boosted the local economies and compensated adequately for the otherwise detestable social manners of these men."[55]

The world over, many communities turn a blind eye to known gangsters as long as they do not interfere with local commerce, but fuel it with goods and money attained on the outside. This is also a traditional asset of the bandit as a social rebel who contributes to the accumulation of local capital:

> What do they do with the rustled cattle, the travelling merchant's goods? They buy and sell. Indeed, since they normally possess far more cash than ordinary local peasantry, their expenditures may form an important element in the modern sector of the local economy, being redistributed, through local shopkeepers, innkeepers and others, to the commercial middle strata of rural society. ... It is therefore a mistake to think of bandits as mere children of nature roasting stags in the greenwood. A successful brigand chief is at least as closely in touch with the market and the wider economic universe as a small landowner or prosperous farmer. Indeed, in economically backward regions his trade may draw him close to that of others who travel, buy and sell.[56]

2.5. No State, No Accumulation, No History: Pirates as "Primitives"?

If we subscribe to Pierre Clastres's division of societies into two main groups, namely "primitive societies, or societies without a State" and "societies with a State,"[1] then the society of golden age pirates clearly falls on the primitive side. This seems even more evident when we also accept Clastres's assessment that "faithless, lawless, and kingless" were the "terms used by the sixteenth-century West to describe the Indians"[2]—after all, the same terms would be used a century later to describe the golden age pirates who "opposed the high and mighty of their day and by their actions became the villains of all nations."[3]

To further strengthen the case for golden age pirates constituting a society without a state, let us consider Marshall Sahlins's definition of a "state society":

> (1) there is an official public authority, a set of offices of the society at large conferring governance over the society at large; (2) 'society

at large,' the domain of this governing authority, is territorially
defined and subdivided; (3) the ruling authority monopolizes
sovereignty—no other person or assembly can rightly command
power (or force) except by sovereign delegation, leave, or consent;
(4) all persons and groups within the territory are *as such*—by
virtue of residence in the domain—subject to the sovereign, to its
jurisdiction and coercion.[4]

None of this applies to the golden age pirate communities. At the same
time, we can draw plenty of startling parallels to so-called primitive societies.
Elman R. Service, for example, calls a primitive or "band society" one with
"no specialized or formalized institutions or groups that can be differenti-
ated as economic, political, religious, and so on."[5] In response to the infamous
Hobbesian assumption about the lives of primitive, stateless people as "nasty,
brutish and short," Service writes that "primitive peoples' lives are usually
short, but not always nasty, and never brutish."[6] This description applies to
many pirates' lives as well.

The absence of written records from pirate ships also allows for interesting
comparisons. It would clearly be too daring to deduce an "archaic culture"[7]
from Captain Johnson's remark that amongst the pirates living in Madagascar
in the 1690s there was not "a man amongst them, who could either read or
write."[8] But to speak of an *oral culture* in the case of the golden age pirates
seems hardly exaggerated. This appears particularly interesting when considering that it was largely the keeping of written records that marked the
moment when "Time became History."[9]

Another notable aspect is community size. Clastres writes:

> In fact it is very probable that a basic condition for the existence of
> primitive societies is their relatively small demographic size. Things
> can function on the primitive model only if the people are few in
> number. Or, in other words, in order for a society to be primitive, it
> must be numerically small. And, in effect, what one observes in the
> Savage world is an extraordinary patchwork of 'nations,' tribes, and
> societies made up of local groups that take great care to preserve
> their autonomy within the larger group of which they are a part,
> although they may conclude temporary alliances with their nearby

'fellow-countrymen,' if the circumstances—especially those having to do with warfare—demand it. This atomization of the tribal universe is unquestionably an effective means of preventing the emergence of the State, which is a unifier by nature.[10]

Once again, this applies almost word for word to the golden age pirate communities.[11] According to Marshall Sahlins, the society of the golden age pirates could be interpreted as a *segmentary tribe*:

> A tribe is specifically unlike a modern nation in that its several communities are not united under a sovereign governing authority, nor are the boundaries of the whole thus clearly and politically determined. ... Such a cultural formation, at once structurally decentralized and functionally generalized, is a primitive segmentary society. ... The segmentary tribe is sharply divided into independent local communities ('primary political segments'). These communities are small. They rarely include more than a few hundred people, usually many less ... [12]

The following description is as apt: "Certain groups may ally for a time and purpose, as for a military venture, but the collective spirit is episodic. When the objective for which it was called into being is accomplished, the alliance lapses and the tribe returns to its normal state of disunity."[13] Finally, Sahlins's explanation of how the tribe maintains its identity through cultural similarity rather than a continuously shared existence is striking with respect to pirate communities:

> Perhaps most critical in giving a tribal people that measure of coherence and identity they do possess is their cultural similarity. The local groups are like each other in custom and speech, even as they often differ in these respects from others. Cut from the same cloth, they have a common destiny or, more technically, a 'mechanical solidarity.' Insofar as these groups are alike, they respond the same way to the world and thus develop an historic identity if not exactly a polity. Also important is the social nexus linking neighboring settlements of a tribe. ... Then there are certain *pan-tribal institutions*, widespread tribal associations: not exactly 'groups' since they do

not act as collectives, but more like fraternal orders with chapters established in different locales—so that for the price of a secret handshake one may be able to cadge a free lunch in another place.[14]

2.6. *"Cultural Contact"*:
Pirates and the Non-European People of the Caribbean

In his study "Frei-Beuter: Charakter und Herkunft piratischer Demokratie im frühen 18. Jahrhundert" ["Freebooters: Character and Origin of Pirate Democracy in the Early 18th Century"], German scholar Rüdiger Haude defines four crucial influences for the democratic organization of the golden age pirates' communities. Apart from "spontaneous emergence," "the school of the sea," and "expatriated radicalism,"[1] Haude also names "cultural contact." Haude's parameters suggest that the parallels drawn between golden age piracy and "primitive" societies above do not just illustrate structural commonalities of stateless people, but possibly indicate an actual influence of Native American/Caribbean culture on the European renegades who formed the buccaneer community.

Here, a lack of sources not only concerning the buccaneers and pirates, but also the lives of people who inhabited the Caribbean realm prior to the Europeans' arrival, prevents the proposal of more substantial theories. Anthropological research on the Caribbean's pre-European societies has largely had to rely on archaeological material (which allows few conclusions on matters of political organization and the social dimensions of intercultural contact) and missionary records (scarcely known for objectivity). Julian Granberry sums up the situation as follows:

> Archaeologists are gradually piecing together the prehistoric backgrounds and migrations of the native peoples of the Caribbean, but even that picture is in a state of flux today. The official Spanish accounts of the time, preserved in the Archives of the Indies in Seville, with few exceptions discuss only the Indies' potential for wealth and the conversion of the native peoples to Christianity. Almost the only interest shown in the people per se was as a source of unpaid, baptized labor. There is some information of ethnographic interest in these early accounts but regrettably little.[2]

In fact, the available material is so sparse that no strict cultural divisions have ever been established. Irving Rouse, a well-regarded specialist on the anthropological history of the Caribbean, distinguished three main ethnic groups in the 1948 *Handbook of South American Indians*: the Arawak (with the Taíno as the biggest subgroup), the Carib, and the Ciboney.[3] Today, this categorization is challenged by various scholars—some preferring to speak of Island-Arawak, Island-Carib, and Guanahatabeys/Guanahacabibes instead, others questioning the three categories altogether.[4] Since most of the literature that discusses contacts between buccaneers/pirates and Indians follows Rouse's classification, and since commonly accepted alternatives are missing, Rouse's terms will be employed here despite the obvious need for future modification.

If the historical records are to be believed, the Carib were the only one of the three mentioned groups that could have had contact with the buccaneers and pirates of the Caribbean. The Arawak, whose society has been described as one of *theocratic chiefdoms*,[5] were reputedly extinguished by the mid-1500s.[6] (This is particularly shocking in light of their numbers having been estimated at several hundred thousand at the time of Columbus's arrival only half a century earlier. It suggests a genocide of enormous proportions.) The Ciboney, who have been described as "hunters and gatherers with a political organization which probably did not develop beyond that of the nomadic band,"[7] might have already been extinct at the time of Columbus's arrival. Groups of Caribs, however, survived and put up fierce resistance to the European settlement on the Leeward Islands of St. Christopher, Nevis, Montserrat, Guadeloupe, and St. Vincent. Eventually the Carib, too, would reach the brink of extinction. Today a couple of hundred Caribs live in a reserve on Dominica, and descendants of Caribs and African slaves, the "Black Caribs" (also called Garifuna), populate the Caribbean coast of Central America.

According to the records, two more Indian peoples apart from the Carib had regular contact with buccaneers and pirates: the Cuna of the Darién (the easternmost region of Panama) whom the buccaneers encountered during their frequent raids on Spanish towns in the area, and the Mosquito Indians, inhabitants of the coast of the same name, in modern-day Honduras and Nicaragua. Contact with the latter was to a large degree maintained via the logwood settlements in the Bays of Campeche and Honduras.

There is certainly evidence for material influences on the European arrivals, most notably in form of the Carib practice of smoking meat in a *buccan*, which supposedly gave the buccaneers their name, the common buccaneer usage of Indian dugout canoes, and the logwood cutters' and other Caribbean renegades' habit of sleeping in hammocks off the ground.[8]

It is interesting to note Stephen Snelders's suggestion that "in reaction [to colonial aggression] the Caribs developed strategies of piracy that resembled those of the buccaneers. In their periaguas, large canoes that carried fifty or sixty warriors, they moved swiftly among distant islands conducting hit and run raids armed mainly with the bow and arrow, with which they were as skilled as the buccaneers with their muskets."[9] It is hard not to wonder whether it was really the Caribs who were influenced by the buccaneers. Could it not have been the other way around? Maybe it was the buccaneers who adopted Carib raiding techniques—techniques which, for all we know, probably preceded the colonial era. Is this just another overlooked gift the Europeans received from American and Caribbean Indians?[10]

Influences on the sociocultural level are much harder to determine, but some parallels are nonetheless striking. While the traditional forms of the Cuna's social organization appear too stratified for a comparison with Caribbean buccaneer and pirate communities,[11] descriptions of both the Caribs and the Mosquito Indians suggest non-authoritarian societies "distinguished by their sense of democracy and taste for equality."[12]

According to Irving Rouse, the Caribs "relied more upon fishing than upon agriculture; their villages were only semipermanent; they had more elaborate canoes [than the Arawak]; placed greater emphasis upon warfare; choosing their leaders by prowess in fighting rather than by inheritance; lacked elaborate ceremonies; had no worship of idols; and were cannibals."[13] It would without doubt be too bold to construe a Carib influence on the practices of certain buccaneer captains who allegedly enjoyed gnawing on their enemies' hearts,[14] but all other points listed by Rouse can also be applied to the buccaneers and pirates (at least if we agree that hunting and raiding are closer to fishing than to agriculture). Rouse even speaks of "elected temporary war chiefs"[15] among the Caribs and claims: "Although he [the Carib chief] was treated with deference, he had little authority. The Carib men were individualists, and they looked down upon the Europeans for taking orders."[16]

Many features reported in connection with the Mosquito Indians— apparently the most regular Indian companions of the buccaneers and pirates[17]—seem to agree deeply with the Caribbean buccaneer and pirate culture as well. Their warfare was reputedly highly organized, the office of their chiefs was not hereditary, and they see, in the description of Paul Kirchhoff, "a man who has been wronged [as a] a coward if he does not avenge himself"[18]—a notion with central significance for golden age pirate ethics.[19]

Whether there were indeed significant sociocultural influences of the Caribbean's Indian peoples on the buccaneers and pirates remains unresolved, though attempting to find answers would certainly make for fascinating research.

3. "Social Origins," or The European Legacy: Golden Age Piracy and Cultural Studies

NOT ALL HISTORIANS HAVE understood the culture of the Caribbean buccaneers and pirates as radically separate from the European culture that provided their backgrounds. Franklin W. Knight, for example, notes:

> Although the buccaneers were essentially stateless individuals, they retained strong links with the general culture and society with which they were familiar. ... The buccaneers did not try, as did the American Maroons, to create a separate culture and society. Buccaneers had their culture and knew their social origins quite well. What they sought—at least for a time—was freedom from the restraints and obligations of that culture and that society. Most of those who survived the occupational hazards of their profession, returned to those societies.[1]

Such an assessment suggests a study of golden age piracy as a European subculture rather than as its own culture. The term *subculture* is of course, as Chris Jenks fittingly put it, "an idea with a highly restricted currency."[2] Subculture Studies build on various different definitions of the concept.[3] It will be used here in its widest common sense: as a cultural form showing distinctive features while remaining heavily influenced and dependent on the majority culture in which it has developed.

3.1. Fashion, Food, Fun, Lingo: Circumscribing the Pirate Subculture

Some general features that often demand initial attention within the study of subcultures are demography, style, and cultural identifiers.

As we have seen, not much is known about the origins of the buccaneering community. Throughout the decades, however, its demography became more apparent and has been described with some consistency. David Cordingly writes that the buccaneers "included soldiers and seamen, deserters and runaway slaves, cutthroats and criminals, religious refugees, and a considerable number of out-and-out pirates,"[1] while Marcus Rediker summarizes as follows: "The early makers of the tradition were what one English official in the Caribbean called 'the outcasts of all nations'—convicts, prostitutes, debtors, vagabonds, escaped slaves and indentured servants, religious radicals, and political prisoners, all of whom had migrated or been exiled to the new settlements 'beyond the line.'"[2] This blend of outsiderdom would later still characterize the golden age pirates who, in the words of Philip Gosse, were "a queer lot,"[3] "a collection of the flotsam and jetsam of the seas."[4]

The average age of the golden age pirate has been estimated at twenty-seven by Cordingly.[5] It must be assumed that it was somewhat higher among the buccaneers—especially if one extends the buccaneer community to their accomplices and beneficiaries ashore: the crooked merchants, smugglers, and prostitutes. It was a community that was predominantly white and almost exclusively male.

The flamboyant pirate fashion prominently featured in Howard Pyle's paintings, in all commercial representations of piracy, and at every Mardi Gras seems to have some historical ground, even though many details are almost certainly fanciful artistic additions. It seems, for example, unlikely that pirates wore earrings, at least not to the degree highlighted in pirate representations of the 20th century. There is also no documentation of golden age pirates being tattooed. Modern Euro-American tattooing only became popular in connection with the European exploration of the South Pacific— an era which had hardly commenced when the golden age of piracy ended.[6] Then again, Europe's own tattooing tradition never died out completely,[7] practices of tattooing and scarification are reported from both Carib and Mosquito Indians,[8] and in 1691 the heavily tattooed Jeoly (Giolo), from the island of Meangis (most probably today's Miangas, Indonesia's northern-most island), arrived with William Dampier's crew in London.[9] So, contrary to what is sometimes argued, it is difficult to imagine that the practice was altogether unknown to golden age pirates.

Most historians seem to agree that pirates wore, at least on occasion, elaborate clothing. Robert C. Ritchie suggests that the golden age pirates "delighted in such brilliant costumes because in Europe the use of luxury fabrics was confined by law to the upper classes. On the peripheries of empire they could indulge themselves and flaunt sumptuary legislation."[10] One of the most detailed summary of the pirates' fashion exploits can be found in Stephen Snelders's *The Devil's Anarchy*:

> At a time when seamen generally wore short blue jackets, checkered shirts, long canvas trousers or baggy breeches, red waistcoats, and scarves around their necks, pirates added all kinds of plundered silks, velvets, and brocades to their outfits—flouting the dress codes of European society, where luxury fabrics were only worn by the upper classes. Labat notes ... that after capturing a caique, Captain Daniel's men 'dressed themselves up in all kinds of fine clothes, and were a comical sight as they strutted around [Aves] Island in feathered hats, wigs, silk stockings, ribbons and other garments.' When Compaen finally returned to Holland his men were 'richly and costly attired,' and his arms were covered with gold jewelry. According to Senior, Compaen's contemporary, the English pirate Kit Oloard, dressed himself 'in black velvet trousers and jackets, crimson silk socks, black felt hat, brown beard and shirt collar embroidered in black silk.' Pirate captains wore flashy adaptations of the costumes of gentlemen in a deliberate flouting of social dress codes that emphasized the pirates' penchant for enjoying the moment and taunting their social 'betters.'[11]

Certain popular representations of gaudy pirate dress might have still been exaggerated. Angus Konstam at least suspects that "the figure of Captain Hook with his wig, ruffed sleeves, and trimmed beard would have been laughed out of the Caribbean."[12] Konstam also challenges the idea that pirates wore fancy clothing even on deck.[13] He sees the practice confined to land excursions and stresses that "at sea, practicality took precedence over elegance"—which suggests that during voyage the pirate appearance would not have been all that different from that of ordinary sailors.[14]

The style of the original Hispaniola buccaneers was a different story altogether. According to Cordingly, "they dressed in leather hides and, with their
butchers' knives and bloodstained appearance, looked and smelled like men
from a slaughterhouse."[15]

As far as other (sub)cultural identifiers are concerned, the three most noted
among the Caribbean buccaneers and pirates concern *food/drink*, *entertainment*, and *language*.

Food/Drink

Pirate cuisine should not be overrated. There are a fair number of "pirate
cookbooks" available, but it is often hard to see how they differ from ordinary Caribbean or Madagascan cookbooks. One dish, however, is commonly
recognized as a pirate special: *salmagundi*. One of the more sophisticated
descriptions reads as follows:

> Meat of any kind—including turtle, duck, or pigeon—was roasted,
> chopped into chunks, and marinated in spiced wine. Imported salted
> meat, herring, and anchovies also were added. When ready to serve,
> the smoked and salted meats were combined with hard-boiled eggs
> and whatever fresh or pickled vegetables were available, including
> palm hearts, cabbage, mangoes, onions, and olives. The result was
> stirred together with oil, vinegar, garlic, salt, pepper, mustard seed,
> and other seasonings.[16]

While this does sound somewhat appealing—at least to omnivores—the
only other notable pirate special does not: "In times of scarcity they would
eat *crackerhash*—broken-up ship's biscuit shaken in a bag with the week's
leftovers."[17] Worth mentioning are also the pirates' table manners—or lack
thereof. Edward Lucie-Smith reports: "One source gives a most graphic
description of piratical table-manners, which bears out the impression of
chaos: 'They eat in a very disorderly manner, more like a kennel of hounds
than like men, snatching and catching the victuals from one another.... It
seemed one of their chief diversions and, they said, looked martial-like.'"[18]

Unsurprisingly—given the popular image—more buccaneer and pirate
focus was laid on drink. Here, a few classics were created, first and foremost,
rumfustian, "a blend of raw eggs, sugar, sherry, gin, and beer ... no rum."[19]
Other popular pirate drinks included: *Sir Cloudesley*, "brandy mixed with

a little beer, frequently sweetened or spiced, with an added touch of lemon juice" (apparently called *flip* without the lemon);[20] *mum*, a "strong beer made of wheat and oat malts and flavoured with herbs";[21] and *bumboo*, according to Jenifer G. Marx, "a concoction of rum, water, sugar, and nutmeg,"[22] though Philip Gosse makes this the teetotaler pirate drink by describing it as nothing but "limes, sugar and water" and suggesting that it was enjoyed by the few "dry" pirates.[23]

Entertainment

There are no indications that buccaneers or pirates excelled in any way in the arts. Most of them reportedly enjoyed music, usually provided by musicians who often joined them as forced men. Musicians among Bartholomew Roberts's arrested crew reported ill-treatment to the degree where "their fiddles and often their heads broke, only for excusing themselves or saying they were tired when any fellow took it to his head to demand a tune."[24]

Apart from music and drinking, "the pirates' only other recreation was to hold mock trials," as Neville Williams put it.[25] This unique type of political satire might certainly count as an artistic innovation. Captain Johnson shares an account "of these merry trials" that he found "diverting" in the *General History*:[26] After the "attorney-general" presents judge and jury "a sad dog, a sad, sad, dog" who "not having the fear of hanging before his eyes ... went on robbing and ravishing man, woman and child, plundering ships' cargoes fore and aft, burning and sinking ship, bark and boat, as if the devil had been in him," the judge turns to the prisoner: "Hearkee me, Sirrah, you lousy, pitiful, ill-looked dog; what have you to say why you should not be tucked up immediately and set a-sun-drying, like a scarecrow? Are you guilty or not guilty?" The prisoner pleads not guilty, upon which the judge replies: "Say so again, Sirrah, and I'll have you hanged without any trial." Attempts by the prisoner to speak in his defense are rejected by the judge, very much to the delight of the attorney-general who reckons: "Right my lord! For if the fellow should be suffered to speak he may clear himself, and that's an affront to the court." The end of the trial is worth quoting at length:

> Pris.: Pray, my Lord, I hope your Lordship will consider—
> Judge: Consider! How dare you talk of considering? Sirrah, Sirrah, I never considered in all my life. I'll make it treason to consider.

Pris.: But I hope your lordship will hear some reason.

Judge: D'ye hear how the scoundrel prates? What have we to do with reason? I'd have you know, rascal, we don't sit here to hear reason; we go according to law. Is our dinner ready?

Attor.-Gen.: Yes, my lord.

Judge: Then heark'ee, you rascal at the bar, hear me, Sirrah, hear me. You must suffer for three reasons; first, because it is not fit I should sit here as judge and nobody be hanged; secondly, you must be hanged because you have a damned hanging look; and thirdly, you must be hanged because I am hungry; for know, Sirrah, that 'tis a custom that whenever the judge's dinner is ready before the trial is over, the prisoner is to be hanged of course. There's law for you, ye dog! So take him away, gaoler.[27]

Language

To develop its own vernacular and jargon is undeniably a strong feature of any subculture, as, in the words of Peter Lamborn Wilson, "a language (however crude and jury-rigged) is a culture, or at least the sure sign of an emerging culture."[28] The Caribbean buccaneers and pirates not only mixed different languages within the multinational buccaneer and pirate communities (Philip Gosse even speaks of a "sort of Esperanto"[29]), but also partook in the distinct language of the seafarers. The resulting idioms were further modified as the Caribbean buccaneers and pirates formed an exclusive community of high sea raiders with "their own slang and code words."[30] Among these, cuss words apparently featured prominently. A passenger on a ship taken by Bartholomew Roberts's crew reports that "there was nothing heard among the pirates all the while, but cursing, swearing, dam'ing and blaspheming to the greatest degree imaginable."[31] In this regard, pirate eloquence might have reached its apex with Captain Fly, the last renowned Anglo-American pirate captain of the golden age. One of his outbursts reported in Captain Johnson's *General History* is directed at a Mr. Atkinson, who, after having been taken prisoner as the passenger of a captured vessel, dared to ask for his freedom:

Look ye, Captain Atkinson, it is not that we care a t-d for your company, G-d d-n ye; G-d d-n my soul, not a t-d by G-d, and that's fair; but

G-d d-n ye, and G-d d-n's b-d and w-ds if you don't act like an honest man G-d d-n ye, and offer to play us any rogues' tricks by G-d, and G-d sink me, but I'll blow your brains out. G-d d-n me, if I don't.[32]

3.2. "Villains of All Nations"? Piracy and (Trans)Nationality

The Caribbean buccaneers' and pirates' relation to the concept of the nation is somewhat curious. They have been described as "supranational"[1] and "multinational"[2]—but also as an "outlaw nation."[3] Obviously, some of these apparent contradictions can easily be resolved by acknowledging different understandings of the term. There is a basic difference in whether "nation" refers to a "nation-state" or to a community of people with a shared destiny. In the latter sense, Frank Sherry's description of the golden age pirates as an "outlaw nation" does make as much sense as Stephen Snelders's or Marcus Rediker's suggestions that the golden age pirates were anti-nationalist because they did not hold the nation-state in high regard.

As this is not the place to venture too deep into a discussion of the meaning and usage of the term, the following analysis will focus only on the relation of the Caribbean buccaneers and pirates to the *nation-state*. This is a crucial part of their history and identity, and one that appears to have created some misunderstandings. The biggest of these is the assertion that the Caribbean buccaneers developed a culture that indeed went beyond the nation-state concept. This seems to have become a commonplace view among radicals sympathizing with the buccaneer and pirate culture, though there is little evidence to support it. In fact, available evidence indicates rather the opposite.

Part of the problem lies in wrong assumptions. The authors of "Pirate Utopias," for example, write: "The Caribbean islands in the second half of the 17th century were a melting pot of rebellious and pauperised immigrants from across the world."[4] This is a rather bold statement. Aside from the controversial description of "rebellious and pauperized," the *vast* majority of the people who migrated to the Caribbean in the 17th century came from Spain, the British Isles, and France. There were small numbers of Dutch and Scandinavians, and a smattering of individuals from other European countries who found their way to the ports of the European Atlantic coast and arranged a passage to the West Indies. Of course, there were the African slaves who arrived in ever greater numbers towards the end of the century, but to count them as part of a "melting pot" and a community of "immigrants" appears almost cynical.

The buccaneer communities reflected the general migrant patterns of the Caribbean. It is true that men of *some* nations united as buccaneers, but there were not many. At least 80 percent of the buccaneers seemed to have been English, French, or Dutch, the rest consisting mainly of Scots, Irishmen, Portuguese, and Scandinavians. Most non-European men who lived among the buccaneers worked for them as slaves. Furthermore, many of the buccaneers united because they shared a common sentiment: namely, "a bitter hatred" of the Spanish.[5] In this sense, calling their union a transnational model would be similar to hailing the allied forces during World War II as transnationalists. Still, some radical commentators appear so convinced of the alleged buccaneer and pirate anti-nationalism that they offer contradictions in terms: "As long as they could hunt Spaniards it didn't matter to them whether they did so with English, French, Dutch, or Portuguese privateering commissions. They were not interested in, and absolutely unwilling to die for, the interstate rivalries of the European powers."[6] The reality of the opportunistic politics in the colonial Caribbean seems much more aptly illustrated by the following anecdote: "[The French and English] combined very amicably in a murderous attack upon the natives, and then fell to quarrelling about the possession of an island to the south."[7]

It appears that national unities among the buccaneers were as pragmatic and ephemeral as national alliances in times of war. It is therefore not surprising that the composition of buccaneer crews changed with the political (colonial) climate in the Caribbean. As Peter Earle writes in connection with the Nine Years War (1689–1697): "Former pirate now fought former pirate as privateers in the service of England, France, Holland, and Spain."[8] Accordingly, many buccaneers—most famously the knighted Henry Morgan—were hailed as national heroes. The related anti-Spanish sentiments are confirmed to this day. Recent US reprints of Philip Gosse's pirate books read on the back cover:

> The author has also endeavored to point out the tremendous influence
> of the buccaneers upon our country and people. Had it not been for
> these picturesque sea rovers, England would have been hard pressed
> to retain her hold in the New World, and the United States might now

be under Spanish rule. The downfall of Spain's sea power was largely due to the sea rovers and, no matter how despicable they were in many ways, we cannot fail to feel a debt of gratitude to the buccaneers.[9]

The buccaneers' national allegiances became particularly obvious after the English takeover of Jamaica in 1655. From this year on, the English and French buccaneers were strongly divided along national lines. Angus Konstam states that "while buccaneers always fought under their national flags, increasingly they did so against fellow buccaneers."[10] In fact, mutual raids become so frequent that "neither the French in Tortuga nor the English in Port Royal could suppress their own pirates unless they could be sure that the other side would do the same."[11] For many decades, "buccaneers did not usually attack the colony from which the leader of the band originated or the citizens related in nationality or culture to the majority of the members."[12] Men like Jérémie Deschamps, who "obtained ... simultaneous commissions from both the English and the French and successfully played one power against the other,"[13] were certainly the exception.

Some buccaneers—mostly those oppressed by the English or French at home—even sided with the Spanish. Irish captains working in the Spanish fleet were particularly prominent, like Don Philip Fitz-Gerald,[14] or John Murphy who guided the Spanish attacks on Tortuga in 1634/35.[15] A historian's description of the crews of Spanish privateers in the 1680s includes "Corsicans, Slavonians, Greeks."[16] Slavonians and Greeks were hardly heard of in the English- and French-dominated buccaneer crews, and the presence of Corsicans among the Spanish would indicate a transposition of their animosity towards the French colonizers of their island into the West Indies.

The eventual rejection of any national allegiance marks the biggest difference between the golden age pirates and the buccaneers who preceded them. Among the golden age pirates, the anti-national notion becomes stronger, not least in the adoption of the Jolly Roger as their truly transnational symbol. Some golden age pirates might have indeed "no longer thought of themselves as English or Dutch or French but as pirates,"[17] and "as people without a nation."[18] When formulated categorically, however, the following assumptions still appear problematic: "Pirates doubly defied the national-ist logic ... first by forming themselves of the 'outcasts of all nations' (mix-ing together the seafarers of all countries, as suggested earlier), and second by attacking vessels regardless of the flag flying at the mainmast, making all nations and their shipping equal prey."[19] First, the composition of golden age pirate crews appears not to have differed all that much from those of buc-caneer crews. Anglo-American sailors, in fact, appeared particularly domi-nant now. If the analysis of David Cordingly is to be believed, then "of the 700 known pirates who were active in the Caribbean between 1715 and 1725, almost all came from the English-speaking Atlantic and Caribbean basin. Englishmen accounted for the majority, at 35 percent; 25 percent were American, 20 percent came from the West Indies, 10 percent were Scottish, and 8 percent were from other seafaring countries, such as Sweden, Holland, France, and Spain."[20] Some historians even suggest that the Cross of St. George was still flown on occasion, alongside the Jolly Roger (and not as a decoy as many other flags were).[21] Second, pirate captains and crews were certainly not beyond national prejudice, especially with respect to the Spanish. Bartholomew Roberts and his crew, for example, were said to hate men from Bristol (I don't know why) as much "as they do the Spaniards."[22] Roberts apparently also held a grudge against the Irish,[23] not to mention the hatred towards folks from Barbados and Martinique documented on his flag that marked two skulls *ABH*, "a Barbadian's head," and *AMH*, "a Martinican's head," respectively.

At the same time, it is without doubt true that "in a world increasingly dominated by the nation-state system, it became an issue of first importance that pirates 'had not any Commission from any Prince or Potentate,'"[24] and that they posed a significant threat to the nation-state—both confirmed by their reputation as "banditti of all nations"[25] and the fact that legal scholars have called piracy the "first international crime."[26] There are also examples of pirate crews that seem to have truly transcended national rivalries. Neville Williams tells us that the crew of Augustino Blanco, a Spanish pirate who operated from the Bahamas for twenty years, "consisted of English, Scots, Spaniards, Portuguese, mulattos and negroes."[27] Furthermore, we must not forget the symbolic significance of a free-roaming community under a non-nation-state flag, especially in light of the ever increasing regulation of migration and border control. The golden age pirates' obvious defiance of any such notions must stand as a powerful reminder of how things ought to be, and as an unrelenting protest against conditions that force millions of people every year to cross borders under hazardous circumstances. Many of these people do not survive these crossings—some of them drown in the very waters that the golden age pirates once proudly roamed. By taunting the nation-state, the golden age pirates expressed a simple truth: namely, that "it signified nothing what part of the World a man liv'd in, so he Liv'd well.'"[28]

3.3. Satanists and Sabbatarians: Piracy and Religion

The hatred expressed by many European powers (and individuals) against the Spanish was often coated in religious terms. For Angus Konstam, the English privateers of the 16th century already combined "religious and national rivalry with greed."[1] Hans Turley calls the hatred of Catholics a "principle" among the buccaneers,[2] to the degree where those tortured and murdered during the raid on Panama in 1671, "were not seen as individuals by Morgan and the other buccaneers [but] were lumped together as Spanish Catholics, hated by late-seventeenth-century English readers leery of 'popish plots.'"[3] Stephen Snelders states that the buccaneers' "motivation was as much lust for booty as hatred of Spaniards and Catholics,"[4] and the introduction to Howard Pyle's *Book of Pirates* adds—in characteristically dramatic manner—that "in this left-handed war against Catholic Spain many of the adventurers were, no doubt, stirred and incited by a grim, Calvinistic, puritanical zeal for Protestantism."[5] It is not surprising then, that the buccaneers have also been referred to as "corsarios luteranos."[6] In this sense, the killing of monks, friars, or priests[7] ought not be interpreted as proof of an anti-Christian, but rather an anti-Catholic, agenda. The religious rivalries even complicated national loyalty, for example when "protestant Frenchmen served aboard English pirate ships."[8]

The anti-Catholic fervor of the Protestant buccaneers was often justified as a reaction to the Spanish oppression of the Indian communities.[9] It is said that Montbars the Exterminator, one of the cruelest buccaneer captains of legend, "joined the buccaneers after reading a book which recorded the cruelty of the Spaniards to the American natives."[10] However, it seems somewhat surprising that people who themselves raided Indian settlements and kept

Indian slaves would have been so scandalized by the Spaniards doing the same. One cannot help but suspect that these stories mostly emerged as part of the so-called Black Legend—the deliberate distortion of Spanish culture, conduct, and politics by their rival powers in the 16th and 17th centuries. The controversy around whether Spain deserved the accusations levied against it, or whether it was the victim of ideological propaganda, remains unresolved. Assumptions that the Spanish were the worst of all European colonizers seem rather simplistic, however, aside from the consideration that the ranking of atrocities is a very dubious act in itself.

Religious adherence among Catholic buccaneers—who often formed their own units[11]—was strong as well. The French Catholic buccaneer crews of the late 17th century were said to keep their own priests.[12] Famous is the story of Captain Daniel shooting a member of his crew who had appeared inattentive during mass and responded to a rebuke with a blasphemy.[13]

John Masefield's suggestion that "no crew put to sea upon a cruise without first going to church to ask a blessing on their enterprise"[14] may be exaggerated, but Christian identity was certainly important for many buccaneers and pirates. Philip Gosse attributes the uprising against Captain Sharp in 1681 (documented in Basil Ringrose's account of the journey[15]) to the captain's "ungodliness."[16] According to Captain Johnson, during the golden age, the articles of each pirate crew were usually sworn upon the Bible,[17] and some pirate captains, most notably the "worshipful Mr. Roberts,"[18] were known "Sabbatarians."[19] (Once, Roberts's crew apparently tried to woo a clergyman traveling on a taken vessel into joining them and, upon his refusal, "kept nothing which belonged to the church, except three prayer books and a bottle-screw."[20]) Protestant-Catholic rivalries had not disappeared either. Captain Condent apparently humiliated captured priests because Condent's master had been a papist.[21] To Nathaniel North, papists still seemed better than infidels, however. After he and his crew had a number of children with Madagascan women, he decided to "place fortunes for them in the hands of some honest priest, who would give them a Christian education (for he thought it better to have them papists, than not Christians)."[22]

There are also references to pirates who ventured into the Red Sea because they meant to attack non-Christian ships: one of them stated at his trial that it seemed "very lawful ... to plunder ships and goods etc., belonging to the ene-mies of Christianity"; another "proposed to mutiny and cruise in the Red Sea, 'for, said he, there can be no harm in robbing those Mahometans';"[23] finally, one Darby Mullins was convinced to engage in piracy by "it being urged that the robbing only of infidels, the enemies of Christianity, was an act, not only lawful, but one highly meritorious."[24] Such arguments were not welcome by all pirates though. Philip Gosse tells us that one pirate crew threw their captain in irons after he had refused to attack a Dutch merchantman and declared that he only wanted to attack "Moorish ships." (Later, the captain's "scruples against taking Christian ships eased enough to permit him to bag a brace of English ships.")[25]

Alongside tales about pirate adaptations of Christianity, there are also those of rejection, ridicule, and derision. The poor French buccaneer killed by his captain for lack of reverence during mass has already been mentioned. David Cordingly tells the story of one Dolzell, "a forty-two-year-old Scotsman described by the Ordinary as pernicious and dangerous, [who] refused to look at the Bible and threatened to tear it up,"[26] and states that "a surprising number of pirates showed defiance at the end and refused to die in the contrite and penitent manner expected of them."[27] Captain Johnson relates that during the mutiny on the *Elizabeth*, one Alexander Mitchel told the captain, "D-n your blood … no preaching," before his co-mutineer and later pirate captain William Fly interfered: "*Damn him, answered Fly, since he's so devilish godly, we'll give him time to say his prayers, and I'll be parson. Say after me. Lord, have mercy on me. Short prayers are best, so no more words, and over with him, my lads.*" Then, "the captain still cried for mercy, and begged an hour's respite only, but all in vain; he was seized by the villains, and thrown overboard."[28] Similar attitudes seemed to have been dominant among the crew of Captain John Gow. According to Johnson, on one occasion one of their victims "desired earnestly to live till he had said his prayers, but the villains not moved thereat, said, *D—n you, this is no time to pray,* and so shot him dead."[29]

These anecdotes portray the pirates in a way in which many radicals fancy them: secular, sacrilegious, anti-clerical. Marcus Rediker suggests that some pirates indeed "embraced Lucifer, the most rebellious of angels,"[30] and Captain Johnson says of Blackbeard that "some of his frolics of wickedness were so extravagant as if he aimed at making his men believe he was a devil incarnate."[31] However, when the pirates "inverted the values of Christianity"[32] and "turned the religious world, like the social world, upside down,"[33] they only confirmed how deeply rooted in the Christian tradition their culture was. The Jolly Roger might illustrate this best: "All of the chosen symbols on the black colors were rooted in the Christian cultures from which most of the pirates came. [Sailors and freebooters] played with these godly symbols, drew on their power, manipulated and inverted them, and gave them new meanings derived from their own maritime experience."[34] Positive or negative, reverent or defiant, earnest or mocking, Christian symbolism stood at the heart of golden age pirate culture. Stephen Snelders's observation that "in a society where all social relationships are laden with religious ideology, heresy and apostacy are both political choices and modes of social rebellion"[35] only confirms this—as does the dependence on the dark side of Christianity to induce fear: "In announcing that they were on their way to hell, pirates affirmed what respectable, God-fearing people never tired saying about them—that they were devils, all bound for hell."[36]

Pirate satanism was, however, not the only possible way to render the pirates' Christian attachments subversive. The rather revolutionary Deism championed by Captain Misson and his "lewd priest"[37] sidekick Caraccioli was probably an invention of Captain Johnson, but with respect to buccaneers the following observation might very well be based in fact: "According to Father du Tertre ... they owed allegiance only to God, except for whom, the earth whereon they lived had no masters than themselves."[38]

3.4. A Colorful Atlantic? Piracy and Race

Paul Gilroy, in his seminal study The Black Atlantic, contends:

> I have settled on the image of ships in motion across the spaces between Europe, America, Africa, and the Caribbean as a central organising symbol for this enterprise and as my starting point. The image of the ship—a living, micro-cultural, micro-political system in motion—is especially important for historical and theoretical reasons that I hope will become clearer below. ... It should be emphasised that ships were the living means by which the points within the Atlantic world were joined. They were mobile elements that stood for the shifting spaces in between the fixed places that they connected. Accordingly they need to be thought of as cultural and political units

rather than abstract embodiments of the triangular trade. They were something more—a means to conduct political dissent and possibly a distinct mode of cultural production.[1]

Considering that Linebaugh and Rediker have pointed out that one aspect of the Atlantic ship of the late 17th century was its potential for "a setting of resistance,"[2] the prospect of an anti-racist pirate ship—arguably, the most resisting ship of them all—becomes tremendously enticing. It could be seen as "a place to which and in which the ideas and practices of revolutionaries ... escaped, re-formed, circulated, and persisted."[3] While some historians have suggested that such anti-racist pirate ships did indeed exist, the question remains whether this suggestion is really convincing. There does not seem to be any disagreement concerning the fact that the buccaneers kept both American/Caribbean Indians and Africans as slaves. Not only are slaves listed as possible payments in Exquemelin's example for a buccaneer contract,[4] but the buccaneering accounts of Exquemelin, Dampier, and Ringrose are all dotted with references to Indians and "negroes" working involuntarily on their boats.[5] In fact, Exquemelin even writes that "the said buccaneers are hugely cruel and tyrannical towards their servants; insomuch that commonly these had rather be galley slaves in the Straits, or saw brazilwood in the rasp-houses of Holland, than serve such barbarous masters."[6] One buccaneer account tells us that some of their indentured laborers "fell sick of a disease called coma, which was a sort of despair from which they surely died, since it was the effect of brutality in treatment and want of rest."[7] It has also been alleged that some regular buccaneer haunts, like the logwood communities along the Mosquito Coast, doubled as early slave trading posts.[8]

Towards the end of the buccaneering era, when many Caribbean islands had been turned into plantation societies and become dependent on the slave trade, so-called slave raids became a prime factor in the feuds between rival buccaneer communities. Maurice Besson writes that in the 1680s, the French buccaneers "so frequently raided Jamaica, where, for the greater profit of the young plantations of Saint Domingue, they made off with negroes and negresses, that on the coast of Saint Domingo ... the island of Jamaica was called simply Little Guinea."[9]

The situation does not appear much different among the golden age pirates. Captain Johnson's stories are dotted with references to Indians and

Africans working under slave-like conditions on pirate ships or onshore pirate rendezvous.[10] His account of Captain Condent, for example, starts with the story of an Indian who threatens to blow up the ship after being beaten by different members of the crew. Once the heroic Condent killed him, "the crew hacked him into pieces, and the gunner ripping open his belly, tore out his heart, broiled and ate it."[11]

The relations between golden age piracy and slavery were particularly pronounced in Madagascar where the pirates "went to war [for local tribes] and were paid in friendship and slaves. Because of their knowledge of local conditions they rapidly became intermediaries in the slave trade. Merchants who desired to enter the trade were advised that an incoming ship could expect to find someone ready to assist. That someone was invariably a pirate."[12] The center of this enterprise was the pirate trading port at St. Mary's, established in 1691 by the former buccaneer Adam Baldridge. Baldridge collaborated closely with the unscrupulous New York businessman Frederick Philipse who turned into the "chief broker for the Madagascar pirates."[13] Captain Johnson describes a typical trip between New York and St. Mary's as a delivery of "wine, beer, etc." and a return journey with "300 slaves."[14] According to Earle, "when the slavers returned to America they usually carried, in addition to their shackled cargo, a score or so of pirates who now wanted to return to civilisation after their years of looting and boozing in the Indian Ocean."[15] In 1697, Baldridge's post was destroyed by locals in resistance to his slave trading endeavors.

It seems that when golden age pirates took slave ships, the slaves were often seen as part of the cargo[16] and presumably sold at the next best opportunity; many an illegal slave trader along the West African coast apparently made good business with the pirates, particularly those who had erected camp at the Sierra Leone River, "men who in some part of their lives have been either privateering, buccaneering or pirating."[17] There are also accounts of slaves being burned with the ships the pirates decided to destroy, most famously when "eighty of those poor wretches" died after Bartholomew Roberts's crew set ablaze the *Porcupine* at Whydah—in Captain Johnson's estimation, "a cruelty unparalleled."[18]

A lot of the anti-slavery sentiments that radicals claim for the golden age pirates seem to rest on wishful thinking. The only pirate captain who ever explicitly condemned the slave trade was Captain Misson—almost certainly a fictional character. There might be a misinterpretation of Marcus Rediker's convincing theory that the golden age pirates posed a threat to the slave trade and "had to be exterminated in order for the new trade to flourish."[19] There is much reason to believe that "the defeat of Roberts and the subsequent eradication of piracy off the coast of Africa represented a turning point in the slave trade and even in the larger history of capitalism,"[20] that "in the immediate aftermath of the suppression of piracy, Britain established its dominance on the western coast of Africa," and that "in the decade of the 1730s England has become the supreme slaving nation in the Atlantic world."[21] The threat that the golden age pirates posed to the slave trade, however, did not come from the pirates' struggle for equal rights or an early abolitionist conviction, but from interrupting its routes, stealing its "cargo," and making its ventures more costly. In fact, it was not even a threat that affected the slave trade per se—it only affected the government-sponsored and -protected slave trade trying to protect its monopoly. The golden age pirates posed a threat to the official slave trade in about the same way in which distributors of pirated porn pose a threat to the San Fernando Valley porn industry. This, too, might be disruptive of corporate capitalism—but it is hardly a noble cause to embrace.

Several stories do tell of good relations and mutual aid between Caribbean buccaneers/pirates and the Indian societies of the region. According to Pérotin-Dumon, "in 1619–20 French corsairs, returning from a failed venture that had led them through the Atlantic and the Pacific, stayed several months with Caribs in Martinique. Their sick and starving crew members were rescued and adopted by the Indians. The evocative account of their stay reveals that it had been a current practice for several decades."[22] Philip Gosse tells us about a Captain Blewfield who, in the 1660s "was known to be living among the friendly Indians at Cape Gratia de Dios on the Spanish Main,"[23] a Captain Bournao who sailed in the same area in the early 1680s and "was much liked by the Darien Indians,"[24] and a Captain Christian who, likewise, "was on very friendly terms" with the Darién Indians some twenty years later.[25] Exquemelin provides similar examples,[26] and Dampier recalls a rather emotive episode in which his crew picks up a Mosquito Indian on a remote Atlantic island after he had been left behind three years earlier.[27] Manuel Schonhorn indicates that pirate captain Francis Spriggs found refuge among the Mosquito Indians in 1726.[28] Finally, there is the famous account of Lionel Wafer who lived among the Cuna for several months in 1681.[29]

Other accounts paint a different picture. Dampier, for example, writes about the Indians on the Pearl Islands: "Here are but a few, poor, naked Indians that live here; who have been so often plundered by the privateers that they have but little provision; and when they see a sail they hide themselves; otherwise ships that come here would take them, and make slaves of them; and I have seen some of them that have been slaves."[30] Given the sometimes euphoric radical embrace of the logwood cutters of the Bays of Campeche and Honduras— many of whom were part-time buccaneers and all of whom maintained strong relations to the buccaneering community—Dampier's account of some of their exploits is even more troubling: "[They] often made sallies out in small parties among the nearest Indian towns; where they plundered and brought away the Indian women to serve them at their huts, and sent their husbands to be sold at Jamaica."[31] Such practices seem confirmed by Exquemelin who tells us about the Indians of Boca del Toro ending business relations with the buccaneers "because the pirates committed many barbarous inhumanities against them, killing many of their men on a certain occasion, and taking away their women."[32]

Exquemelin's writings also offer an insight into what was probably a rather typical buccaneer attitude towards the Indians of the Caribbean. He calls the Indians of the De las Perlas Islands "properly savages" in comparison to "civil people" (purportedly including the buccaneers).[33] In a more general comment, he refers to Indians as "a barbarous sort of people, totally given to sensuality and a brutish custom of life, hating all manner of labour, and only inclined to run from place to place, killing and making war against their neighbours, not out of any ambition to reign, but only because they agreed not with themselves in some common terms of language."[34]

Radical buccaneer and pirate sympathizers seem to frequently misunderstand the occasional alliances between buccaneers and Indian communities when interpreting them as proof of the buccaneers' decency and openness. Most of these alliances were based on the buccaneers and the Indians fighting a common enemy: the Spanish. While this shared animosity may have created unions between English, French, and Dutch, it is not clear just how close the allied communities felt or how much they respected each other. These were opportunistic unions caused by contingent historical circumstances,[35] and concluding that Indians in the Caribbean were treated well by the buccaneers because they assisted them in raiding Spanish towns[36] is like concluding that Indians in North America were treated well by the French because they assisted them in their wars against the British.

Things look even more troubling when we consider that some of the Indian communities with whom the buccaneers were most friendly, like the Cuna or the Mosquito, apparently also assisted them in slave trading operations. Anthropologists have suggested that among the Cuna, the "object of waging war was evidently to take slaves"[37] (presumably primarily for their own use, albeit it seems likely that they would have traded with Europeans), and that "the Mosquito took prisoners to be sold as slaves to the Whites."[38]

The occasional alliances between pirates and the native people of Madagascar have to be seen in a similar light. They, too, were mainly fostered by pragmatic interests: many locals appreciated the pirates' firepower when fighting their rivals, while the pirates appreciated the supply of slaves that such assistance promised them. However, more than once, pirates were "committing such outrageous acts that they came to an open rupture with the natives."[39] This corresponds to the situation along Africa's west coast where the relations between pirates and Africans mostly concentrated on trade, often enough in slaves. Violent confrontations erupted here as well.[40]

There is also confusion about the presence of Indians on buccaneer and pirate ships. Mosquito Indians especially seemed to have been popular companions among the buccaneers and "through the frequent converse and familiarity these Indians have with the pirates ... [they] sometimes [went] to sea with them, and remain[ed] among them for whole years, without returning home."[41] However, no account would give the impression that they sailed as equal members of the crew. They might not have had the status of slaves, but their popularity mainly seemed to rest on their qualities as superb lookouts, expert fishermen (in Dampier's famous assessment, "one or two of them in a ship, will maintain 100 men"[42]), and mean fighters.[43] As Peter Earle puts it: "No wonder pirates liked to have one or two of these paragons in their crews."[44]

The evidence is unclear about the role of Africans on pirate ships. The observation that "'Negroes and Molattoes' were present on almost every pirate ship"[45] means for many that they were integral parts of the crew. This, however, is less evident than it may seem. Some Africans might have indeed been full crew members (Caesar of Blackbeard's crew is a famed example[46]), but many might have been used as laborers, some as slaves, and some might have been simple "plunder." The seventy-five Africans captured on Bartholomew Roberts's ships in 1722, for example, were not put on trial for piracy (like all the Europeans) but rather sold into slavery.[47] This might only indicate the prejudices of the British officials, but it more likely suggests that most Africans on pirate ships were known to be laborers or slaves rather than full crew members.

Even if some stories of prominent black members in buccaneer and pirate crews are based in fact, the overall picture still seems to point to these as exceptions rather than the anti-racist rule; certainly, there are no popular images of black pirate captains. Marcus Rediker's suggestion that "Black pirates also made up part of the pirates' vanguard, the most trusted and fearsome members of the crew who boarded a prospective prize,"[48] and Kenneth J. Kinkor's claim that "Blacks are accordingly found as leaders of predominantly white crews"[49] are therefore surprising. Rather, we might concur with David Cordingly, who writes: "The pirates shared the same prejudices as other white men in the Western world. They regarded black slaves as commodities to be bought and sold, and they used them as slaves on board their ships for the hard and menial jobs: working the pumps, going ashore for wood and water, washing and cleaning, and acting as servants to the pirate captain."[50]

This is not to say, however, that the complex history of piracy and race contains no encouraging examples. Hugh Rankin's assertion that pirates "did not seem *too* concerned about color differences"[51] might be very well true, not least because of the undeniable truth that "shared feelings of marginality are a solvent which can ameliorate racial ... barriers."[52] Kinkor's assessment that "it would seem that the deck of a pirate ship was the most empowering place for blacks within the eighteenth-century white man's world" rings equally true.[53] It can finally be assumed with Frank Sherry that "blacks, who usually feared a return to slavery even more than they feared death, were often far more willing than white pirates to fight and die in defense of their ships and their freedom."[54]

The potential prospect of living a relatively free life on a pirate ship would have been inspiring for many slaves on the Caribbean Islands and a motivation for revolt. Apparently, authorities in the American colonies did indeed fear alliances of pirates and revolting slaves. Frank Sherry tells of at least one occasion: "The largest recorded mass escape of black slaves at this time took place in Martinique, where fifty blacks, supposedly stirred up by a white man, had risen against their French master and had fled the island 'to seek a career in piracy.'"[55] Still, there might be not enough reason for the enthusiasm expressed in the following conclusion—even if it truly was the perfect pirate answer to the ship allegory laid out by Paul Gilroy:

> Piracy clearly did not operate according to the black codes enacted and enforced in Atlantic slave societies. Some slaves and free blacks found aboard the pirate ship freedom, something that, outside of the maroon communities, was in short supply in the pirates' main theater of operations, the Caribbean and the American South. Indeed, pirate ships themselves might be considered multiracial maroon communities, in which rebels used the high seas as others used the mountains and the jungles.[56]

Regardless of the exact levels of racism and anti-racism among the Caribbean buccaneers and pirates, and regardless of whether it is really apt to call them maroon communities,[57] there is one aspect that such optimistic estimations will always cloud: no matter how subversive, how rebellious or how countercultural the buccaneers and pirates might have been, they were still part of a colonial enterprise of oppression, enslavement, and genocide. This cannot be denied, no matter the angle of analysis. Whatever their exact role, the buccaneers and pirates were overwhelmingly of European origin and, along with their fellow European settlers, took possession of lands and resources that they stole from other people. This is true not only in the case of those who, like many buccaneers, were directly involved in the European colonial expansion, but also of those who, like many golden age pirates, sabotaged certain aspects of it. A history of genocide still haunts the Caribbean— and so does the buccaneers' and pirates' part in it.

3.5. Anne Bonny, Mary Read, and a Co-opted Myth: Piracy and Gender

As stated earlier, the buccaneer community preceding the golden age pirates was almost exclusively male. Some historians have even called the buccaneers "woman-haters" to whom "women and comfort spelt softness and defeat,"[1] and who were "loathing the sight of a kirtle as intensely as any cloistered monk."[2] While such an assumption seems surely exaggerated, the following description might, unfortunately, come close to the truth: "For them women had but the single attraction of their sex; they were playthings to be used and cast aside."[3] Ulrike Klausmann and Marion Meinzerin, authors of *Women Pirates*, agree: "Their attitude towards women was also no different from that of the other invaders. For the buccaneers, women were simply goods to be robbed, traded, or shared in 'brotherly' fashion."[4]

Whatever the individual buccaneers' attitudes towards women were, their community remained exclusively male throughout the 17th century and this exclusivity extended into the pirates' golden age. We know of exactly two female pirates who sailed on golden age pirate ships (even though there might have been more who remained undetected): Mary Read and Anne Bonny.

While the story of Read and Bonny is definitely an inspiring story of liberation, the political credit often seems misplaced. It has been suggested repeatedly that their story proved the potential that pirate society offered to individuals—"even women"—to liberate themselves. Had it been up to the pirates, however, Read and Bonny would not have even been allowed on their ships, and their presence did not indicate a subversion of patriarchal norms. They had to enter pirate society disguised as men and had to maintain their right to be part of it by "acting as men." How much they seemed to identify with this role is piercingly expressed in Anne Bonny's comment on the execution of her former lover, John "Calico Jack" Rackam: "she was sorry to see him there, but if he had fought like a man, he need not have been hanged like a dog."[5] Mary Read and Anne Bonny's story confirms that "just as freedom meant noble status for a man, it meant male status for a woman"[6]—among golden age pirates as much (or more so?) as in other communities. What makes their story a story of liberation is the remarkable strength and perseverance they demonstrated in a male-dominated world. In other words, Mary Read and Anne Bonny owe their achievements to *themselves* and not to pirate society. Yes, they "proved that a woman could find liberty beneath the Jolly Roger,"[7] but this in spite of, not thanks to the pirates. In this sense, assertions that make them part of a "utopian experiment beyond the reach of the traditional powers of family, state, and capital"[8] are misleading and suggest an unmerited progressiveness of pirate communities while diminishing the feat of two determined women who defied the odds.

Read and Bonny's story is special—and better known than those of other women defying the odds by passing as men—because of its sensationalist pirate frame. Other than that, there is nothing characteristically piratical about it, not even the respect they gained from fellow pirates for their "man-like" qualities; everyone respected them for that. They have created a "many-sided and long-lasting legacy"[9] within mainstream society because "Anne Bonny's life at sea, in particular, seems to have followed the career of the archetypal female warrior as a 'high-mettled heroine who disguises herself as a soldier or sailor and goes to war for her beloved.'"[10] Along these lines, Marcus Rediker sums up the two most compelling aspects of the story of Mary Read and Anne Bonny well when he writes that "their very lives and subsequent popularity represented a subversive commentary on the gender relations of their own times as well as 'a powerful symbol of unconventional womanhood' for the future."[11]

Aside from the glamorous story of Read and Bonny, the search for other images of women in the context of golden age piracy seems to prove John C. Appleby's remark that studies of individual heroines "inflate the importance of women's role in piracy and piratical activity."[12] Some individual examples notwithstanding,[13] there seems to be no real-life pirate "named Pussycat, who was truly the meanest of all the pirates."[14] The most common connection between piracy and the fate of women is that "wherever piracy flourished so did the business of prostitution."[15]

The buccaneer diaries as well as Captain Johnson's *General History* abound with tales of women being mistreated and raped. Exquemelin tells us about the Cape of Gracias à Dios: "The custom of the island is such that, when any pirates arrive there, every one has the liberty to buy for himself an Indian woman, at the price of a knife, or any old axe, wood-bill or hatchet."[16] Captain Johnson reports that Edward England's crew "forced [women] in a barbarous manner to their lusts";[17] that after Thomas Anstis's crew had taken a female prisoner, "twenty-one of them forced the poor creature successfully, afterwards broke her back and flung her into the sea";[18] that after two girls had been taken by members of John Gow's crew, they "were hurried onboard, and used in a most inhumane manner";[19] and that after Thomas Howard had retired from pirate life and married an (Asian) Indian woman, "being a morose ill-natured fellow, and using her ill, he was murdered by her relations."[20]

These stories correspond with the picture of the general social traits of the buccaneers and pirates. Common sense suggests that David Cordingly is right in claiming that "in the tough, all-male regime of the pirate community, many of the men cultivated a macho image which was expressed in hard drinking, coarse language, threatening behaviour and casual cruelty."[21] Ulrike Klausmann and Marion Meinzerin remark that "the band of buccaneers were no less racist or sexist than the rest of the world in the eighteenth century."[22]

Despite all this, the world of the golden age pirates does hold a fascination for many radical women. Some historians provide curious explanations of this phenomenon, first and foremost David Cordingly:

> As all women know and some men can never understand, the most interesting heroes of literature and history have always been flawed characters. ... So it is with the pirates. They are seen as cruel, domineering, drunken, heartless villains, but it is these very vices which make them attractive. A degenerate and debauched man is a challenge which many women find hard to resist.[23]

A more palatable theory is that the appeal of the pirates' reach for freedom is strong enough to shatter the gender conventions of the pirates themselves. This does not make the real pirate community of the golden age any better than it was; but, as Klausmann and Meinzerin tell us in the opening pages of *Women Pirates*, it allows a group of radical feminists to occupy a luxury yacht under the Jolly Roger. This is a perfect example of the radical potential of golden age piracy that this book tries to highlight, a potential that lies in relating to the anti-authoritarian and rebellious spirit that lies at golden age piracy's core, elevating it beyond its cultural context, and situating it within contemporary struggles. In this sense, there are without doubt many women pirates out there, some certainly "leaping about and looking for booze and doing whatever pirate girls do regardless of what they're supposed to be doing."[24]

3.6. On Sodomites and Prostitutes: Piracy and Sexuality

Given the all-male character of the Caribbean buccaneer and pirate communities, lively discussions among historians about the frequency of homosexual encounters abound. These were further fueled by the *matelotage* system of the Hispaniola and Tortuga buccaneers in which two men united to live and share their possessions together. This system must not be over-interpreted, however. Exquemelin's original description of *matelotage* reads as follows:

It is a general and solemn custom amongst them all to seek out for a
comrade or companion, whom we may call partner, in their fortunes,
with whom they join the whole stock of what they possess, towards
a mutual and reciprocal gain. This is done also by articles drawn and
signed on both sides, according to what has been agreed between
them. Some of these constitute their surviving companion absolute
heir to what is left by the death of the first of the two. Others, if they
be married, leave their estates to their wives and children; others to
other relations.[1]

This sounds mostly like a sophisticated, yet predominantly pragmatic
union between buddies, and not much like "a kind of homosexual union."[2]
In fact, some *matelots* were known to share their wives after women arrived
on Tortuga in 1666 (they were French prostitutes meant to be bought as
wives by the buccaneers—this was part of a scheme to "civilize" them). Cruz
Apestegui relates an amusing account of the event:

The men had formed a semicircle on the beach; many had shaved.
The women were brought to land in groups of ten. ... They did not
dare look at the men ... and the men seemed indifferent. Suddenly,
one of the brothers stepped out and, leaning on his rifle, began a long
ceremonious, grandiloquent speech. He spoke of good behaviour, of
honesty, of loyalty and even of redemption. He ended by telling the
women that since they had chosen this line of conduct they should
continue at all costs and correct their bad instincts. The sale took
place without incident.[3]

According to Angus Konstam, the *matelotage* system died out in the 1670s.[4]
This, of course, does not answer the question of whether homosexual
encounters among Caribbean buccaneers and pirates were more frequent
than those within other all-male societies, like prison populations, army
units, or crews of common sailors. In his candidly titled *Sodomy and the Pirate
Tradition*, B.R. Burg strongly argues for the existence of a buccaneer culture
(extending into the period of golden age piracy) in which "homosexual contact" was not only "the ordinary form of sexual expression,"[5] but "the only
form of sexual expression engaged in,"[6] while "heterosexual contact" was
considered "a genuinely exotic manner of sexual expression."[7]

The opinions of other historians on Burg's suggestion are rather uniform. David Cordingly diplomatically states that "it is an interesting theory and there may be some truth in it, but there is little evidence to prove things one way or the other."[8] Peter Earle writes that "the argument rests on the fanciful deduction from the undoubted fact that most pirate ships were all-male institutions, and no real evidence is given to support the assertion."[9] Robert C. Ritchie states that "although I agree that homosexuality existed, there is too much evidence of pirate heterosexuality in too many sources for me to accept this thesis."[10] And Hans Turley, who also exploits the homo-erotic theme in his *Rum, Sodomy and the Lash*, concludes that "the evidence for piratical sodomy is so sparse as to be almost nonexistent."[11]

All this is rather persuasive. Burg's theory, while alluring, offers little in terms of evidence and some of its sociopsychological considerations are rather dubious. There is no reason to believe that the ratio between homosexuals on the one hand and hetero- or bisexual men engaging in homosexual practices on the other would have been significantly higher among the Caribbean buccaneers and pirates than in other all-male communities. As P.K. Kemp and Christopher Lloyd matter-of-factly put it: "Since cruises often lasted a year or more, homosexuality was common. Such was the custom of the coast."[12]

Further, the accounts that reach us of the buccaneers' and pirates' sexual life ashore indicate a predominantly heterosexual orientation. Hans Turley quotes from a 1740 *History of Jamaica*: "Wine and women drained their [the buccaneers'] wealth to such a degree that in a little time some of them became reduced to beggary. They have been known to spend 2 or 3000 pieces of eight in one night; and one of them gave a strumpet 500 to see her naked."[13] Cruz Apestegui says that the famed buccaneer captain "[Henry] Morgan blamed the prostitutes for the state of poverty in which his men lived."[14] Captain Johnson speaks of Blackbeard's crew and the "liberties he and his companions often took with the wives and daughters of the plant-ers,"[15] of Edward England's and Olivier La Buse's crews "making free with the negro women,"[16] of Captain Cornelius's crew falling ill because of "being too free with the women,"[17] and of Captain North's crew living in Madagascar as "polygamists."[18]

Even if the buccaneer and pirate crews did not include an above average number of homosexuals, however, the acceptance of same-sex encounters within them seemed much stronger than in comparable groups. While "the Royal Navy periodically conducted savage antibuggery campaigns to repress homosexual practices among men who might often be confined at sea for years,"[19] "it is ... significant that in no pirate articles are there any rules against homosexuality."[20] Even if the occasional maltreatment of a pirate engaging in homosexual acts is reported,[21] it might very well be true that "life in the pirate settlements offered greater latitude of individual behavior than anywhere else."[22] It might also be true that for homosexual exploits, the pirate crews were "probably just about the safest place you could be."[23] In this sense, there are implications of Burg's theory that seem convincing: "Among the men of this seafaring community, there was no need to hide sexual orientation, and the anxieties, psychological disruptions, and psychopathological difficulties that often result from this type of guilt and repression did not emerge."[24] And:

> The almost universal homosexual involvement among pirates meant homosexual practices were neither disturbed, perverted, exotic, nor uniquely desirable among them, and the mechanisms for defending and perpetuating such practices, those things that set the modern homosexual apart from heterosexual society, were never necessary. The male engaging in sexual activity with another male aboard a pirate ship in the West Indies three centuries past was simply an ordinary member of his community, completely socialized and acculturated.[25]

According to Michel Foucault, the general history of homosexuality in European society begins in the early 18th century (right around the golden age of piracy) with homosexuality becoming "one of the forms of sexuality when it was transposed from the practice of sodomy onto a kind of interior androgyny, a hermaphrodism of the soul. The sodomite had been a temporary aberration; the homosexual was now a species."[26] Foucault concludes that

> it is the agency of sex that we must break away from, if we aim— through a tactical reversal of the various mechanisms of sexuality—to counter the grips of power with the claims of bodies, pleasures, and knowledges, in their multiplicity and their possibility of resistance. The rallying point for the counterattack against the deployment of sexuality ought not to be sex-desire, but bodies and pleasures.[27]

3.7. Escaping Discipline and "Biopolitics": The Pirate Body

If, as Foucault suggests, the control exerted over the individuals in European societies since the 18th century is to a significant degree exerted as a control over their bodies, it is worth comparing the body of the pirate with the body of the controlled and disciplined European worker. This comparison becomes particularly revealing when tying Foucault's analysis to Marcus Rediker's descriptions of the merchant ship.

With respect to the control of the proletariat, Foucault points out that "there had to be established a whole technology of control," namely "schooling, the politics of housing, public hygiene, institutions of relief and insurance, the general medicalization of the population, in short, an entire administrative and technical machinery."[1] An important part of this control was the regulation of space:

> Disciplinary space tends to be divided into as many sections as there
> are bodies or elements to be distributed. One must eliminate the
> effects of imprecise distributions, the uncontrolled disappearance
> of individuals, their diffuse circulation, their unusable and danger-
> ous coagulation; it was a tactic of anti-desertion, anti-vagabondage,
> anti-concentration. Its aim was to establish presences and absences,
> to know where and how to locate individuals, to set up useful commu-
> nications, to interrupt others, to be able at each moment to supervise
> the conduct of each individual, to assess it, to judge it, to calculate its
> qualities or merits. It was a procedure, therefore, aimed at knowing,
> mastering and using. Discipline organizes an analytical space.[2]

Foucault calls this process focusing on the control of the individual an "anatomo-politics of the human body."[3] This politics is soon accompanied— and eventually surpassed—by a "bio-politics of the population,"[4] described by Foucault as

> something new emerging in the second half of the eighteenth
> century: a new technology of power, but this time it is not disciplin-
> ary. ... Unlike discipline, which is addressed to bodies, the new
> nondisciplinary power is applied not to man-as-body but to the
> living man, to man-as-species. To be more specific, I would say that
> discipline tries to rule a multiplicity of men to the extent that their

multiplicity can and must be dissolved into individual bodies that can
be kept under surveillance, trained, used, and, if need be, punished.
And that the new technology that is being established is addressed
to a multiplicity of men, not to the extent that they are nothing more
than their individual bodies, but to the extent that they form, on the
contrary, a global mass that is affected by overall processes characteristic of birth, death, production, illness, and so on. So after a first
seizure of power over the body in an individualizing mode, we have
a second seizure of power that is not individualizing but, if you like,
massifying, that is directed not at man-as-body but at man-as-species.
After the anatomo-politics of the human body established in the
course of the eighteenth century, we have, at the end of that century,
the emergence of something that is no longer an anatomo-politics of
the human body, but what I would call a 'biopolitics' of the human
race.[5]

Marcus Rediker's brilliant study of seamen culture in the 17th and 18th
centuries, *Between the Devil and the Deep Blue Sea*, provides many examples
that confirm Foucault's theory. Rediker illustrates the original disciplining of
individuals in the context of the 17th-century "expansion of the world capitalist economy and its need for new types of authority and discipline" when
pointing out

> that any worker who came from a workshop, a farm, or an estate to
> the ship entered not only one of the great technological wonders of
> the day but a new set of productive relations as well. The seaman was
> confined within a spatially limited laboring environment, forced to
> cultivate regular habits and keep regular hours, and place in coopera-
> tive relationships with both other workers and the supervisors of his
> labor. In all of these ways, the seaman's experience foreshadowed
> that of the factory worker during the Industrial Revolution. New
> patterns of authority and discipline were crucial to the process of
> industrialization.[6]

Confirming Foucault's timeline, Rediker writes "that questions of authority and labor discipline at sea took on special significance after 1690."[7] He
also describes the gradual shift from anatomo-politics to bio-politics within

the authoritarian institution of the ship: "The ship was a 'total institution' in which the captain had formal powers over the labor process, the dispensing of food, the maintenance of health, and general social life on board the ship. Such formal and informal controls invested the captain with near-dictatorial powers and made the ship one of the earliest totalitarian work environments."[8] And: "Control over physical punishment and food equaled a measure of control over health, a matter of special importance among men who notoriously suffered from yellow fever, malaria, dysentery, and scurvy. A fully documented case from 1731 reveals how these issues of discipline, food, and health intertwined in an intricate spiral of power and authority."[9]

Through various shifts and modifications, these processes have continued to define our politics to this day, leading Giorgio Agamben to conclude that "only because politics in our age had been entirely transformed into biopolitics was it possible for politics to be constituted as totalitarian politics to a degree hitherto unknown."[10] Adding that, "from this perspective, the camp—as the pure, absolute, and impassable biopolitical space (insofar as it is founded solely on the state of exception)—will appear as the hidden paradigm of the political space of modernity,"[11] the subversive imagery of the pirate ship comes alive. While as a "total institution" any ship can resemble a camp, as an archetype, it remains opposed to any such notion: it indicates movement, floating, the crossing of borders; it defies the "disciplining" of space. In this context, the organization of the pirate ship differed radically from the rigid regime on navy and merchant ships by all accounts. Instead of disciplined individual sailors assigned to certain times, places, and duties, we encounter a wild variety of bodies and "a regime that was relaxed and easy-going."[12] Christopher Hill describes the difference as one "between a factory and a co-operative,"[13] which gives yet another boost to the pirate ship's anti-disciplinary and anti-bio-political symbolism. While "Western civilization has had persistent trouble in honoring the dignity of the body and diversity of human bodies,"[14] it seems that the golden age pirates escaped this flaw.

3.8. Eye Patches, Hook Hands, and Wooden Legs: Piracy and Disability

It must be one of the most notable achievements of the Caribbean buccaneers and pirates that they are about the only communities in Western history that have managed to make physical disabilities look cool.[1] Many kids have gone through strenuous efforts to sport peg legs and hook hands at Halloween, while the much more easier applied eye patch is a perennial costume favorite.

Even though the presence of peg legs, hook hands and eye patches was certainly exaggerated by popular representations of the pirates in the 20th century, there are indications that they were a fairly common reality among buccaneers and pirates. Some successful buccaneer captains, like the Dutch Cornelis Corneliszoon Jol or the French François le Clerc, wore peg legs. So did the pirate vouching for the captured Captain Mackra in one of the best-known episodes from Johnson's *General History,*[2] and William Phillips, a pirate standing trial in Boston in 1724.[3] Peter Earle also cites documents that mention one "John Fenn, 'a one-handed man,'"[4] and "'Domingo Fort, a lame man whom the Court deem'd an object of pity.'"[5] Furthermore, the declaration of loyalty that Captain Tew received from his crew in the *General History* seems telling: "A gold chain, or a wooden leg, we'll stand by you."[6]

The implications of readily embracing physical disabilities in the pirate context are not all rosy, of course. The main reason that pirates lift disability beyond deficiency is that they render it as proof of manliness, courage, and audacity. As documented in the eye-opening volume *Disabled Veterans in History*, this has always distinguished disabled war veterans— "often…sentimentally lionized in the abstract as heroes"[7]—from other disabled men and women in Western societies to the point of causing rifts in the movement for disability rights (especially since disabled veterans were often not perceived as the recipients of welfare but of "a reward for…service"[8]). Obviously, this points to a political ambivalence. While the acceptance of disability itself must be uncompromisingly welcomed, the underlying values must not. The 2005 documentary film *Murderball*, dedicated to disabled quad rugby players, strikingly exemplifies the problem: while the players' attitudes towards their disabilities are tremendously uplifting, the film's underlying values of traditional masculinity are deeply troubling. What remains nonetheless remarkable in the pirate context is that those who did suffer a permanent disability were often provided for by their crew. While the articles of the buccaneer crews already included payments for injuries that led to permanent disabilities, these payments were compensations rather than actual social service. The golden age pirate crews introduced the latter. Article number six of the pirate crew sailing under Captain George Lowther promised not only compensating payment for "he that shall have the misfortune to lose a limb" but also to "remain with the company as long as he shall think fit."[9] Even pirate historians bereft of all romanticism concede: "While injured naval ratings were cast ashore to beg or starve, pirates looked after their own. Pirate codes were revolutionary social charters for their time."[10] In Marcus Rediker's words, the golden age pirates "anticipated a modern idea that many consider one of the most humane of our times: creating their own social security system."[11]

An exciting, yet enormously challenging project would be to relate the discussion of pirate homosexuality to that of pirate disability, providing a fascinating case study for the relatively new field of Crip Theory whose most prominent exponents declare that "compulsory heterosexuality is contingent on compulsory able-bodiedness, and vice versa."[12] If, as Robert McRuer suggests in *Crip Theory: Cultural Signs of Queerness and Disability*, "Crip Theory comes along to show that another world is possible,"[13] then maybe the golden age pirates provided first glimpses in this respect. The subversive dimensions of the acceptance of physical disability within their ranks seem clear. While "Western nations embraced capitalism, a system predicated on able-bodied ideals,"[14] the pirates' embraced plunder and zero-production, a system predicated on multi-bodied ideals.

The difference between the two arguably best-known disabled characters in the history of Anglo-American literature, Louis Stevenson's Long John Silver and Herman Melville's Ahab, is striking. Long John Silver, though hardened and fearsome, is an entertaining and cheerful fellow. Ahab is bitter and dedicates his entire life to revenge on the creature he holds responsible for his disability. Rosemarie Garland Thomson, author of the groundbreaking *Extraordinary Bodies: Figuring Physical Disability in American Culture and Literature*, locates Ahab's anger in the fact that, in his mind, he is "not a self-made man, but a whale-made man."[15] This makes him "the quintessential disabled figure in American literature"[16] whose "disabled body exposes the illusion of autonomy, self-government, and self-determination and underpins the fantasy of absolute able-bodiedness."[17]

If there is truth in this analysis, it would render the acceptance of physical disability among the golden age pirates a simultaneous rejection of this illusion and an acknowledgment of our individual incompleteness and dependence on others—a truly revolutionary concept in the face of the cutthroat individualism that has become the ideological foundation of Western life.

4. "Ni dieu, ni maître":
Golden Age Piracy and Politics

4.1. From "Brethren of the Coast" to a
"Commonwealth of Outlaws": Pirate Organization

A LOT HAS BEEN written about the egalitarianism and democratic character—or "the defiant, stateless, peripatetic collectivity"[1]—of the Caribbean buccaneer and pirate communities. Even non-radical historians concede that the "pirate communities were ... democracies. A hundred years before the French Revolution, the pirate companies were run on lines in which liberty, equality and brotherhood were the rule rather than the exception."[2] The buccaneers' society has been called "the most democratic institution in the world of the seventeenth century"[3] and "essentially communistic in its organisation."[4] Maritime metaphors like "floating democracy"[5] or "floating republic"[6] abound.

According to Jenifer G. Marx, "the Tortuga buccaneers began to call themselves the Brethren of the Coast about 1640. To become a member of this democratic confraternity a man vowed to subscribe to a strict code called the Custom of the Coast."[7] It is worth quoting Exquemelin's version of the code at length:

> They [the buccaneers] agree upon certain articles, which are put in writing, by way of bond or obligation, which every one is bound to observe, and all of them, or the chief, set their hands to it. Herein they specify, and set down very distinctly, what sums of money each particular person ought to have for that voyage, the fund of all the payments being the common stock of what is gotten by the whole expedition; for

otherwise it is the same law, among these people, as with other pirates.
No prey, no pay. In the first place, therefore, they mention how much
the captain ought to have for his ship. Next the salary of the carpenter,
or shipwright, who careened, mended and rigged the vessel. This commonly amounts to one hundred or a hundred and fifty pieces of eight,
being, according to the agreement, more or less. Afterwards for provisions and victualling they draw out of the same stock about two hundred pieces of eight. Also a competent salary for the surgeon and his
chest of medicaments, which usually is rated at two hundred or two
hundred and fifty pieces of eight. Lastly they stipulate in writing what
recompense or reward each one ought to have, that is either wounded
or maimed in his body, suffering the loss of any limb, by that voyage.
Thus they order for the loss of a right arm six hundred pieces of eight,
or six slaves; for the loss of a left arm five hundred pieces of eight, or
five slaves; for a right leg five hundred pieces of eight, or five slaves;
for the left leg four hundred pieces of eight, or four slaves; for an eye
one hundred pieces of eight, or one slave; for a finger of the hand the
same reward as for the eye. All which sums of money, as I have said
before, are taken out of the capital sum or common stock of what is
got by their piracy. For a very exact and equal dividend is made of the
remainder among them all. Yet herein they have also regard to qualities and places. This the captain, or chief commander, is allotted five
or six portions to what the ordinary seamen have; the master's mate
only two; and other officers proportionate to their employment. After
whom they draw equal parts from the highest even to the lowest mariner, the boys not being omitted. For even these draw half a share, by
reason that, when they happen to take a better vessel than their own,
it is the duty of the boys to set fire to the ship or boat wherein they are,
and then retire to the prize they have taken. They observe amongst
themselves very good orders. For the prizes they take, it is severely
prohibited to every one to usurp anything in particular to themselves.
Hence all they take is equally divided, according to what has been said
before. Yea, they make a solemn oath to each other not to abscond, or
conceal the least thing they find among prey. If afterwards any one is
found unfaithful, who has contravened the said oath, immediately he
is separated and turned out of the society.[8]

The most noteworthy aspects of this account seem to be: 1. the collective and egalitarian character of formulating the articles and agreeing on them; 2. the relative equality in shares; 3. the communal arrangement of provisions; 4. the compensation for injuries; 5. the high value put on honesty and justice; 6. the punishment by exclusion; 7. the mentioning of slaves as currency.

What distinguishes the buccaneers' articles most notably from those of the golden age pirates are the division of shares (they would become more equitable in the golden age), and the temporal character of the contract that remains bound to a certain expedition rather than constituting a design for possible long-term company. The listing of slaves as potential currency hints at a general problem of the buccaneer society (later—albeit under different circumstances—reproduced by the golden age pirates): while "brotherhood" and solidarity are emphasized *among* the buccaneers, others remain excluded from their moral universe. This, however, does not change the fact that "the buccaneer vessels were autonomous units operating on a democratic regime,"[9] and that "there should ... be no doubt that, where a sailor on a 'normal' ship was subject to a despotic regime, among the Brethren of the Coast he was considered a man among equals with a full vote in the adoption of decisions."[10]

Many of the buccaneers' principles later got translated into the articles of the golden age pirates. Captain Johnson lists three detailed sets of articles: those of the companies of Captain Bartholomew Roberts, Captain George Lowther, and Captain John Phillips. Johnson writes that the articles of Captain Phillips were "taken *verbatim*,"[11] while those of Bartholomew Roberts only constitute "the substance of the articles, as taken from the pirates' own informations,"[12] since, before being captured, "they had taken care to throw overboard the original they had signed and sworn to."[13] There is no specification with respect to the origins of Captain Lowther's articles, quoted here:

> I. The Captain is to have two full shares; the master is to have one share and a half; the doctor, mate, gunner and boatswain, one share and a quarter.
> II. He that shall be found guilty of taking up any unlawful weapon on board the privateer or any prize by us taken, so as to strike or abuse

one another in any regard, shall suffer what punishment the Captain
and majority of the Company shall think fit.

III. He that shall be found guilty of cowardice in the rime of engagement shall suffer what punishment the Captain and the Majority shall
think fit.

IV. If any gold, jewels, silver etc., be found on board of any prize or
prizes, to the value of a piece-of-eight, and the finder do not deliver it
to the quartermaster in the space of 24 hours, shall suffer what punishment the Captain and the Majority shall think fit.

V. He that is found guilty of gaming, or defrauding another to the
value of a shilling, shall suffer what punishment the Captain and
majority of the Company shall think fit.

VI. He that shall have the misfortune to lose a limb, in time of
engagement, shall have the sum of £150 sterling, and remain with the
company as long as he shall think fit.

VII. Good quarter to be given when called for.

VIII. He that sees a sail first, shall have the best pistol or small arm on
board her.[14]

   All of these articles are confirmed by those of Phillips and Roberts. Their
articles are more specific, however, when it comes to the sort of punishment
handed out—"death or marooning"—and include some interesting details
not found among Lowthers's: Phillips's articles announce punishment
for those who sign up with another pirate ship "without the consent of our
company," for those who "strike another whilst these articles are in force," for
those who "smoke tobacco in the hold without a cap to [the] pipe, or carry a
candle lighted without a lanthorn," and for those who "shall not keep [their]
arms clean, fit for an engagement." They end with the threat that "if at any
time you meet with a prudent woman, that man that offers to meddle with
her, without her consent, shall suffer present death"—a remark interesting
as much for its apparent necessity and the no-nonsense punishment as for
the troubling specification of "prudent" women.[15] Roberts's articles stipulate
the need "to keep [the] piece, pistols and cutlass clean and fit for service," and
include some further specifics, especially with respect to the democratic and
communal structures on board: "Every man has a vote in affairs of moment;
has equal title to the fresh provisions or strong liquor at any time seized, and

[may] use them at pleasure unless a scarcity … make it necessary for the good of all to vote a retrenchment." The articles also include a punishment for theft from a fellow company member that is reminiscent of the buccaneers' original practice: "slitting the ears and nose of him that was guilty, and set him on shore, not in an uninhabited place but somewhere where he was sure to encounter hardships." Furthermore, "no boy or woman" was allowed among the men, and "if any man were found seducing the latter sex, and carried her to sea disguised, he was to suffer death." Also, "lights and candles [were] to be put out at eight o'clock" and "if any of the crew after that hour still remained inclined to drinking, they were to do it on the open deck." (A measure, as Captain Johnson comments, that meant to "give a check to [the pirates'] debauches" but "proved ineffectual.") "The musicians," finally, were "to have rest on the sabbath day, but the other six days and nights none, without special favour."[16]

Overall, the articles indicate a radically egalitarian and democratic community—a characteristic that to many defines the backbone of the golden age pirates' social experiment. It is worth quoting Robert C. Ritchie's interpretation of this at length:

> The marauders wandered the seas, dividing and coalescing like amoebas. They lived in small self-contained democracies that usually operated by majority vote, with the minority asked (or forced) to leave in order to keep the remaining crew in happy consensus. The marauders raided fishing vessels, towns, ships—virtually anything ashore or afloat—in search of supplies or loot. Every so often they would return to a safe port to sell their goods and enjoy themselves. Shortly thereafter they would go back to sea again. Many men remained at sea for years, or retired to small settlements in out-of-the-way places, or else crossed into non-European societies. In this sense they were marginal men freed from social conventions, living beyond restraint except for the few rules they set for themselves. Few ever returned home again; the sea, hunger, thirst, disease, and fighting all took their toll and most of the survivors preferred the free life of the pirate to the restrictive conventions of European society. By the end of the seventeenth century the deep-sea marauders were increasing in number and extending their range. As we shall see, changing values, prosperity,

and defense needs made piracy less and less attractive to officials and merchants, who gradually withdrew their sponsorship. The field was left to marauders, who continued to cluster around the periphery of empire.[17]

One important aspect of the golden age pirates' organization—also in comparison to that of the buccaneers—was the role of the quartermaster, attractively described by Captain Johnson: "The quartermaster's opinion is like the mufti's among the Turks. The captain can undertake nothing which the quartermaster does not approve. We may say the quartermaster is a humble imitation of the Roman Tribune of the people; he speaks for and looks after the interest of the crew."[18] He was also appointed by the crew. A court transcript of a pirate trial tells of one John Archer who, "being asked how he came to be quartermaster, answered that the company thought him the fittest man for a quartermaster and so chose him."[19] It seems that the pirate crews made a conscious effort to, first, reduce the considerable gap that still existed between captain and crew among the buccaneers, and, second, keep the captain in check (almost like one of Clastres's "mechanisms" employed by Indian communities to avoid the formation of authoritarian chiefdom). According to Joel Baer, the encroachment on the captain's privileges was also expressed in the physical features of the pirate ship itself: "The upper work on a pirate ship was sometimes removed, cabin and all, primarily to improve its agility but also to eliminate class differences among its crew."[20]

All important decisions were made by the pirates' council. Marcus Rediker suggests that "the decisions the council made were sacrosanct. Even the boldest captain dared not challenge its power. Indeed, councils removed a number of captains and other officers from their positions."[21] Rediker also illustrates the democratic founding moments of a pirate company: "In their founding moment, after a mutiny or when the crew of an overcrowded vessel split and formed a new pirate ship, the crew came together in a council to elect their captain, draw up their articles, and declare to be true to each other and their flag, all amid merriment, festivity, eating, drinking, and the firing of cannon."[22]

The versions of the pirate articles that existed on different ships appeared so similar in essence that they indeed constituted a common golden age pirate culture or, in Frank Sherry's words, a *commonwealth*: "Because of

the similarity of these ships' articles, pirates—like the citizens of any commonwealth—always shared a general understanding of what was acceptable
and unacceptable behavior, no matter what port they might be visiting or
what ship they might be serving on."[23] This, without doubt, contributed to
the strong sense of community shared across the various golden age pirate
companies. For one, "meeting brother pirates suspended their sense of isola-
tion."[24] But there was more to it: "There was the joy of meeting another pirate,
saluting him with the great guns and celebrating in days of 'mutual civilities'
the solidarity of the pirate community, 'l'ensemble du peuple pirate,' in its
war against all the world."[25] Marcus Rediker sums up this sense of pirate solidarity in *Villains of All Nations*:

> Pirates did not prey on one another. Rather, they consistently showed
> solidarity for each other, a highly developed group loyalty. Here I turn
> from the external social relations of piracy to the internal in order to
> examine this solidarity for their 'fellow creatures' and the collectiv-
> istic ethos it expressed. Pirates had a profound sense of community.
> They showed a recurring willingness to join forces at sea and in port,
> even when the various crews were strangers to each other.[26]

Frank Sherry, in his usual dramatic manner, suggests that "in the course
of their war, fought over millions of square miles of ocean from Madagascar
to the Bahamas to the steamy west coast of Africa, the pirate outlaws became
fused into a loose-knit but powerful confederacy—a rough-and-ready republic of rebels, robbers, and rovers";[27] a "true 'Republic of Rogues'"[28] whose
members "met each other again and again, on ships and in safe ports, working
together and drifting apart."[29]

Marcus Rediker has done formidable work on tracing this community in
more detail. He comes to the conclusion that about 4,000 pirates roamed the
sea during the golden age's heyday from 1716 to 1726, with about 1,500–2,400
sailing in about 20 to 25 ships at a time.[30] Most of these, as an impressive chart
in *Villains of All Nations* illustrates,[31] were in some concrete way connected
to one another through shared experiences as crew members or amicable
splits of pirate companies. According to Rediker, "it was primarily within
and through this network that the social organization of the pirate ship took
on its significance, transmitting and preserving customs and meanings, and
helping to structure and perpetuate the pirates' social world."[32]

As Captain Johnson relates through his protagonist Captain Misson, the strong sense of solidarity among the golden age pirates was also an expression of "the necessity of living in unity among themselves, who had the whole world for enemies."[33] This implied strong commitment. Certain pirates—as Frank Sherry suggests, out of sheer "loyalty ... to their fellow outlaws"[34]— attacked "the shipping of places where pirates had been tried and hanged, Blackbeard for instance making a habit of destroying ships from New England for this reason."[35] Captain Johnson tells of Captain Condent's crew cutting off the ears and noses of some Portuguese fellows because they had taken pirates prisoners along the Brazilian coast.[36] Among themselves, their sense of solidarity with one another was expressed in unconditional support. This had already been true for the buccaneers: "The buccaneers were true to each other and as time went on their organisation became astonishingly sound. Those afloat could rely upon the integrity of those ashore and vice versa. Indeed, they formed a community of singularly united villains."[37] These assumptions are confirmed by Exquemelin: "Among themselves, and to each other, these pirates are extremely liberal and free. If any one of them has lost all his goods, which often happens in their manner of life, they freely give him, and make him partaker of what they have."[38] Given the reason why some of the crew members were left without means at the end of the journey documented by Basil Ringrose, his account provides an astonishing example of such generosity: "Hereupon we agreed among ourselves to give away, and leave the ship to them of our company who had no money left of all their purchase in this voyage, having lost it all at play; and the to divide ourselves into two ships, which were now bound for England."[39]

Conflicting opinions among pirate crew members often led to cordial separation rather than to infighting and disharmony. Marcus Rediker writes that it was such separations that helped the "radical democratic social order and culture" of the pirates to spread, "hydralike."[40] Not all separations were harmonious of course. There exist a fair number of accounts in which minorities were simply marooned rather than provided with a fair share of the company's riches. On occasion, the principle of "might is right" probably outweighed all democratic culture. Nonetheless, the following words of Rediker remain convincing:

> The social organization constructed by pirates was flexible, but
> it could not accommodate severe, sustained conflict. Those who

had experienced the claustrophobic and authoritarian world of
the merchant ship cherished the freedom to separate. The pirates'
democratic exercise of authority had both negative and positive
effects. Although it produced a chronic instability, it also guaranteed
continuity; the very process by which new crews were established
helped to ensure a cultural continuity among the pirates.[41]

According to Rediker, the progressive character of social organizing on
the pirate ship can be traced to elements inherent in general seamen culture
of the 17th century: "Building on the lower-class/lower-deck values of collectivism, anti-authoritarianism, and egalitarianism, the pirates realized,
through their social order, tendencies that had been dialectically generated
and in turn suppressed in the normal course of alienated work and life at
sea."[42] Rediker even calls piracy "a 'structure' formed upon a 'foundation'
of the culture and society of Anglo-American deep-sea sailors in the first
half of the eighteenth century."[43] He specifically lists the following values:
1. *Collectivism*—specified as a "collectivity formed among the common tars,
constituted in the confrontation with capital, created over and against the
logic of discipline and cooperation for the sake of profit. Collective labor
passed easily into collective self-defense as seamen sought to protect themselves from harsh conditions, excessive work, and oppressive authority."[44] 2.
Anti-authoritarianism—maybe best described by those most frightened by it:
"When the authorities came into contact with the pirates, they were often
shocked by their democratic tendencies. The Dutch governor of the stopover
colony of Mauritius commented after meeting a pirate crew, 'Every man has
as much say as the captain and each man carries his own weapons in his blan-
kets.'"[45] 3. *Egalitarianism*—according to Rediker, "institutionalized aboard
the pirate ship,"[46] and explained as follows: "The seaman's egalitarianism
was of a piece with other aspects of his culture. It was an essential part of
an emphasis on hospitality and cooperation, reciprocity and mutuality, and
generosity over accumulation."[47]

The term *brotherhood* has been used extensively to describe the strong sense
of loyalty, solidarity, and community among buccaneers and pirates. The
buccaneers have been called an "autarchic 'Brotherhood'"[48] or a "brotherhood
of sea-sharks,"[49] the golden age pirates an "outlaw brotherhood"[50] or a
"transnational brotherhood."[51] The problem with such appellations is that

two troubling features are tied into almost all praises of brotherhood: masculinity and exclusivity. After all, stories of extraordinary generosity and solidarity can also be told of boy scouts, right-wing fraternities, neo-Nazi gangs, Marines, or Hell's Angels.[52] The notion of *standing by someone*, "a favorite among pirates,"[53] tops most virtue lists in such communities— and gives some plausibility to Cordingly and Falconer's deriding description of the pirate articles as "a living example of 'honour amongst thieves.'"[54] Equally prominent is another integral virtue of male bonding, namely that of "courage"; according to Rediker, "a principal means of survival"[55] among pirates, and "the antithesis of law."[56] In this context it is not surprising that the governor of New England would say after a particularly audacious raid by Bartholomew Roberts that "one cannot withhold admiration for his bravery and daring."[57] "Real men" think alike. And they bar others from their exclusive communities. As strong as the commitments of buccaneers and pirates were to each other, their conduct outside of their communities was bound by few moral considerations. For Stephen Snelders—who appears very sympathetic to the buccaneers and pirates—the account of Jan Erasmus Reyning "exposes the atrocities they committed on outsiders."[58]

Understanding oneself as part of a vanguard is a double-edged sword. When Marcus Rediker writes that "by walking 'to the Gallows without a Tear,' by calling themselves 'Honest Men' and 'Gentlemen,' and by speaking self-servingly but proudly of their 'Conscience' and 'Honor,' pirates flaunted their certitude,"[59] this certainly conveys an inspiring sense of rebellion. After all, the pirates held no positions of institutionalized power and were "outcasts" and "outlaws." At the same time, flaunting their certitude towards their victims (most of whom were not worldly or clerical authorities), to common sailors, women, and Indians, had nothing to do with rebellion and everything to do with a despicable exercise of power.

A peculiar understanding of pirate loyalty, solidarity and community has been voiced in the early 1980s in a German essay, entitled "Parasitäre Piraten" ["Parasitic Pirates"]. Heiner Treinen, the essay's author, asserts that the pirates' "solidarity" was rather opportunistic than value-driven:

> The decision to join the pirates as a particular form of 'organization'
> was exclusively based on the calculated gains of every individual.
> This was the only reason that made cooperation and acceptance of

the collective power structure possible. This structure was endured because it promised the satisfaction of individual goals. ... The investment in a social structure among the pirates was inherently temporary.[60]

Treinen suggests that even the relative lack of racial or national discrimination among pirate crews was merely the consequence of their individualism:

> While out there raiding, racial and religious discrimination did not occur, even though the raiding was often justified on racial or religious grounds. The absence of discrimination is no utopian anarchist ideal. It exists when, as in the case of the pirates, the individuals who work together do not really have an interest in living together; when there are no actual common goals.[61]

Treinen's views may appear cynical, but Captain Johnson's *General History* contains passages that also portray pirate togetherness as serving primarily tactical purposes, i.e. as something imposed by a crew's specific existential circumstances rather than by political or ethical convictions. One example concerns the situation of Captain North's crew among the Madagascan natives:

> They thought, and very justly, that unity and concord were the only means to warrant their safety; for the people being ready to make war on one another upon the slightest occasion, they did not doubt but they would take the advantage of any division which they might observe among the whites, and cut them off whenever a fair opportunity offered. North often set this before them, and as often made them remark the effects of their unanimity, which were, the being treated with great respect and deference, and having a homage paid them as to sovereign princes. Nature, we see, teaches the most illiterate the necessary prudence for their preservation, and fear works changes which religion has lost the power of doing.[62]

Of course, Johnson's account might be purely fictional, and Treinen's analysis might simply be false (or in any case too negative). In fact, one might even argue that all displays of social virtues are essentially ego-driven since this is how human beings work—in which sense the pirates' mutual aid would not lose any value, even if it was indeed only based on the fact that "the harshness of life at sea made mutual aid into a simple survival tactic."[63] Still, both Treinen's reflections and the passage from Johnson's *General History* seem to reveal a problem inherent in golden age pirate society: namely, that their "brotherly" ideals were not framed by a wider social and political vision or ambition. We will return to this problem frequently.

4.2. Flying the Black Flag: The Jolly Roger

The golden age pirate brotherhood, commonwealth, or confederacy was most tangibly expressed by its menacing flag, the Jolly Roger. No other pirate symbol—and not many symbols overall—have had such a lasting impact on the Western mind and its popular culture.

The origins of the Jolly Roger are not entirely clear. It was first reported by navy officers chasing French pirate captain Emanuel Wynn in the Cape Verde Islands in 1700. Wynn's flag was described as "a sable ensign with crossbones, a Death's head and an hour glass"[1] against a black background. This design—albeit with variations—soon became a standard signifier for pirate ships. As David F. Marley writes, "when the Spanish War of Succession ended thirteen short years later, most pirates were using a black background for their personal standards."[2] This means that "within 15 years, pirates frequently used black flags and, by 1714, they were a clearly recognized symbol."[3]

Although the Jolly Roger did come in different varieties, all of them shared the same basic themes, in essence symbols associated with death: skull and crossbones,[4] skeletons, hour glasses, cutlasses, bleeding hearts.[5] "The primary symbolism of the flag was straightforward. Pirates intended its symbols—death, violence, and limited time—to terrify their prey, to say, unequivocally, to merchantmen that their time was short, they must surrender immediately, or they would die a bloody death."[6]

There are different theories about the origin of the name. The two most common and convincing are: 1. *Jolly Roger* is an English corruption of the French *la jolie rouge*, which referred to the red flags hoisted by maritime crews to announce battle. 2. *Jolly Roger* is a variation of *Old Roger*, which was a common moniker for the devil.[7]

Whatever the origin of its name, the Jolly Roger defines the era of piracy studied in this book (the golden age) and confirms the sense of unity that must have existed among its pirate crews. Marcus Rediker writes:

> When pirates created a flag of their own, as they did for the first time in the early eighteenth century, they made a new declaration: they would use colors to symbolize the solidarity of a gang of ... outlaws, thousands strong and self-organized in daring ways, in violent opposition to the all-powerful nation-states of the day. By flying the skull and the crossbones, they announced themselves as 'the Villains of all Nations.'[8]

Rediker also confirms that "the flag was very widely used; no fewer, and probably a great many more, than twenty-five hundred men sailed under it."[9] In Chris Land's analysis, "the pirates' choice of flag made explicit their rejection of the nation-state as a foundation for community and their challenge to its monopoly on violence. ... Once the Jolly Roger was raised the pirates broadcast their rejection of the very foundation of the contemporary geo-political order, placing themselves outside its sphere of government and justice."[10]

At a Paris rally in 1880, Louise Michel carried—in protest against the hypocrisy of the official socialist movement—a black flag instead of a red one and created one of the most characteristic and renowned anarchist symbols. Louise Michel might not have thought of the golden age pirates. Nonetheless, it is hard to believe that her choice of color was purely coincidental.

4.3. Is This Anarchy? Matters of Definition I

The associations of golden age piracy with anarchy are legion. In fact, it seems impossible to read a book about piracy without at least one reference to anarchy, no matter the author's political persuasion. We can read about "anarchic behaviour,"[1] "anarchic crews,"[2] "anarchic strains,"[3] "sexual and cultural anarchy,"[4] "anarchy with no form of self-discipline,"[5] "ordered anarchy,"[6] "a cacophonous floating anarchy,"[7] "the very picture of anarchy,"[8] "mini-anarchies,"[9] or "the life of a buccaneer [which] could in some ways be seen as anarchistic."[10] A recent academic essay on piracy even introduces the term "an-*arrgh*-chy."[11]

What can we make of this? Apart from the fact that some of these attributes are negative ascriptions by conservative writers, the critical question is: were the golden age pirates really anarchists?

There appear to be two main ways to respond: 1. If being anarchistic means to live outside the control of the nation-state, or any form of institutionalized authority, then the golden age pirates were surely anarchistic—as much as the nomadic and "primitive" people they have been compared to. 2. If being anarchistic means to consciously attempt to realize social ideals of universal equality and justice, then the golden age pirates were hardly anarchistic. Too many indications exist that they had no social ideals at all, or at least none that extended beyond a community of "brothers" who pledged loyalty to one another.

If there was an anarchism of golden age pirates, it hence lay in their rejection of institutionalized authority and in attempts at egalitarian community building. This is summed up well by Chris Land:

> By signing up to these articles a sailor joined the pirate community
> and agreed to the practices that enabled it to be sustained despite the
> absence of a transcendent law—such as national law or religion—that
> might impose order from without. In this sense the organization of
> the pirate ship in the early 18th century was an experiment in radical,
> anarchistic forms of democratic organizing which were explicitly
> opposed to the systems of authority on conventional sailing vessels.[12]

At the same time, there was no anarchist fight for the benefit of *all*. Often enough, the pirates' actions would have sabotaged any such fight. Nonetheless, both their uncompromising anti-authoritarianism and their truly utopian micro-democratic experiment are of tremendous importance and lie at the heart of radical adaptations of piracy to this day.

4.4. The War Machine: Reading Piracy with Deleuze and Guattari

It is never easy to employ the term *war* analytically. However, the common references to the "war" that the golden age pirates were engaged in as well as fitting theoretical concepts operating with the notion of war—most notably by Michel Foucault, Gilles Deleuze, and Félix Guattari—demand some reflection.

The importance of Foucault's contribution lies in his interpretation of all historical struggle as war, and of war as "a principle for the analysis of power relations."[1] In this sense, we are confronted with a war that never ends. What we call *peace* only marks a certain phase of the underlying war: "Society, the law, and the State are [not] like armistices that put an end to wars, or ... the products of definitive victories. Law is not pacification, for beneath the law, war continues to rage in all the mechanisms of power, even in the most regular. War is the motor behind institutions and order. In the smallest of its cogs, peace is waging a secret war."[2] Foucault explains in conclusion: "Why do we have to rediscover war? Well, because this ancient war is a ... permanent war. We really do have to become experts on battles, because the war has not ended, because preparations are still being made for the decisive battles, and because we have to win the decisive battle."[3]

The significance of these notions for golden age piracy becomes obvious when Foucault describes a 17th century shift in the understanding of war: from warring against a representation of power (most commonly a king) to warring against "culture" or "civilization":

> From the seventeenth century onward, ... the idea that war is the uninterrupted frame of history takes a specific form: The war that is going on beneath order and peace, the war that undermines our society and divides it in a binary mode is, basically, a race war. ... It is this idea that this clash between two races runs through society from top to bottom which we see being formulated as early as the seventeenth century.[4]

Foucault's employment of the term *race* in this context must be controversial. However, what he means seems pertinent: namely that—instead of the war waged between two (economically defined) classes—the decisive war is the one waged between two categories ("races") of people who are defined as "civilized" and "savage." It is not coincidental that this shift in discourse correlates with the onset of the colonial European enterprise. Certain people needed to be "dehumanized." This meant non-Europeans as much as Europeans who fell outside the norms of their own society. As Rediker reports, pirates were "denounced ... as sea monsters, vicious beasts, and a many-headed hydra—all creatures that ... lived beyond the bounds of human society."[5] Indeed, as late as the early 20th century, some would call pirates "monsters in human form"[6] or "an odd mixture of human trash."[7]

Piracy has always been associated with war. The frequency of war references rivals that of anarchy references. Most famous is Captain Johnson's repeated declaration that pirates had declared *war against all the world*.[8] Since then, historians have written about "the final battles of the pirate war on the world,"[9] shared the observation that "many perceived piracy as an activity akin to war,"[10] or, like Peter Earle, have dedicated the titles of their books to the theme (in this case *The Pirate Wars*).

The French philosopher-psychoanalyst duo Gilles Deleuze and Félix Guattari introduced the concept of the *nomadic war machine* in their 1980 book *A Thousand Plateaus*. To them, "the war machine is like the necessary consequence of nomadic organization."[11] It is "exterior to the State apparatus."[12] What is important in their theory is that "the war machine has an extremely variable relation to war itself."[13] It does "not in fact have war as its primary object, but as its second-order, supplementary or synthetic objective, in the sense that it is determined in such way as to destroy the State-form and city-form with which it collides."[14] It is only when the state "appropriates the war machine" that it takes "war for its direct and primary object" and that "war becomes subordinated to the aims of the State."[15] As long as the war machine is in the hands of the nomads, it "has as its object not war, but the tracing of a creative line of flight, the composition of a smooth space and of the movement of people in that space."[16]

This last aspect explains the relevance of the concept for the golden age pirates. In Deleuze and Guattari's terminology, the golden age pirates constituted a nomadic war machine as an inevitable aspect of their struggle for freedom from state and capitalist oppression. The "creative line of flight," the "composition of a smooth space" and the "movement of people in that space" were all literal aspects of the pirate existence during the golden age. Their war machine did not mean to establish totalitarian orders—it meant to destroy the state and its cronies. In this sense the following rings very true:

> Each time there is an operation against the State—subordination,
> rioting, guerilla warfare or revolution as act—it can be said that a
> war machine has revived, that a new nomadic potential has appeared,
> accompanied by the reconstitution of a smooth space or a manner of
> being in space as though it were smooth. ... It is in this sense that the
> response of the State against all that threatens to move beyond it is to
> striate space.[17]

Even if the nomadic war machine does "not in fact have war as its primary object," the pirates' warfare was more than merely "metaphoric" or "symbolic."

Although the violence of the Caribbean buccaneers and pirates has probably been historically exaggerated for different reasons,[18] they were no flower-sniffin' hippies either. Stephen Snelders is one of many authors who confirms that the buccaneers "paid close attention only to their most prized possessions and tools, their firearms and cutlasses."[19] Angus Konstam has compiled an impressive overview of the weapons used by the buccaneers,[20] and there are stories about engagement in battle as pirate initiation rites. Marcus Rediker, for example, tells us that "pirate captain Thomas Cocklyn apparently felt that the 'new-entered men' would not truly be part of the pirate community until they had seen action in battle."[21]

If we accept the concept of the nomadic war machine and its application to the anti-statist tradition developed by the Caribbean buccaneers and brought to bloom by the golden age pirates, *and* if we accept the conclusions of Pierre Clastres, then the buccaneers' and pirates' readiness to go to war would indicate a necessary and effective means of preventing falling under the brutal power of the state, since "Clastres [identifies] war in primitive societies as the surest mechanism directed against the formation of the State: war maintains the dispersal and segmentarity of groups, and the warrior himself is caught in the process of accumulating exploits, a process which leads him on to solitude and a prestigious death, but without power."[22]

One aspect of Deleuze and Guattari's analysis that is of particular significance for Caribbean buccaneers and pirates is the war machine's adaptation by the state. This for two reasons. First, the nomadic war machine created by the buccaneers became appropriated for the state's ends every time they were sent out as privateers to bolster the colonial enterprise and inter-state rivalry. This led Alexander Winston to conclude his book on privateering with the prophetic words: "If privateering is ever needed, it will be back."[23] Second, war machines created by the state became uncontrollably "nomadic" once they served their purpose and were abandoned by the state. The latter especially is of extreme importance for Caribbean history. There is a lot of truth in Janice E. Thomson's simple observation that "the practice of privateering produced the problem of piracy."[24] This is confirmed by considerations expressed in contemporaneous sources. Captain Johnson formulated the problem in the following manner:

> Yet the observation is just, for so many idle people employing them-
> selves in privateers for the sake of plunder and riches, which they

always spend as fast as they get, that when the war is over and they can have no farther business in the way of life they have been used to, they too readily engage in acts of piracy; which being but the same practice without a commission, they make very little distinction betwixt the lawfulness of one, and the unlawfulness of the other.[25]

Edmund Dummer, running a mail service to the Caribbean just after the outbreak of the War of the Spanish Succession, remarked that "it is the opinion of every one this cursed trade [privateering] will breed so many pirates that, when peace comes, we shall be in more danger from them than we are now from the enemy."[26] According to Philip Gosse this is exactly what happened after the war ended in 1713:

> Thousands of privateersmen were thus thrown out of employment, and there was not nearly enough merchant shipping to give honest work to all the crews. Some men no doubt settled down on shore to one kind of work or another, but hundreds of the roughest sort were still without means of making a living. The consequence was that these formed companies and went to sea as before, but now without a commission. To such desperate men nothing came amiss, and in truth was it said that they had 'declared war upon all nations.'[27]

This, without doubt, contributed decisively to golden age piracy reaching its zenith only a short time later.

The contemporary parallels are striking. From US-trained and sponsored "Islamic fundamentalists" who have turned against their former mentors, to Latin American contras continuing their terror campaigns after their employment by political interest groups has ended, to militias formed from the remains of former state socialist security agencies, to the government-equipped Janjaweed of Sudan's Darfur region, to the thousands of guerrillas-turned-bandits in all corners of the earth—the state creating its own worst enemy is a recurring theme. The reason is that it depends on a violence it cannot always control. This, once again, reminds us of the pirate as a politically ambiguous figure: while all the mentioned defectors can potentially turn into freedom fighters, they can also all turn into callous assassins. It is not always clear where on this spectrum we can place the golden age pirate.

4.5. Tactics: Pirates and Guerrilla Warfare

According to Stephen Snelders, the golden age pirates, after the end of the still land-based buccaneering tradition, "reverted to guerrilla tactics, preying on the sea routes of the West Indies, Africa, and the Arabian and Indian coasts."[1] The choice of words here ought not be considered arbitrary. In its methods and tactics, the golden age pirates indeed engaged in guerrilla warfare as laid out by some of the great guerrilla warfare theorists, in particular Mao Zedong, Che Guevara, and Carlos Marighella. Their nomadic war machine was a guerrilla war machine.

The parallels begin with striking structural similarities. When Mao says that "guerrilla warfare … is a weapon that a nation inferior in arms and military equipment may employ against a more powerful aggressor nation,"[2] then this accurately describes the pirate situation, only that we must replace the "inferior" nation with a "non-nation" and the "more powerful" nation with "all nations." It is important, however, to stress that the parallels between golden age pirates and guerrillas concern methods and tactics, not politics. Politically, the golden age pirates' *war against all the world* would not qualify as a guerrilla war. First, it lacks the political consciousness that all theorists of guerrilla warfare see as a defining feature. Marighella, for example, stresses that "we must avoid the distortion of [the] political objective and prevent the guerrilla, urban or rural, from transforming itself into an instrument of banditry, or unifying with bandits or employing their methods."[3] Second, the golden age pirates lack a people and its assistance. For Mao, "guerrilla warfare basically derives from the masses and is supported by them."[4] For Che Guevara, "guerrilla warfare is war by the entire people against the reigning oppression."[5] The war of the golden age pirates never was such a war. In fact, in Guevara's judgment, this makes them "robber bands" rather than guerrilla units:

> For the individual guerrilla, then, wholehearted help from the
> local population is the basis on which to start. Popular support is
> indispensable. Let us consider the example of robber bands that roam
> a certain region. They possess all the characteristics of a guerrilla
> band—homogeneity, respect for their leader, bravery, familiarity with
> the terrain, and frequently even thorough understanding of tactics.
> They lack only one thing: the support of the people.[6]

One could, of course, try to make a case for alleged bandits or robbers being a legitimate part of a people's struggle against oppression. In fact, Mao did make such provisions in his guerrilla army concept:

> The seventh [and last] type of guerrilla organization is that formed from bands of bandits and brigands. This, although difficult, must be carried out with utmost vigour lest the enemy use such bands to his own advantage … It is only necessary to correct their political beliefs to convert them. In spite of inescapable differences in the fundamental types of guerrilla bands, it is possible to unite them to form a vast sea of guerrillas.[7]

Whether this applies to the golden age pirates will be discussed in the subsequent sections of this chapter. The following pages will—by the use of original quotes from guerrilla handbooks and corresponding passages from pirate histories—try to illustrate the methodical and tactical parallels between pirate warfare and guerrilla warfare. (In the case of Marighella, the specification of *urban* guerrilla warfare has been omitted in the quotations as it does not seem relevant to the systematic comparisons drawn here.) Apart from some minor exceptions—like Guevara's demands of "alcohol is out" or "on the march, strict silence"[8]—the similarities are striking.

Basics

☠ Marighella's descriptions of the "technique of the … guerrilla" and the advantages he has in his struggle could be used word for word to define the pirates' situation:

> The technique of the … guerrilla has the following characteristics: 1. it is an aggressive technique, or in other words, defensive action means death for us. Since we are inferior to the enemy in firepower and have neither his resources nor his power base, we cannot defend ourselves against an offensive or a concentrated attack by the gorillas. And that is the reason why our urban technique can never be permanent, can never defend a fixed base nor remain in any spot waiting to repel the circles of reaction; 2. it is a technique of attack and retreat by which we preserve our forces; 3. it is a technique that aims at the development of urban guerrilla warfare, whose function will be to wear out,

demoralize, and distract the enemy forces. ... The initial advantages
[of the guerrilla] are: 1. he must take the enemy by surprise; 2. he
must know the terrain of the encounter better than the enemy; 3.
he must have greater mobility and speed than the police and other
repressive forces; 4. his information service must be better than the
enemy's; 5. he must be in command of the situation and demonstrate
a decisiveness so great that everyone on our side is inspired and never
thinks of hesitating, while on the other side the enemy is stunned and
incapable of responding.[9]

☠ In this context, Marighella's description of the guerrilla's training makes
Hispaniola sound like a guerrilla warrior boot camp:

The ... guerrilla can have strong physical resistance only if he trains
systematically. ... Useful forms of physical preparation are hiking,
camping, the practice in survival in the woods, mountain climbing,
rowing, swimming, skin diving, ... fishing, harpooning, and the hunting of birds and of small and big game.[10]

Shooting

☠ Marighella: "The ... guerrilla's reason for existence, the basic condition in
which he acts and survives, is to shoot. ... In unconventional warfare, in
which ... guerrilla warfare is included, the combat is at close range, often
very close. To prevent his own extinction, the ... guerrilla has to shoot
first and he cannot err in his shot."[11]

☠ David Marley: "The rovers' rise to world-wide predominance during the
second half of the seventeenth century can be attributed primarily to one
factor: firepower. No matter how few in numbers, most pirate bands felt
they could carry any objective through guile, mobility and superior mus-
ketry. ... With the exception of Saint-Domingue's *boucaniers* and other
such sharpshooting hunters, most privateersmen waited until they could
unleash volleys from close range during battle."[12]

☠ Stephen Snelders: "One advantage of the Brethren's independence of
spirit was that they were excellent skirmishers."[13]

Arms

- ☠ Marighella: "Light arms have the advantage of fast handling and easy transport."[14]
- ☠ Mao: "In regard to the problem of guerrilla equipment, it must be understood that guerrillas are lightly armed attack groups, which require simple equipment."[15]
- ☠ Stephen Snelders: "basis of [the buccaneers'] way of life, their most common characteristic and in a sense their raison d'être, lay in their expertise with small firearms: muskets, blunderbusses, and pistols. With these weapons they stalked the island in small bands of five or six hunters."[16]

Supplies

- ☠ Mao: "The equipment of guerrillas cannot be based on what the guerrillas want, or even what they need, but must be based on what is available for their use."[17]
- ☠ Guevara: "Keep in mind that the guerrilla's most important source of supply is the enemy himself."[18]
- ☠ Cordingly and Falconer: "The clothes, arms and ships of these motley bands, composed of the adventurers of all nations, depended on the loot they acquired."[19]

Expropriation

- ☠ Marighella: "As to the vehicle, the ... guerrilla must expropriate what he needs. When he already has resources, the ... guerrilla can combine the expropriation of vehicles with other methods of acquisition. Money, arms, ammunition and explosives ... must be expropriated. And the ... guerrilla must rob banks and armories and seize explosives and ammunition wherever he finds them. None of these operations is undertaken for just one purpose. Even when the assault is for money, the arms that the guards bear must also be taken."[20]
- ☠ As has been highlighted earlier, the golden age pirates were completely dependent on "expropriation." The eccentric "gentleman pirate" Stede Bonnet is known as the only pirate who "showed such a nicety of feeling" as to buy his own ship.[21]

Traps

☠ In his article "Street Fighting," James Connolly describes the significance of a "defile" for the guerrilla struggle: "A street is a defile in a city. A defile is a narrow pass through which troops can only move by narrowing their front, and therefore making themselves a good target for the enemy."[22]

☠ In *Patterns of Pillage*, Paul Galvin explains the significance of Tortuga for the buccaneers in its "hold over maritime choke points" and "vulnerable bottlenecks."[23]

Speed

☠ Régis Debray: "In time of war questions of speed are vital, especially in the early stages when an unarmed and inexperienced guerrilla band must confront a well-armed and knowledgeable enemy."[24] Mao also speaks of "lightning-like tactical decisions."[25]

☠ Cordingly and Falconer: "Speed was essential for a pirate ship to enable her to make a successful attack and a rapid getaway."[26]

☠ Douglas Botting: "Speed and surprise were of the essence."[27]

Surprise

☠ Marighella: "To compensate for his general weakness and shortage of arms compared to the enemy, the … guerrilla uses surprise."[28]

☠ Mao: "Although the element of surprise is not absent in orthodox warfare, there are fewer opportunities to apply it than there are during guerrilla hostilities. In the latter, speed is essential. The movements of guerrilla troops must be secret and supernatural rapidity; the enemy must be taken unaware, and the action entered speedily. There can be no procrastination in the execution of plans; no assumption of a negative or passive defence; no great dispersion of forces in many local engagements. The basic method is the attack in a violent and deceptive form."[29]

☠ Guevara I: "The way a guerrilla army attacks is also different: a sudden, surprise, furious, relentless attack, then, abruptly, total passivity. … An unexpected lightning blow is what counts."[30]

☠ Guevara II: "Some disparaging people call this 'hit and run.' That is exactly what it is! Hit and run, wait, stalk the enemy, hit him again and run, do it all again and again, giving no rest to the enemy. Perhaps this smacks of not facing up to the enemy. Nevertheless, it serves the goal of guerrilla warfare: to conquer and destroy the enemy."[31]

☠Angus Konstam: "Stealth and surprise were the key elements in buccaneer attacks."[32]

☠Douglas Botting: "Essentially, they were hit-and-run raiders, and their tactics were designed to that end."[33]

☠Cordingly and Falconer: "When there was a fight, the most popular ploys were stealth, surprise and trickery."[34]

☠The following summary by Marighella again applies word for word to what we know about the Caribbean buccaneers' and pirates' warfare:

> The technique of surprise is based on four essential requisites: 1. we know the situation of the enemy we are going to attack, usually by means of precise information and meticulous observation, while the enemy does not know he is going to be attacked and knows nothing about the attacker; 2. we know the force of the enemy that is going to be attacked and the enemy knows nothing about our force; 3. attacking by surprise, we save and conserve our forces, while the enemy is unable to do the same and is left at the mercy of events; 4. we determine the hour and the place of the attack, fix its duration, and establish its objective. The enemy remains ignorant of all this."[35]

"Smooth Space"

☠Mao: "When the situation is serious, the guerrillas must move with the fluidity of water and the ease of the blowing wind. Their tactics must deceive, tempt, and confuse the enemy. They must lead the enemy to believe that they will attack him from the east and north, and they must then strike him from the west and the south. They must strike, then rapidly disperse."[36]

☠Régis Debray: "At the beginning they keep out of sight, and when they allow themselves to be seen it is at a time and place chosen by their chief."[37]

☠David Cordingly: "The navy also had the problem which has always faced the forces of law and order when confronted by well-armed rebels, guerillas or terrorists: knowing when and where the next attack might take place."[38]

☠ Paul Galvin: "Their movements were less predictable than those of their piratical predecessors, and they were difficult to catch."[39]

Terrain

☠ Marighella I: "The ... guerrilla's best ally is the terrain and because this is so he must know it like the palm of his hand."[40]

☠ Marighella II: "It is an insoluble problem for the police in the labyrinthian terrain of the ... guerrilla, to get someone they can't see, to repress someone they can't catch, to close in on someone they can't find."[41]

☠ Guevara I: "When we analyse the tactics of guerrilla warfare, we see that the guerrilla must possess a highly developed knowledge of the terrain on which he operates, avenues of access and escape, possibilities for rapid manœuvre, popular support, and hiding places."[42]

☠ Guevara II: "The guerrilla must ... know the theater of operations like the palm of his hand."[43]

☠ Peter Earle I: "As in the earlier campaigns, they [the pirates] knew the waters where they cruised better than their pursuers and were often able to use that knowledge to their advantage."[44]

☠ Peter Earle II: "On one occasion HMS *Mermaid* was chasing a sloop commanded by the pirate Low and with a good wind was catching up fast. 'But it happened there was one man on board the sloop that knew of a shoal ground thereabouts who directed Low to run over it; he did so; and the man-of-war who had so forereached him as to sling a shot over him ... ran a ground upon the shoal and was dismasted."[45]

Mobility

☠ Marighella I: "The ... guerrilla should always be mobile."[46]

☠ Marighella II: "Face to face with the enemy, he must always be moving from one position to another, because to stay in one position makes him a fixed target and, as such, very vulnerable."[47]

☠ Mao: "When we discuss the terms 'front' and 'rear', it must be remembered, that while guerrillas do have bases, their primary field of activity is in the enemy's rear areas. They themselves have no rear."[48]

☠ Guevara I: "The guerrilla relies on mobility. This permits him quickly to flee the area of action whenever necessary, constantly to shift his front, to evade encirclement (a most dangerous situation for the guerrilla), and even to counter-encircle the enemy."[49]

☠Guevara II: "One cannot conceive of static guerrilla warfare. ... The withdrawal must be swift."[50]

We can recall several passages quoted in earlier sections on golden age pirate life here:

☠Stephen Snelders: "All pirates knew themselves to be homeless."[51]
☠Robert C. Ritchie: "Anarchistic marauding involved leaving behind the base of operation and wandering for months—even years—at a time."[52]
☠David Cordingly: "A study of the tracks of the pirate ships shows many zig-zagging all over the place without apparent reason."[53]

Organization
☠Marighella I: "Leadership in our organization, and in the coordination and command groups in particular, is very simple and is always based upon a small number of comrades who, in order to merit confidence, distinguish themselves in the most hazardous and responsible actions by their capacity for initiative and their intransigence in the defense and application of the revolutionary principles to which we are committed."[54]
☠Marighella II: "Guerrillas, on the contrary, are not an army but small armed groups, intentionally fragmented."[55]
☠Mao I: "In all armies, obedience of the subordinates to their superiors must be exacted. This is true in the case of guerrilla discipline, but the basis for guerrilla discipline must be the individual conscience. With guerrillas, a discipline of compulsion is ineffective."[56]
☠Mao II: "In a revolutionary army, all individuals enjoy political liberty and the question, for example, of the emancipation of the people must not only be tolerated but discussed."[57]
☠Mao III: "Officers should live under the same conditions as their men, for that is the only way in which they can gain from their men the admiration and confidence so vital in war."[58]
☠Guevara: "Food was distributed share and share alike. This is important, not only because the distribution of food is the one regular daily event,

but also because the soldiers are sensitive to fancied injustices and displays of favouritism."[59]

Again, several passages on golden age pirate life can be recalled:

☠ David Cordingly: "Pirate communities were ... democracies."[60]

☠ Marcus Rediker: "The decisions the council made were sacrosanct. Even the boldest captain dared not challenge its power."[61]

☠ Marcus Rediker: "The social organization constructed by pirates was flexible ... "[62]

☠ Frank Sherry: "For the most part pirates chose their captains on the basis of merit."[63]

☠ Stephen Snelders: "Regardless of how pistol-proof, bold, terrifying, or beloved a pirate captain might be, all hierarchy and authoritarianism were constantly questioned."[64]

☠ Robert C. Ritchie: "The marauders ... lived in small self-contained democracies that usually operated by majority vote"[65]

Initiative

Finally, a number of passages from the guerrilla handbooks confirm the overall sense of pirate initiative expressed throughout this volume:

☠ Marighella I: "The small initial group of combatants is oriented toward construction of an infrastructure that will permit action, instead of worrying about building a hierarchical structure through meetings of delegates or the calling together of leaders of the old conventional parties."[66]

☠ Marighella II: "Office has no value. In a revolutionary organization there are only missions and tasks to complete."[67]

☠ Marighella III: "The ... guerrilla has no mission other than to attack and retreat."[68]

☠ Mao: "The tactics of defence have no place in the realm of guerrilla warfare."[69]

☠ Mao II: "The attack must be made on guerrilla initiative; that is, guerrillas must not permit themselves to be manœuvred into a position where they are robbed of initiative and where the decision to attack is forced upon them."[70]

☠ Guevara I: "Another characteristic of the individual guerrilla is his initiative. In contrast to the rigidity of classical warfare, the guerrilla invents his own tactics for each moment of battle and constantly surprises his enemy."[71]

☠ Guevara II: "Combat comes as a welcome relief from this drudgery and leaves the band with freshened spirits. It begins at the right moment, upon discovering an enemy encampment sufficiently weak to be wiped out, or upon entry of a hostile column into guerrilla territory."[72]

☠ Guevara III: "Combat is the climax of guerrilla life. Though each individual encounter may be only of brief duration, each battle is a profound emotional experience for the guerrilla."[73]

In conclusion, it seems significant that Lenin talks about guerrilla warfare as a "form of struggle [that] was adopted as the preferable and even *exclusive* form of social struggle by the vagabond elements of the population, the lumpen proletariat and anarchist groups."[74] Both lumpen proletariat and anarchist groups point towards the golden age pirates—whose guerrilla tactics were, if we believe the authors of "Pirate Utopias," far from ineffective: "They launched raiding parties so successful that they created an imperial crisis, attacking British trade with the colonies, and crippling the emerging system of global exploitation, slavery and colonialism."[75] Did this make the golden age pirates revolutionaries despite a lack of revolutionary consciousness?

4.6. Revolutionary, Radical, and Proletarian Pirates? Matters of Definition II

The question of what constitutes a revolutionary identity often turns into a mere fight over words. As with the question of what constitutes an anarchist identity, much depends on matters of definition. If being revolutionary requires a conscious all-encompassing political agenda—i.e. an agenda to fundamentally change all of society's organizational structures—then it appears unlikely that many golden age pirates would qualify, as such an agenda seems missing. Yet if being revolutionary means contributing to a disruption of society's organizational structures that pose a fundamental threat to the political order, then golden age pirates did have revolutionary traits and their actions could indeed be described as revolutionary.[1] After these clarifications, the question becomes how much sense such descriptions make.

Not all historians deny the golden age pirates political consciousness. Marcus Rediker claims that they "self-consciously built an autonomous, democratic, egalitarian social order of their own, a subversive alternative to the prevailing ways of the merchant, naval, and privateering ship and a counterculture to the civilization of Atlantic capitalism with its expropriation and exploitation, terror and slavery,"[2] and adds:

> Pirates perceived themselves and their social relations through a
> collectivistic ethos that had been forged in their struggle for survival,
> first as seamen, then as outlaws. They had reasons for what they did,
> and they expressed them clearly, consistently, confidently, and even,
> on occasion, with a degree of self-righteousness. In and through their
> social rules, their egalitarian social organization, and their notions of
> revenge and fairness, they tried to establish a world in which people
> 'were justly dealt with.'[3]

Hans Turley offers a somewhat weaker form of such claims when writing that "unlike the buccaneers and the privateers, the golden-age pirates not only chose to live outside the parameters of social conventions, but … *embraced* a life that challenged those conventions."[4]

There are examples among the records on golden age piracy that support the theory of a self-conscious political aspect to their actions. One document names merchant captain Thomas Checkley who reported that pirates referring to themselves as "Robin Hoods Men" had taken his ship.[5] According to Captain Johnson, some members of Bartholomew Roberts's crew commented on their death sentences by alluding that "they were poor rogues … and so hanged, while others, no less guilty in another way, escaped,"[6] while another pirate crew returned what they had taken from a ship after they had found out that most of the booty belonged to "innocent children."[7] Johnson also relates one of the most socially conscious declarations of a famed pirate, when Mary Read approves of capital punishment for her kind because otherwise "many of those who are now cheating the widows and orphans, and oppressing the poor neighbours who have no money to obtain justice, would then rob at sea, and the ocean would be crowded with rogues like the land."[8] There were also, during the last phases of golden age piracy, the courts of justice meted out against merchant captains of taken vessels.[9] Finally, political authorities were freely mocked: victims of an attack by Bartholomew Roberts's crew recalled that "they [the pirates] often ridiculed and made a mock at king George's acts of grace with an oath, that they had not got money enough, but when they had, if he then did grant them one, after they sent him word, they would thank him for it."[10] Still, none of these examples seems to suggest a particular political or social vision in the golden age pirates' self-consciousness as "poor rogues." Even if certain victims might have been regarded as more honorable targets than others, the overall picture suggests a pretty indiscriminate pattern of those who were targeted. The records seem to refute any claim that golden age pirates attacked only the rich, or behaved benevolently towards the poor. They much rather fit the picture of the *social bandit* laid out by Eric Hobsbawm, discussed in a later section of this chapter.

The best-known attempt at finding traces of conscious political activism in the Caribbean buccaneer and pirate communities has been undertaken by Christopher Hill who, in 1984, published the essay "Radical Pirates?"

It is noteworthy that some pirate-passionate radicals have shown a tendency to ignore the question mark at the end of the essay's title. Hill ends his essay with the cautious comment: "I suggest … that it might be worth investigating more carefully the West Indies as a refuge for political radicals after the defeat of the [English] Revolution."[11] In this sense, Hill makes no claims, he only points to tantalizing research opportunities. He also, however, suggests, "we may conclude that the survival of some radical ideas among the pirates whom Defoe [Captain Johnson] describes is not impossible: it is, indeed, likely."[12] This is certainly what got many radicals excited.

To recapture the main points of Hill's essay: Hill suggests that with Cromwell's expedition to the West Indies in 1654/55 (which, most significantly, brought England Jamaica as a colony—and a buccaneer headquarters) a number of radicals moved to the West Indies. There they either found their way into buccaneer and pirate ranks, or helped create a social climate in which dissident ideas could grow and inspire others to join. In particular, Hill mentions adherents of the Ranters and Quakers, anti-clerical Christian rebels. He also cites the presence of "faded red coats of the New Model Army"[13]—the military wing of England's republican revolution in the mid-17th century—within the ranks of the buccaneers. What are we to make of this?

The Ranters would fit wonderfully into this volume with their libertarian pantheism, especially when we consider Hill's description that "theirs was 'a heroic effort to proclaim Dionysus in a world from which he was being driven.'"[14] The problem is that not only do we lack records of Ranters traveling to the West Indies (let alone establishing themselves there as a recognized community), we lack reliable records about the Ranters movement in general—which has led some historians to argue that there never really was a Ranters movement:

> The primacy of the indwelling spirit, the pantheistic sense that God is in possession of or infuses all things, the *frisson* of millenarian perception, the juggling of inversions, these common features of the mid-seventeenth-century landscape of spiritual enthusiasm cannot be confined to a Ranter group and, accordingly, they are not adequate discriminators for identifying such a group. … Such evidence as there is, therefore, suggests that the Ranters did not exist either as a small group of like-minded individuals, as a sect, or as a large-scale, middle-scale or small movement. … There was a Ranter sensation.[15]

Even if we assume that a Ranters movement existed and reached the Caribbean, there seems to be hardly any indication that it would have influenced buccaneers and pirates. One perpetually cited example is that of "Ranter Bay" in Madagascar, where one James Plantain established himself as a "Pirate King" around 1720.[16] To conclude, however, that this proves a Ranter strain in the pirate community, seems rather daring. For one thing, all the standard dictionaries list *to rant* as a common 17th- and 18th-century term for "talking foolishly" or "raving."[17] Ranter Bay hence seems a likely self-ironic name for a pirate post without any political connotations—especially when considering that this post was established 70 years after the Ranter movement had its short (real or alleged) moment. Another possibility is that the name derived from the Dutch word *ranten*—meaning much the same as *to rant*. Cross-lingual variations were common among the English-French-Dutch alliances of buccaneers and pirates, as the cases of *boucanier/buccaneer*, *zeerover/sea rover*, *jolie rouge/Jolly Roger* and others demonstrate. A Dutch pirate presence on Madagascar is recorded.[18] Most importantly, however, John Plantain's self-proclaimed status as a king, his self-declared rule over the native population, his involvement in the slave trade, and the "harem" of native women he supposedly kept, can hardly allow us to go gung-ho over the name he gave *his* bay, whatever its origins or allusions.[19]

Quakers definitely settled in the Caribbean. In fact, like Rhode Island on the North American coast, Barbados soon developed into a Quaker center in the so-called New World. The suggestion that Quakerism could have had an impact on the Caribbean buccaneer and pirate societies, however, seems hardly convincing for several reasons: 1. Quakerism simply arrived too late to influence the buccaneers' *Custom of the Coast*, the foundation of the Caribbean buccaneer and pirate culture. The custom was well established in the 1650s when the first Quakers appeared on the Caribbean scene. 2. George Fox, Quakerism's most prominent early figure, did visit Barbados and Jamaica for several months in 1671. No connections—in whatever way—between him and the buccaneer community are recorded. 3. Despite expressing noble ethical ideals, including early condemnations of slavery, Quakerism did little to challenge economic injustices—a political ambition of the golden age pirates if there was any. One of Barbados' early and most active Quaker leaders was in fact "a wealthy sugar-planter, who was a great friend of the governor."[20] 4. As far as the Quakers' noble ethical ideals are concerned, it was pacifism that soon occupied the most prominent role, not piratism. This is clearly expressed in the account of the Quaker Captain Knot in the *General History*: Knot was the commander of a "very peaceable ship," one that "had neither pistol, sword nor cutlass on board." Some pirates of Captain Walter Kennedy's crew thought they could use his ship as a cover to reach the shores of the American colonies—only to be disclosed by Knot and hanged.[21] 5. The ethical antagonism between Quakers and pirates seems particularly pronounced when we consider the fate of those Quakers we might call political activists. Some of them shared their fate with that of many pirates and ended on the gallows. Not for robbery and murder, however, but for principled pacifist defiance—like the Barbadian William Leddra who became one of the four *Boston Martyrs* when, one year after Mary Dyer, he was hanged in 1661 by the Massachusetts authorities for violating the Quaker entry ban. This, I believe, is where we find the Quaker spirit of the West Indies, not underneath the Jolly Roger.

As far as the "faded red coats of the New Model Army" go, Hill references the 1961 book *Brethren of the Coast: Buccaneers of the South Seas* by P.K. Kemp and Christopher Lloyd. Kemp and Lloyd twice make references to these coats as part of the Morgan expedition to Panama. They do not cite a direct source, but it can be assumed that one of the sources they list at the end of their book gave reason to the remark. In any case, whether the coats were worn by some buccaneers or not seems politically rather irrelevant. Since the expedition sent to the West Indies by Cromwell in 1654 marks an important step in the history of English settlement in the West Indies, it should not be surprising if New Model Army coats found their way across the Atlantic as well. How much this said about the political consciousness of those who wore them—especially 15 years later—is another question altogether. Most importantly, however, the political legacy of the New Model Army itself remains controversial. Although radical elements, Levelers and others, certainly played their part, in Ian Gentles's perspective "Calvinistic puritanism"—and not "libertarian antinomianism"—was the driving force behind and within the army.[22] Oliver Cromwell's "Speech at the Opening of Parliament 1656" would confirm this. Cromwell used the speech to call the Spaniard a "natural enemy" and the "head of the Papal interest" (which he equated with an "anti-Christian interest")—someone "you could not have an honest nor honourable peace with," and who has "an enmity put into him by God" that stands "against all that is of God ... in you."[23] Needless to say, the Irish—to name just the most obvious example—have always had a hard time swallowing the radical romanticization of the New Model Army.

Mentioning the Irish hints at another aspect that seems problematic in Hill's account. A large part of the English expedition to the Caribbean consisted of Irish and Scottish prisoners of war who were used as indentured laborers.[24] They must have constituted the likeliest recruiting force for the English-speaking buccaneers and pirates. However, given both the national and religious rivalries of the region, not too many of these indentured laborers found a place among them—or wanted to. If they managed to escape their situation, they often ended up in the service of the Spanish. Somewhat ironically, it must be assumed that out of the indentured laborers arriving in the Caribbean as part of the 1654/55 expedition, the most rebellious groups might have joined the Spanish forces, while the likeliest group to join the buccaneers were the English royalists. The political consciousness they would have added to their ranks can only be imagined.[25]

Hill lists a few other disputable indications for the putative presence of politically conscious forces among the Caribbean buccaneers and pirates.[26] One is the alleged presence of "theorists among pirates" which he finds "suggested by the fact that at trial they were denied benefit of clergy."[27] I imagine there could have been a number of reasons why clergy would have been denied to pirates. Hill further points to the fact that "we find... expressions of sympathy for Monmouth's rebellion made by West Indian pirates and privateers."[28] Even if this were true, the radical implications of the Monmouth Rebellion seem as questionable as those of the New Model Army—unless each and every Protestant and anti-Catholic rebellion of the 17th-century was considered "radical."

Hill also offers an explanation for the absence of any hard evidence suggesting that the radical ideas that swept England in the mid-1650s did indeed travel to the Caribbean: "The dependence of the West Indian economy on slaves and subjected Indians must have made these ideas hard to sustain, especially when piracy seemed to offer the only means of livelihood."[29] This is a curious statement for two reasons. First, Hill seems to suggest that by turning pirate, a radical gave up his ideas—this, however, would undermine his very thesis, namely the influence of these ideas on piracy. Second, with all due respect to the difficulties posed by dire economic circumstances, it seems doubtful that they ever eradicate solid political ideas; they might force people to compromise their ideas, but politically conscious people forced to compromise their ideas out of economic necessity usually reflect upon, explain and (convincingly or unconvincingly) justify this. No such debates among buccaneers or pirates seem to be on record.

In fact, not only is there a lack of solid indications for a political pirate consciousness, but there are also a fair number of indications suggesting that such a consciousness simply did not exist (to the point where it might be true that pirate captains like Bartholomew Roberts fought a "personal war against the world"[30] more than anything else). The complete lack of political declarations on part of the golden age pirates—and the buccaneers, for that matter—seems indeed stunning; at least if it is fair to assume that any self-consciously political pirate would have, at least at some point, felt the urge to share an articulated explanation of his exploits with the world. This, however, apparently never happened. There seem to be no records of political declarations at pirate trials that go beyond the faint references to social injustice quoted above. The same goes for their executions. There is no pirate equivalent to, say, August Spies's declaration on the day of the Haymarket Martyrs' death that "the day will come when our silence will be more powerful than the voices you strangle today." Closest come some remarks of the pirates hanged in New Providence in 1718 under the eyes of many of their former companions. Dennis Macarty recalled "the time when there were many brave fellows on the island who would not have suffered him to die like a dog,"[31] and, according to Philip Gosse, Humphrey Morrice accused the reformed pirate onlookers of "'pusillanimity and cowardice' because they did not rescue him and his fellow-sufferers."[32] However, as much as these sentiments express disappointment at the lack of "brotherly loyalty," they do not indicate any particular political ideals one way or another.

Certainly no one in the crowd demonstrated rebellious political consciousness. This seems telling for the overall political consciousness of the pirate community insofar as the several hundreds of pirates who had accepted the King's pardon and Woodes Rogers's governorship constituted around half of the pirates frequenting New Providence at the time of Rogers's arrival.[33] This would indeed indicate that vast parts of the pirate community did not see themselves as part of a revolutionary vanguard but had taken to piracy as a matter of circumstance or because they had fallen in with a crowd to which they did not really want to belong.

Of course, half of the New Providence pirates had refused to give up their pirating ways, but did they do so for self-conscious political reasons? Although they certainly were "those renegades who possessed the greatest pugnacity,"[34] they were probably more concerned about their personal freedom (a very political motivation in a certain way—not in another) than in saving mankind. Some, in fact, might have simply mistrusted the pardon. It was known that the authorities would often enough, usually by means of strictly legalistic interpretations of the terms, persecute them nonetheless.[35] The only political declarations that reach us from their ranks appear neither anarchistic nor revolutionary but concern a quarrel between royals. Some golden age pirate crews gave their ships Jacobite names—*King James, Royal James* or *Queen Anne's Revenge*"[36]—in honor and support of the deposed House of Stuart.[37]

Apart from the debate about a political pirate consciousness, there is an interesting discussion about whether pirates were part of an underprivileged, proletarian class. It is once again Marcus Rediker who endorses such a notion most prominently. He not only calls the golden age pirates "proletarian outlaws"[38] and interprets their "self-rule and social order" as part of a "volatile, serpentine tradition of opposition ... within both maritime and working-class culture,"[39] but he even suggests that pirates were engaged in an "undeclared class war,"[40] and were indeed "class-conscious."[41] These suggestions have been picked up enthusiastically by some radicals. The authors of "Pirate Utopias," for example, suggest that "piracy was one strategy in an early cycle of Atlantic class struggle" and that "pirates were perhaps the most international and militant section of the proto-proletariat constituted by 17th and 18th century sailors."[42]

How useful are such descriptions? Within Marxist theory, *class* is surprisingly one of the concepts that have never been "systematically defined and elaborated."[43] In most interpretations, however, they seem at least in some way connected to people's status within the process of economic production. Within this logic, pirates—not being part of any such process—would rather constitute a *non-class*.[44] Yes, their exploits might have been "rooted in a rejection of the class system of European society,"[45] and their social order might have expressed a "levelling of class inequalities,"[46] but not because they assumed the working class' revolutionary agenda—rather because they rejected class society altogether. In this light, it becomes understandable why Hans Turley would call Rediker's argument "overdetermined."[47] The golden age pirates—as a people with no recorded history—seem once again closer to so-called primitive communities than to the Euro-American proletariat: "It is said that the history of peoples who have a history is the history of class struggle. It might be said, with at least as much truthfulness, that the history of peoples without a history is the history of their struggle against the State."[48]

Perhaps there was neither anarchist nor revolutionary consciousness among the pirates of the golden age—but they certainly carried anarchist and revolutionary momentum.

4.7. Pirates as Social Bandits: Homage to Eric Hobsbawm

Golden age piracy as a form of social resistance[1] might best be studied within the analytical framework of social banditry provided by Eric Hobsbawm. While applying criteria of self-conscious political movements to the golden age pirates might give the impression that there was nothing revolutionary about them at all, analyzing them as social bandits might help tease out the revolutionary implications of their actions.

Many authors have commented on the startling parallels between golden age pirates and the bandit communities analyzed by Hobsbawm.[2] Most of these comments have been in passing. This might partly be due to an obvious difficulty that needs to be overcome in order to relate Hobsbawm's analysis to golden age piracy in more detail. After all, Hobsbawm analyzes social banditry as a peasant phenomenon. Obviously, golden age pirates were no peasants. Still, we can concur with Kenneth J. Kinkor, who writes that golden age piracy was "'social banditry' carried out in a maritime context."[3] This is echoed by Marcus Rediker's observation that "pirates, of course, were not peasants, but they fit Hobsbawm's formulation in every other respect."[4]

The Framework

In his highly popular study, *Bandits*, Eric Hobsbawm explains that "in this book we shall be dealing only with some kinds of robbers, namely those who are *not* regarded as simple criminals by public opinion."[5] This certainly fits the perception of golden age pirates. Edward Lucie-Smith is just one who raises questions like the following: "Granted that piracy is really no more than robbery at sea, how did the crime come to acquire the aura of sinister glamour that still clings to it, an aura which sets the pirate apart from other and more commonplace malefactors?"[6] In its simplicity, Philip Gosse's answer might point at the heart of the explanation: "Piracy may be a blot on civilization and its practitioners criminals whom it is a duty to extirpate. Yet there will always be a sympathetic response in the human heart to the appeal of the adventurer who dares go to far and dangerous places and in defiance of all organized respectability take his courage in both hands to carve out his fortune."[7]

The "sympathetic response" that Gosse evokes also explains why he would find a significant difference between the pirates of the golden age and those of other eras. He calls, for example, the pirates of the 19th century (who were, as some historians suggest, more numerous and successful than those of the golden age[8])

> worse than any ... that existed before. The earlier pirates, with all
> their black faults and their cruelty, were not without some trace of
> humanity, and on occasion could fight bravely. These new pirates were
> cowards without a single redeeming feature. Formed from the scum
> of the rebel navies of the revolted Spanish colonies and the riff-raff of

the West Indies, they were a set of bloodthirsty savages, who never
dared attack any but the weak, and had no more regard for innocent
lives than a butcher has for his victims. The result is a monotonous
list of slaughterings and pilferings from which scarcely one event or a
single character stands out to strike a spark from the imagination.[9]

In a very similar vein, Peter Lamborn Wilson would write many decades
later that "sea-going muggers who prey on the poor, and murder them as well,
would seem to have forfeited all claim to consideration as social bandits or
even 'real pirates.'"[10]

There are clear indications that the golden age pirates were, in the eyes
of many, "social bandits [who] are considered by their people as heroes,
as champions, avengers, fighters for justice, perhaps even leaders of liberation, and in any case as men to be admired, helped and supported."[11] There
remains the question, of course, who the pirates' people were. Even though
the pirates "had spies and sympathisers throughout the West Indies,"[12] and
"not a few … of those on shore who received their goods … aided them,"[13]
these folks did not constitute the tight-knit peasant communities that the
social bandits analyzed by Hobsbawm could retire to and count on. We will
return to this question below. First, let us consider some of the most obvious
parallels between Hobsbawm's definition of social banditry and golden age
piracy in Hobsbawm's own words:

> It is a commonplace that brigands flourish in remote and inaccessible
> areas such as mountains, trackless plains, fenland, forest or estuar-
> ies with their labyrinth of creeks and waterways, and are attracted
> by trade-routes and major highways, where pre-industrial travel is
> naturally both slow and cumbrous.[14]

> Socially it seems to occur in all types of human society which lie
> between the evolutionary phase of tribal and kinship organization,
> and modern capitalist and industrial society.[15]

> Banditry tended to become epidemic in times of pauperization and
> economic crisis.[16]

> The robber band is outside the social order which fetters the
> poor, a brotherhood of the free, not a community of the subject.

Nevertheless, it cannot opt out of society. Its needs and activities, its very existence, bring it into relations with the ordinary economic social and political system.[17]

All this means that bandits need middlemen, who link them not only to the rest of the local economy but to the larger networks of commerce.[18]

If they had any model of social organization, it was the male brotherhood or society.[19] (*This quote refers to the haiduks of the Balkans, a prime example of the bandits analyzed by Hobsbawm. Hobsbawm adds—in light of the Mary Read and Anne Bonny story—an interesting explanation with respect to the women who had joined the haiduk: "it seems that for the time of their haiduk life, these runaway girls were men."[20]*)

Banditry is freedom ... [21]

There are many other and more specific aspects in Hobsbawm's analysis that reveal similar parallels. Hobsbawm, for example, places certain bandits "on the turbulent frontier between state and serfdom on the one hand, the open spaces and freedom on the other,"[22] and sees them moving in "open spaces ... where lordships, serfdom and government had not yet arrived."[23] It is notable who makes up an important part of the bandits' ranks: "escaped serfs, ruined freemen, runaways from state or seignorial factories, from jail, seminary, army or navy, men with no determined place in society ... among such marginals, soldiers, deserters and ex-servicemen played a significant part."[24] As those who are "in some ways the most important category of potential bandits," Hobsbawm names

men who are unwilling to accept the meek and passive social role of the subject ... the stiffnecked and recalcitrant, the individual rebels ... the 'men who make themselves respected' ... These are the men who, when faced with some act of injustice or persecution, do not yield meekly to force or social superiority, but take the path of resistance and outlawry. ... They may be the toughs, who advertise their toughness by their swagger, their carrying of arms, sticks or clubs, even when peasants are not supposed to go armed, by the casual and rakish costume and manner and costume which symbolizes toughness.[25]

Finally, Hobsbawm describes a general sociopolitical pattern that can be applied word for word to the history of golden age piracy:

> Where the state is remote, ineffective and weak, it will indeed be tempted to come to terms with any local power-group it cannot defeat. If robbers are successful enough, they have to be conciliated just like any other centre of armed force. Every person who lives in times when banditry has got out of hand knows that local officials have to establish a working relationship with robber chiefs ... The only difficulty is that the closer a bandit comes to the people's ideal of a 'noble robber,' i.e. to being the socially conscious champion of the rights of the poor, the less likely it is that the authorities will open their arms to him. They are much more apt to treat him as a social revolutionary and hunt him down. This should normally take them not more than two or three years, the average span of a Robin Hood's career...[26]

Three types of bandits

Hobsbawm defines three main types of bandits: "the *noble robber* or Robin Hood, the primitive resistance fighter or guerrilla unit of what I shall call the *haiduks*, and possibly also the terror-bringing *avenger*."[27] Golden age pirates represented all three.

☠ Robin Hood

We have already seen that members of at least one golden age pirate crew called themselves *Robin Hoods men*.[28] According to Marcus Rediker, Henry Every was referred to as a "maritime Robin Hood."[29] In Hobsbawm's definition, the Robin Hood bandit "does not seek to establish a society of freedom and equality."[30] His role is rather "that of the champion, the righter of wrongs, the bringer of justice and social equity."[31] This seems reflected both in what is known about the golden age pirates' real-life activities and in their mythical reputation: they were not out to create any particular kind of society for all, they were out to live independently, take a stand, and bring justice to their enemies. It is in this sense that the golden age pirate is, in Edward Lucie-Smith's words, "a symbol of equality, a leveller."[32]

⚑ Guerrilla

Hobsbawm states that "guerrilla movements ... are obliged to follow substantially similar tactics as social bandits."[33] He uses the example of the Balkan haiduks—impoverished peasants who formed militia units both to fight Ottoman rule and secure a livelihood—to describe the bandit as guerrilla more specifically. While the haiduk "would see himself, above all, as a free man—and as such as good as a lord or a king; a man who had in this sense won personal emancipation and therefore superiority,"[34] he would, at the same time, "not automatically [be] committed to rebellion against all authority." The haiduks could accept—and even make arrangements with—authority as long as this did not interfere with their personal freedom. In Hobsbawm's words: "They could, as in some parts of Hungary, become attached to lords whom they provided with fighters against a recognition of their status as free men."[35] The same is true for both the Caribbean buccaneers (clearly) and the golden age pirates (who dealt with many corrupt officials). Concerning their social organization, the haiduks shared the buccaneers' and pirates' egalitarian sensitivities: "Freedom implied equality among haiduks and there are some impressive examples of it. For instance, when the King of Oudh tried to form a regiment of Badhaks, much as the Russian and Austrian emperors formed haiduk and cossack units, they mutinied because the officers had refused to perform the same duties as the men."[36] An important parallel lies also in Hobsbawm's judgment that the haiduks, in their guerrilla-like organization and operations, constituted a kind of "permanent and formalized banditry" and were "therefore automatically ... potentially more 'political'"[37] than the noble robber. In other words: "Haiduk banditry was therefore in every respect a more serious, a more ambitious, permanent and institutionalized challenge to official authority than the scattering of Robin Hoods."[38] Hobsbawm calls haiduk banditry "the highest form of primitive banditry, the one which comes closest to being a permanent and conscious focus of ... insurrection."[39]

⚑ Avenger

Hobsbawm introduces his third social bandit type with the following observation:

> It is at first sight strange to encounter bandits who not only practice
> terror and cruelty to an extent which cannot possibly be explained as

mere backsliding, but whose terror actually forms part of their public image. They are heroes not in spite of the fear and horror their actions inspire, but in some ways because of them. They are not so much men who right wrongs, but avengers, and exerters of power; their appeal is not that of the agents of justice, but of men who prove that even the poor and weak can be terrible.[40]

If we agree with the following assertion of Marcus Rediker, then golden age pirates fit this picture well: "In truth, pirates were terrorists of a sort. And yet we do not think of them this way. They have become, over the years, cultural heroes, perhaps antiheroes, and at the very least romantic and powerful figures in an American and increasingly global popular culture. Theirs was a terror of the weak against the strong."[41] Christopher Hill, intentionally or not, uses Hobsbawm's exact words when he says that "some pirates must have seen themselves as egalitarian avengers."[42] Hobsbawm explains this by stating that "killing and torture is the most primitive and personal assertion of ultimate power."[43] This is strongly connected to the fact that "cruelty is inseparable from vengeance, and vengeance is an entirely legitimate activity for the noblest of bandits."[44] Vengeance, in turn, lies at the heart of the golden age pirates' concept of justice and will be examined in a later section of this chapter.

How is it possible to get around the main problem in applying Hobsbawm's analysis to golden age piracy, namely that Hobsbawm sees his bandits rooted in peasant society? It cannot suffice to simply widen the peasant identity or to replace the peasant community with another. Besides, there is no community in connection with the golden age pirates that could serve as a substitute. The golden age pirates do not represent any particular community—they are outcasts, separated from all society, warring against *all* the world.

Or are they? Obviously, many folks throughout the centuries have not seen them as their enemies, but rather as symbols with which to identify. Symbols that all appear in connection with Hobsbawm's social bandits: *free men, strong men, noble men, levellers, avengers, rebels*. In fact, this is possibly truer for golden age pirates than for any other group of outcasts who have challenged the rules of law and order. It might be that the golden age pirate—for whatever reason: his elusiveness, the powerful metaphor of the ship and the sea, the exotic location of his tales, the ideals of equality and democracy that he represents—has become *the* bandit of the Western world. He is a sort of archetypical bandit, a *social* or *primitive rebel* (to use other terms employed by Hobsbawm) who almost all of us, in some way, can relate to and find sympathy with. Hobsbawm himself says that "the bandit is not only a man, but a symbol."[45] Maybe we *all* are the golden age pirates' people. Hobsbawm writes that "the country which has given the world Robin Hood, the international paradigm of social banditry, has no actual record of social bandits after, say, the early seventeenth century."[46] Is this is because the buccaneers and pirates took over that role?

Hobsbawm himself concedes that a shift away from the close connection of the social bandit to peasant communities might have been inevitable given the industrialization process that undermined the very identity of peasant communities. In his own words: "In a broader sense 'modernization,' that is to say the combination of economic development, efficient communications and public administration, deprives any kind of banditry, including the social, of the conditions under which it flourishes."[47] Yet among the population a psychological need for images of social bandits remained. Did this mean an ever-stronger shift of the social bandit to his symbolic side? Hobsbawm compares the social bandits of the peasantry to what he calls "the criminal underworld of urban or vagrant elements":[48]

> Criminal bands thus lacked the local roots of social bandits, but at the same time they were not confined by the limits of the territory beyond which social bandits could rarely venture in safety. They formed part of large, if loose networks of an underworld which might stretch over half a continent, and would certainly extend into the cities which were *terra incognita* for peasant bandits who feared and hated them. For vagrants, nomads, criminals and their like, the kind of area within which most social bandits lived out their lives, was merely a location for so many markets or fairs a year, a place for occasional raids, or at most (for instance if strategically placed near several frontiers) a suitable headquarters for wider operations. Nevertheless, criminal robbers cannot be simply excluded from the study of social banditry.

In the first place, where for one reason or another social banditry did
not flourish or had died out, suitable criminal robbers might well be
idealized and given the attributes of Robin Hood, especially when
they concentrated in holding up merchants, rich travellers, and others
who enjoyed no great sympathy among the poor.[49]

If we follow this analysis, golden age pirates might have been the "suitable
criminal robbers" who have taken on this role—so suitable, in fact, that they
took on this role not only for peasants and the poor, but for all of us. Given the
universal appeal that the golden age pirates have always exerted, this seems
like a compelling proposition. The fact that, according to this theory, only
a symbolic social bandit remains does not make his influence any less real.
Many fictional and mythical heroes have very real influence on people and
their cultures: Barbie, Spiderman, the Easter Bunny...

What is the political significance of the golden age pirate as a (symbolic)
social bandit? Is there any?

Hobsbawm has been taken to task by many radicals for his assumptions
that "social banditry has next to no organization or ideology," is "totally
inadaptable to modern social movements," proves "ineffective" (even in "its
most highly developed forms, which skirt national guerrilla warfare"),[50]
and remains "a modest and unrevolutionary protest."[51] The critics have
pointed out—probably rightfully so—that these assumptions are based
on Hobsbawm's own ideological biases which veer towards more orthodox
(some would say "authoritarian") strains of the left.

As far as Hobsbawm's political analysis of social banditry (without the ideological implications) is related to golden age piracy, though, his comments
seem convincing. Golden age piracy had "next to no organization or ideology," can hardly be described as a "social movement," and—in the sense of
establishing long-lasting alternative social orders—was "ineffective." As with
the haiduks, it can probably also be said of the golden age pirates that "class-
consciousness was not normally the motive which drove [them]."[52]

However, some might say that it is a good thing that "banditry is a rather
primitive form of organized social protest, perhaps the most primitive we
know."[53] The lack of ideology, organization, and class-consciousness can
certainly be seen as refreshing, even liberating. As far as social movements
go—aren't they kind of boring? And effectiveness? Isn't a Temporary

Autonomous Zone (no italics) in the form of a pirate utopia much more effective than tedious party politics? Maybe the "mentality of roving insurgents" that entered the Red Army due to Mao's inclusion of "outlaws" and "declassed elements" should have never been "remedied [through] intensified education"?[54] Maybe the whole point of being revolutionary is to "prove that justice is possible, that poor men need not be humble, helpless and meek," since no one will ever completely "abolish oppression"?[55] Maybe it is better to be "activists and not ideologists or prophets, from whom novel visions or plans of social and political organization are to be expected"?[56]

It should be possible to find answers to these questions that lie somewhere between a yes and a no. On the one hand, some of Hobsbawm's judgments can easily be perceived as too strong. For example: "What part, if any, do bandits play in ... transformations of society? As individuals, they are not so much political or social rebels, let alone revolutionaries ... *En masse*, they are little more than symptoms of crisis and tension in their society—of famine, pestilence, war or anything else that disrupts it."[57] Reducing people who refuse to obey the political and/or clerical authorities and who partake in the creation of alternative social orders by virtue of stepping outside the dominant social orders to "symptoms" of social developments and categorically denying them any revolutionary identity seems disrespectful, even condescending. Yet some of Hobsbawm's conclusions are compelling and appear applicable to the golden age pirates:

> They right wrongs, they correct and avenge cases of injustice, and in doing so apply a more general criterion of just and fair relations between men in general, and especially between the rich and the poor, the strong and the weak. This is a modest aim, which leaves the rich to exploit the poor (but no more than is traditionally accepted as 'fair'), the strong to oppress the weak (but within the limits of what is equitable, and mindful of their social and moral duties). It demands not that there should be no more lords...[58]

"Bandit-heroes are not expected to make a world of equality. They can only right wrongs and prove that sometimes oppression can be turned upside down."[59] Equally applicable to the situation of the golden age pirates is the following passage (even if the golden age pirates did not drive Cadillacs): "Paradoxically therefore the conspicuous expenditure of the bandit, like the gold-plated Cadillacs and diamond-inlaid teeth of the slum-boy who has become world boxing champion, serves to link him to his admirers and not to separate him from them; providing that he does not step too far outside the heroic role into which the people have cast him."[60] With many golden age pirates—and certainly with many buccaneers—in mind, it becomes easy to conclude with Hobsbawm that "the more successful he is as a bandit, the more he is *both* a representative and champion of the poor *and* a part of the system of the rich."[61]

Still, Hobsbawm might underestimate the revolutionary connotations of the social bandit's activities and rate them too strongly against his own ideas of political resistance, which he reveals in passages hailing the power of "political organizations" and conclusions that "there is no future" for those who—like the social bandits—"do not take to the new ways of fighting."[62] In other words, even though Hobsbawm himself admits that "social banditry has an affinity for revolution,"[63] he refuses to accept the implications of this concession. In *Bandits*, for example, Hobsbawm states that social bandits are people "who, in their own limited way, have shown that the wild life in the greenwood can bring liberty, equality and fraternity to those who pay the price of homelessness, danger, and almost certain death."[64] How can setting such an example not be revolutionary? In *Primitive Rebels*, Hobsbawm writes: "Only the ideals for which they fought, and for which men and women made up songs about them, survive, and round the fireside these still maintain the vision of the just society, whose champions are brave and noble as eagles."[65] Again, how can the power of inspiration expressed in this quote stop short of being revolutionary power?

It seems that their role as social bandits confirms the revolutionary moment and potential of the golden age pirates—after all, a wild life is not reduced to the greenwood, it can be had on the oceans too. Whether this is enough to make them *revolutionaries* remains a matter of definition. It should matter little to us. The golden age pirates are gone. Their moment and their potential, however, are not.

4.8. Libertalia: Another Reading

No story has occupied radical minds fascinated by pirates like that of Captain Misson's utopian community Libertalia, told in the second volume of Captain

Johnson's *General History of the Pirates*. Johnson divides the story into two parts, "Of Capt. Misson and his Crew" and "Of Capt. Tew and his Crew." The latter contains the foundation of Libertalia. It is commonly accepted today that the story is fictional.[1] This does not deter politically interested pirate scholars from discussing its political significance. Peter Lamborn Wilson raises an interesting point by suggesting that the story remained unchallenged at the time of its publication because it seemed "inherently believable" and hence "*could* have been real," and that this should form the basis for our discussions.[2] Other authors have argued that Libertalia was "based upon the realities of pirate organizations during the golden age,"[3] and that "because Johnson's chapter 'Of Captain Misson' is a history, and because Misson is a product of Johnson's imagination, the liberty espoused by Misson is a literary—or fictional—reality."[4] Marcus Rediker explains in more detail:

> Was [Libertalia] fiction? Since a man named Misson and a place
> named Libertalia apparently never existed, the literal answer must
> be yes. But in a deeper historical and political sense Misson and
> Libertalia were not simply fictions ... Libertalia was a fictive expres-
> sion of living traditions, practices and dreams of an Atlantic working
> class, many of which were observed, synthesized and translated into
> discourse by the author of *A General History of the Pyrates*. A mosaic
> assembled from the specific utopian practices of the early eighteenth-
> century pirate ship, Libertalia had objective bases in historical fact.[5]

Chris Land draws the convincing conclusion that "the historical veracity of *Of Captain Misson* is perhaps not as important as its lasting influence ... on the insurrectionary imagination."[6] William Burroughs's *Ghost of Chance*, featuring a lemur- and (no surprises there) drug-loving Captain Misson, is just one example.

Marcus Rediker also links the inspiring utopian aspect of Libertalia to the subversive social trajectory that he and Peter Linebaugh defined as *Hydrarchy* in the modern-day classic *The Many-Headed Hydra*:

> Our discussion of Hydrarchy and Libertalia raises questions about
> the process by which subversive popular ideas and practices are kept
> alive, underground and over water, for long periods of time. Indeed,
> the pirates' alternative social order might be seen as a maritime

continuation of the traditional peasant utopia, in England and
continental Europe, called 'The Land of Cockaygne.' The dislike
of work, the abundance of food, the concern with good health, the
levelling of social distinctions and the turning of the world upside
down, the redivision of property, the ease and the freedoms—all of
the elements of primitive communism that informed the medieval
myth were expressed in Libertalia and at least partially realized on the
pirate ship. And yet if Hydrarchy and Libertalia echoed the dreams of
Cockaygne in centuries gone by, so did they speak to the future, to the
development of mass radical-democratic movements. Hydrarchy and
Libertalia may be intermediate popular links between the defeated
republicans of the English Revolution and the victorious republicans
of the age of revolution more than a century later. The relative absence
of piracy in the Atlantic between 1750 and 1850 may in the end owe
something to the utopian prospect of an earlier age and the ruthless
repression they called forth. But so too might the age of revolution
owe something to the utopian dimensions of earlier popular struggles.
Maybe pirates themselves may have died upon the gallows, defeated,
but Hydrarchy and Libertalia had many victories yet to claim.[7]

The gist of this utopian prospect and its legacy are perhaps best expressed
in Larry Law's introduction to his charming mini-edition of the Misson story:

> As with Robin Hood there is more than a trace of wishful thinking
> in the story of Misson. But the wish was there and if nothing else the
> story of Misson stands as a tribute, over 250 years' old, to the concept
> of a society run on a system of co-operation and mutual aid, which
> cared for its old and disabled, was merciful to its malefactors, ran its
> own affairs and needed neither money nor policemen.[8]

Stephen Snelders sees this concept rooted in the Caribbean buccaneer
culture:

> In linking the European mercenary traditions to the discontent of
> oppressed sailors, the Brotherhood of the Coast became a sanctuary
> for dropouts, deserters, outcasts and social failures, and so created
> a myth of freedom and independence that eventually developed

into the dream of Libertalia. In their rough way they kept the ideals
of Liberty, Equality, and Fraternity that exploded the world of the
Ancien Regime more than a century later.[9]

It seems persuasive that it does not matter much whether Libertalia was
real or not. What matters is the story's political significance and strength. It is
curious, however, that a closer look at the story, as told by Captain Johnson,
does not necessarily provide much ground for radical euphoria.

In the story, Captain Misson is a young Frenchmen from a wealthy family who travels to Rome for a proper Christian education. Soon disillusioned
with the Catholic Church, he meets an equally disillusioned and eloquent
Italian student by the name of Caraccioli, who becomes Misson's life-long
companion and ideological mentor. The two end up going to sea together,
sail to the Caribbean, and, after the captain, second captain and the three
lieutenants of their ship are killed in an engagement with an English man-of-
war, Misson is elected captain.[10] He eventually leads his men to Madagascar,
while propagating a number of noble causes related to individual freedom
and the equality of men in elaborate speeches. In Madagascar he meets with
(the very non-fictional) Captain Thomas Tew, convinces him to become his
cohort, and founds the utopian settlement of Libertalia, which after some
time is destroyed by native Madagascans. While sailing towards France con-
templating his future, Misson and his crew die in a storm.

Several aspects of this story seem to have received no attention in radical
circles, or have been played down and misrepresented.

1. Misson and Caraccioli make it clear that they do not want to be pirates.
According to Captain Johnson,

> Caraccioli objected that they were no pirates, but men who were
> resolved to assert that liberty which god and nature gave them, and
> own no subjection to any, farther than was for the common good of
> all. That indeed, obedience to governors was necessary, when they
> knew and acted up to the duty of their function, were vigilant guard-
> ians of the people's rights and liberties, saw that justice was equally
> distributed, were barriers against the rich and powerful when they
> attempted to oppress the weaker.[11]

For these reasons, Caraccioli also objects to the Jolly Roger as their flag:

> As we then do not proceed upon the same grounds with pirates, who
> are men of dissolute lives and no principles, let us scorn to take their
> colours. Ours is a brave, a just, an innocent, and a noble cause; the
> cause of liberty. I therefore advise a white sign, with Liberty painted
> in the fly, and if you would like the motto, A *Deo a Libertate*, for God
> and Liberty, as an emblem of our uprightness and resolution.[12]

These are serious declarations. In fact, the passages reveal the role of
Misson's tale in Captain Johnson's *General History*: it is the moral antipode to
the exploits of the pirate captains, the warning index finger, conscience rising
above selfishness. Citing Captain Misson as golden age piracy's most shining example drastically corrupts the story. A simultaneous embrace of golden
age piracy *and* Captain Misson seems impossible. Rather, we have to make
a choice: either we believe in the revolutionary virtue of a band of outlaws
under the black flag—or we believe in the revolutionary virtue of a man of
principle under the white flag. You can't eat your cake and have it, too.

2. How revolutionary were Caraccioli and Captain Misson's principles
and demands? The passages quoted above already confirm that they objected
neither to governors per se (Caraccioli praises a good governor as "a real
father"[13]) nor to distinctions between the "rich and powerful" on the one
hand and the "weaker" on the other, as long as there existed institutional
"barriers" to prevent oppression. (How can oppression be avoided in an economically unjust society?) What, then, defines the progressiveness of Misson
and Caraccioli? Misson is democratic: "He then gave the sentiments of those
who were against him, and their reasons, and begged that every one would
give his opinion and vote according as he thought most conducive to the good
of all; that he should be far from taking it ill if they should reject what he
had proposed, since he had no private views to serve."[14] Misson would "force
no man."[15] Misson objects to slavery: "For his part, and he hoped he spoke
the sentiments of all his brave companions, he had not exempted his neck for
the galling yoke of slavery, and asserted his own liberty, to enslave others."[16]
Misson advocates common property, "telling… all should be in common
and the particular avarice of no one should defraud the public."[17] Misson is
a humanist who

was under an obligation to recommend to them a brotherly love to
each other; the banishment of all private piques and grudges, and a
strict agreement and harmony among themselves. That in throwing off
the yoke of tyranny ... he hoped none would follow the example of the
tyrants, and turn his back upon justice; for when equity was trodden
under foot, misery, confusion and mutual distrust naturally followed.[18]

Misson objects to the death penalty, "a barbarity by which he would not
purchase his security."[19] Misson treats his prisoners justly: "He then enquired
into the circumstances of every particular [prisoner] and what they had lost, all
of which he returned."[20] Misson abides by the virtues of grace and forgiveness:
"He was averse to everything that bore the face of cruelty and thought a bloody
revenge, if necessity did not enforce it, spoke a groveling and timid soul."[21] All
these sentiments together shape Misson's unique sea robbing agenda:

Self-preservation, therefore, and not a cruel disposition, obliging him
to declare war against all such as should refuse him the entry of their
ports, and against all, who should not immediately surrender and give
up what their necessities required; but in a more particular manner
against all European ships and vessels, as concluded implacable
enemies. *And I do now,* said he, *declare such war, and, at the same time,
recommend to you my comrades, a humane and generous behaviour
towards your prisoners, which will appear by so much more the effects of
a noble soul, as we are satisfied we should not meet the same treatment
should our ill-fortune, or more properly our disunion, or want of courage,
give us up to their mercy.*[22]

This of course is all very noble, extremely remarkable for its time, and
certain aspects—especially the final declaration—must surely be considered
radical. Still, does it make Misson a revolutionary? Or rather a mixture of
a holy man, a social reformer, and a Robin Hood? Could such a mixture
be revolutionary? Maybe Misson's own resolution—the settlement of
Libertalia—provides the answer.

3. The aim of Libertalia is never in doubt: it is supposed to be a social
order with a government and coercive laws. In other words: the objective of
establishing Libertalia is to establish a *state,* complete with naval force and

all. Captain Johnson explicitly confirms that the "great many wholesome laws ... enacted" were "registered in a State book," while Caraccioli fills the position of "Secretary of State." Government is deemed a "necessity to ... conservation," the coercive laws considered indispensable because otherwise "the weakest would always be the sufferers, and everything must tend to confusion." Both government and law are the answers to "men's passion [which is] blinding them to justice, and making them ever partial to themselves."[23] At this point it becomes utterly clear that Misson's ideas build on the assumptions of Thomas Hobbes, the ideological godfather of the modern nation-state. Libertalia then simply becomes a Leviathan with humanitarian coating. Such Leviathans define today's political landscape. Are they really "working-class dreams"?[24]

It has been suggested that Libertalia was communistic and anti-capitalist.[25] These assumptions seem somewhat baffling given Captain Johnson's outline of Libertalia's economy: "The treasure and cattle they were masters of should be equally divided, and such lands as any particular man would enclose should, for the future, be deemed his property which no other should lay any claim to, if not alienated by a sale."[26] Accordingly, "an equal division was made of their treasure and cattle, and everyone began either to enclose land for himself or his neighbor, who would hire his assistance."[27] Does this not just sound like plain old petty-bourgeois liberalism?

The most radical aspects of Libertalia were its governing council, consisting "of the ablest among them, without distinction of nation or colour," and the fact that "the different languages began to be incorporated, and one made out of many"[28]—which corresponds to the name of Libertalia and "the name of Liberi to his people, desiring ... that might be drowned the distinguished names of French, English, Dutch, Africans, etc."[29] Still, Libertalia was a state and all states are coercive, no matter how council-based; after all, soviet means council, too.

That the governing council of Libertalia took its coercing role seriously is revealed in the following episode of the Libertalia story. Some months prior to its establishment, Tew's former quartermaster led a group of renegade crew members who separated from their captain and established their own Madagascan settlement. When Libertalia's governing council discussed the proposal of inviting the group to join them, we find "the council rejecting this, alleging that as they deserted their captain, it was a mark of mutinous temper, and they might infect others with a spirit of disorder."[30] Since when do the dreams of radicals condemn "mutinous temper" or a "spirit of disorder"?

Stephen Snelders, however, seems to be the only radical author who discusses this part of the Libertalia story. (Peter Lamborn Wilson also speaks of the "'anarchist' schism" caused by Tew's former quartermaster, but only in passing.[31]) Snelders writes:

> If we compare the chapter on Misson with what we have learned
> about the organization on board the pirate ships, the radically dis-
> sident pirates appear more typical of the politics of Old Roger than
> Libertalia's proto-democracy, with its Lockean original contract and
> movement towards the formation of a liberal state with private prop-
> erty and formal democracy to protect it. The anarchists who refuse
> to accept the democratic pirate utopia and have no use for laws of any
> kind may be the truest reflection of the pirate ethos.[32]

It is hard to see the basis for such claims in Captain Johnson's text; Snelders's conclusion appears as curious as the romanticization of Libertalia, and by far the most puzzling in his outstanding *The Devil's Anarchy*. According to Johnson, after the council rejects the dissidents, Captain Tew is granted permission to see them nonetheless in order to give notice about Libertalia: "If, they made it their earnest entreaty to be admitted, and would desert the quartermaster, it should be granted as a particular favour done to them at the instance of the admiral [Tew], and upon his engaging a parole of honour for their quiet behaviour."[33] Tew makes the journey to the settlement, is received "mighty civilly" by the quartermaster, and tells him about Libertalia. (Why he would talk to the one person who, according to the council, needs to be deserted as a condition for the others to join, remains a mystery.) The quartermaster tells him "that he could see no advantage to themselves in changing their present situation,... that they... enjoyed all the necessaries of life, were free and independent of all the world, and it would be madness again to subject themselves to any government which, however mild, still exerted some power."[34] So far into the story, Snelders's interpretation would make sense.[35]

This perception changes, though, when the quartermaster continues:

> However, if you will go to America or Europe and shew the
> advantages which may accrue to the English by fixing a colony here,

out of love we bear for our country, and to wipe away the odious
appellation of Pirates, with pleasure we'll submit to any who shall
come with a commission from a lawful government. But 'tis ridiculous
to think we will become subjects to greater rogues than ourselves.[36]

In other words, the community that represents for Snelders "the truest
reflection of the pirate ethos" not only wants to rid itself of the "odious appellation of Pirates," but would also be ready to function as a colonial English
outpost, among other reasons because "a settlement here would be a curb on
Pirates and a protection as well as a great conveniency to our east India ships,
who might here be stored with fresh or salt provisions." This is formulated in
a letter that the quartermaster fetches before Tew's departure, urging him to
present it to the English authorities back in America. The letter lists a number of arguments for granting colony status to their settlement. Among these
arguments, we find not only the quoted condemnations of piracy, but also the
following calculation:

> Negroes in Barbadoes are at £30, £40, or £50 a head, and I dare answer
> to 10 s. in European goods will purchase a negro slave at Madagascar,
> since we have purchased one for an old coat, a lusty fellow. Food is very
> dear at Barbadoes and here you may feed a slave, as well as yourself
> without expense, consequently he will do more work than a Barbadoes
> slave, who is, by the dearness of provision, half-starved.[37]

In the end, the tale of Libertalia features two political options: a democratic-
liberal state (whose utopian notion never really exceeded that of Thomas
More[38]), and a rough-and-ready colonial station. Neither option appears ter-
ribly attractive for radical politics.

4.9. Safe Havens, Onshore Settlements, Pirate Utopias: Pirates on Land

In comparison to the most probably fictional Libertalia, an illustration of the
pirate settlements whose existence is beyond doubt will better help explore
their political dimensions. What is certain is that these settlements scared
the authorities. As Linebaugh and Rediker state: "Some among the powerful
worried that pirates might 'set up a sort of Commonwealth' in areas where
no power would be able 'to dispute with them.' Colonial and metropolitan

merchants and officials feared incipient separatism in Madagascar, Sierra Leone, Bermuda, North Carolina, the Bay of Campeche, and Honduras."[1] Snelders calls these areas "illegal autonomous zones"[2] and "border areas of civilization"[3]—both apt descriptions and much more fitting than "quasi-states."[4]

Caribbean

The Caribbean buccaneers and pirates used various land bases from the 1620s to the 1720s. Providence Island was an early privateering station for the English in the 1630s, Martinique developed into a center for French buccaneers and pirates some decades later, and the Virgin Islands (in particular Saint Thomas) were a regular rendezvous for pirates from many nations throughout the century. The most important centers, however, were Hispaniola, the stomping ground of the early buccaneer community; Tortuga, the "buccaneers' 'acropolis'"[5] across a strait of Hispaniola's northwestern tip where most of the buccaneers moved once they had turned from hunters to sea robbers; Petit-Goâve on western Hispaniola, where most of the Tortuga buccaneers returned in the 1660s; Port Royal, Jamaica, which, in the words of David Cordingly and John Falconer, developed into "a paradise for buccaneers"[6] after the English takeover in 1655; the Bays of Campeche and Honduras, centers of the notorious logwood cutters during the last decades of the 17th century; and New Providence, which served as the golden age pirates' "sanctuary"[7] for two short years from 1716 to 1718.

Hispaniola

Descriptions of everyday life on western Hispaniola during the buccaneer heyday make life sound like a step short of a primitivist Eldorado. Father du Tertre, an early missionary in the Caribbean, writes about an "unorganized rabble of men from all countries" who "would not suffer any chiefs":

> In general they were without any habitation or fixed abode, but only rendezvoused where the cattle were to be found, and some sheds cov-ered with leaves to keep off the rain and to store the hides of the beasts they had killed until some vessel should pass to barter with them for wine, brandy, line, arms, powder, bullets, and cooking vessels which they needed and which were the only moveables of the buccaneers.[8]

Du Tertre also remarked: "You would say that these are the butcher's vilest servants who have been eight days in the slaughterhouse without washing themselves."[9] A graphic illustration is also provided by Clark Russell:

> The Island of San Domingo, or Hispaniola as it was then called, was
> haunted and overrun by a singular community of savage, surly, fierce
> and filthy men. ... These people went dressed in shirts and panta-
> loons of coarse linen cloth, which they steeped in the blood of the
> animals they slaughtered. They wore round caps, boots of hogskin
> drawn over their feet, and belts of raw hide, in which they stuck their
> sabres and knives ... They were hunters by trade, and savages in their
> habits ... They ate and slept on the ground, their table was a stone,
> their bolster the trunk of a tree, and their roof the hot and sparkling
> heavens of the Antilles.[10]

This community of hunters was driven from Hispaniola by the Spaniards who killed off the game in the 1630s. Most buccaneers moved across a small strait to the island of Tortuga off Hispaniola's northwestern tip.

Tortuga

Tortuga probably had some semi-permanent settlers (mostly traders) starting in the 1620s. The island then experienced a rather turbulent colonial history and changed hands between the English, French, and Spanish a few times, until the French established a hold over it in 1642 with governor Jean le Vasseur fortifying the island and turning it into a strong sea-raiding base. Despite continued Spanish attacks, the French and the buccaneers remained (with short interruptions) until the 1770s before the last buccaneer generation established itself around the thriving settlement of Petit-Goâve on Hispaniola.

Philip Gosse has called Tortuga "a buccaneer republic, where the seamen made their own laws and cultivated the land for sugar-cane and yams,"[11] while John Masefield suggests that the Tortuga buccaneers "soon became so numerous that they might have made an independent state had they but agreed among themselves."[12] A vivid description of Tortuga in its heyday comes from Basil Fuller and Ronald Leslie-Melville:

> The Brethren of the Coast lived a life which was an extraordinary
> mixture of idealism and savagery. Gradually their haven became more

prosperous. A better harbour and better defences were built. The standard of living in Tortuga rose as wealth flowed into it in ever increasing tides. But still no attempt was made to add to the luxury of the haven. Amazingly the buccaneers maintained their determination to eschew comforts, fearful to their softening effects. So Tortuga was raised from the insignificant island it had once been to the dignity of a dangerous lair, over which ministers in far-away Whitehall scratched their heads, and Spanish grandees fumed and cursed. The secret of the success of the haven lay in the true 'brotherhood' of its people, who realised to an astonishing degree, considering what stamp of men they were, the truth of the old tag 'united we stand, divided we fall.' The buccaneers stuck to each other with a loyalty which compels our admiration.[13]

Petit-Goâve

Petit-Goâve, located in Hispaniola's southwest, served as the base of the French buccaneers during the dying phases of the community from the 1670s to the 1690s. Described as the capital of "a population of tramps and rebels,"[14] hundreds of buccaneers were based there until the late 1680s.[15] By 1700, however, the town had become "a sleepy French colonial backwater."[16]

Port Royal

When the restoration of Charles II in 1660 brought an increase in privateering licenses on Jamaica, the harbor town of Port Royal developed into the major center for English buccaneers, many of whom flocked into the new English colony from Hispaniola and Tortuga. By 1665, the town counted more than 2,000 buccaneers who regularly embarked on journeys from its port.[17] When the English stopped using privateers in the 1680s, the buccaneer community came to an end. This did not stop the "mushroom growth" of Port Royal, though, which "immediately before the earthquake that destroyed it in June 1692 ... was nearly twice as large as New York at the same period."[18] Many saw the earthquake itself as a kind of divine intervention, since Port Royal had a "hell-raising reputation":[19] "It was, according to one righteous visitor, the 'Sodom of the New World.' A clergyman claimed, 'its population consists or pirates, cut-throats, whores and some of the vilest persons in the whole of the world.'"[20] Port Royal has further been described as the "the wickedest town in America,"[21] "the most corrupt and debauched town in all His

Majesty's dominions,"[22] "the Gomorrah of the times,"[23] and "the receptacle of vagabonds, the sanctuary of bankrupts, and a close-stool for the purges of our prisons."[24] Somewhat more informative is of Neville Williams's description:

> Port Royal developed very rapidly as a bleary-eyed town of unashamed debauchery, where seamen of every rank seemed only too happy to be parted from their money. There were more dram shops there than in London, almost as many brothels as in Paris and more sudden deaths than in the whole of Scotland. The men who sailed into Port Royal after only a moderately successful cruise for plunder threw their money about with incredible prodigality.[25]

Bay of Campeche/Bay of Honduras

The Bays of Campeche and Honduras developed into the center of the English logwood cutters in the 1670s. The logwood cutters were tightly connected to the buccaneers who also served as important trading partners. Many of the logwood cutters were ex- or part-time buccaneers themselves. Logwood was used for dying clothes, and the cutters—all in all no more than "260 to 270 men" in Dampier's estimation[26]—made good money living in conditions similar to those of the early buccaneers on Hispaniola: "The logwood cutters had a reputation not unlike that of the original buccaneers who hunted cattle on the island of Hispaniola: hard men earning a difficult living in primitive conditions, unfettered by the constraints of civilized society."[27] In fact, the logwood cutters engaged in hunting expeditions on the side—as we have seen previously, they also engaged in raids on Indian communities. Nonetheless, Linebaugh and Rediker have called them part of "a landed extension of hydrarchy" exercising a kind of "primitive communism."[28] Given the fact that we have hardly any documentation of life in these communities other than the notes taken by Dampier, which sketch a tough male frontier society, this appears somewhat idealistic.[29]

New Providence

For two short years, from 1716 to 1718, the island of New Providence in the Bahamas became, in the words of one historian, "the pirate capital of the New World."[30] The island had already served as a pirate base in the 1690s, but it was only with the reemergence of piracy in 1713 (after the end of the War of the

Spanish Succession) that pirate crews started flocking en masse to what was perceived to be a perfect pirate haven. There they created, depending on which fanciful phrase we prefer, a "nest of pirates,"[31] a "colony of rogues,"[32] a "rough-and-ready republic,"[33] or an "outlaw state."[34] In Stephen Snelders's estimation, "between 1716 and 1718 ... the pirate brotherhood was numerically as strong as the old Brotherhood of the Coast had been."[35] Neville Williams writes that "within a few months this 'Pirate Republic' boasted a population of some 2,000 desperate men. New Providence was both a retreat for outlaws, where ships could careen and water in safety, and a first-class operational base."[36]

David F. Marley explains why New Providence made such a formidable pirate base: "Its harbour was too shallow and tricky for heavy men-of-war to enter easily, while the surrounding hills afforded excellent vantage points for espying passing ships. Furthermore, the island's reefs teemed with lobster, fish and turtle, and the well-wooded interior featured fresh-water springs and an abundance of fruit and game."[37] In the lofty words of Douglas Botting, New Providence was "the most felicitous haven that ever met the squinting gaze of an outlaw seaman." Besides, "there was no law in Nassau except that of the fist and cutlass. ... In that part a pirate felt truly unfettered; he was cut from the moorings of social constraint."[38]

According to Jenifer G. Marx, "whores and outcasts, mangy dogs, and multiplying rats added to the fluctuating population. Merchants and traders were drawn to the settlement. They catered to the outlaws' needs and purchased their plunder, much if which was smuggled to the colonies for resale."[39] A graphic illustration, worth quoting at length, also comes from Frank Sherry:

> The town of Nassau, once a torpid waterside hamlet, had by 1716 become the capital city of the reborn pirate confederacy. Nassau reflected both the values and the style of the brigands who made it their headquarters: impermanent, licentious, and chaotic. A shanty-town—a zany collection of stores, shacks, whorehouses, and saloons, cobbled together from driftwood and canvas with palm thatch for roofs—stretched in a half circle along the sandy shore of the harbor. The wreckage of captured prizes lay rotting on the beach, their ribs exposed like long-dead carcasses. Dozens of vessels—pirate sloops and captured merchants—crowded the harbor, their masts looked like a leafless forest from the shore. In this place, their own crazy

metropolis, the pirates of the western world drank, argued among themselves, gambled away fortunes, paid in stolen coin for the bodies of the prostitutes who flocked to the town, and lived in an uproarious present until their coin was gone and they had to go to sea once more. It was said that the stench from Nassau—a combination of roasting meat, smoke, human offal, rum, unwashed bodies, and rotting garbage, all stewing together under the tropical sun—could be detected far out to sea, long before the island itself was visible. New Providence and its wild harbor town were in many ways a pirate heaven as well as a pirate haven. Free from all laws other than the laws of piracy, it made available all the rough joys that the outlaw brotherhood held dear.[40]

As far as these "laws of piracy" are concerned, it has been suggested that the island was "ruled by a council of captains and quartermasters, just as if it had been a very large pirate ship,"[41] but there seems little evidence for such a level of organization. As far as the reference to New Providence as a "pirate heaven" goes, the image apparently did indeed enter the pirates' own mythology: "It was said that every pirate's wish was to find himself not in heaven after death but back on that island paradise where the resting rovers could laze in their hammocks beneath the palms, swinging gently in the fanning breezes. There were whores aplenty, continuous gambling, the camaraderie of fellow rovers, and unlimited drink."[42]

Some historians challenge the notion of a pirate paradise, however. Neville Williams writes:

> There was little romance about the pirate's life ashore for the base on New Providence developed as a fiendish shanty town to which only Hogarth could have done justice. The men were spendthrift, and most shares were frittered away on liquor and on half-bred women; the idea of buried treasure is a myth, for the dram shops and the brothels took every available piece of eight.[43]

David Mitchell's judgment is similar: "Nassau was a shanty town of driftwood and palm fronds and old sails draped over spars to make tents. … Every other hovel was a grog shop or a brothel with Negro and mulatto prostitutes. … The general atmosphere resembled that of Hogarth's Gin Lane in balmy climate, or of a resurrected and even sleazier Port Royal."[44]

For a more diplomatic description we may finally quote Paul Galvin:

> The piratical fraternity of New Providence ... has often been painted
> (one might say with decidedly romantic license) as a near-utopian,
> ultra-democratic or anarchistic haven: a brutish yet noble 'Pirate
> Republic' ... There is an element of truth to this myth, but the reality
> of the pirates' settlement was probably closer to Woodbury's 'marine
> hobo jungle ... a place of temporary sojourn and refreshment for a
> literally floating population.'[45]

The pirate hold over the island ended in 1718 with the arrival of Governor Woodes Rogers.

Madagascar

Probably none of the pirate strongholds—including New Providence—received as much romantic attention as the island of Madagascar, which developed into a central base for American and Caribbean pirates in connection with their excursions into the Indian Ocean.

Most significantly, Adam Baldridge, a former buccaneer, established a trading post at the island of St. Mary's on Madagascar's northeast coast in 1691. Baldridge's post soon served both pirates and slave traders. A similar post was established a few years later by Abraham Samuel on the southern tip of Madagascar at Fort Dauphin. St. Mary's remained the center of the pirate community, though, and David F. Marley suggests that in the late 1690s it was inhabited by around 1,500 Europeans.[46] Cordingly and Falconer's estimate is more conservative; according to them, no more than several hundred pirates settled on Madagascar at any one time.[47] Peter Earle concurs: "After 1695, the most pirate-infested year, there were seldom more than six pirate ships operating in the Indian Ocean and some six or seven hundred men in their crews or enjoying themselves somewhere ashore, but these men made a great noise in the world."[48]

The reasons for the attention the Madagascan pirates received despite their rather modest numbers were, according to Cordingly and Falconer, the following:

> The mystery of the island (little-known despite its size), its exotic
> reputation and the absence of other European settlers caused it to be

seen as a 'pirate island' in the popular imagination. Soon stories of pirate chiefs living in tropical splendour and ruling whole tribes of natives began to filter back to Europe, endowing the pirates with a lifestyle and riches few of them can have known.[49]

The stories were impressive enough to worry the English authorities who, in 1704, released a parliamentary warning that if the Madagascar pirates' "numbers should be increased, they may form themselves into a settlement of robbers, as prejudicial to trade as any on the Coast of Africa & should be enticed to come home for love of country, otherwise children will be 'foreign English.'"[50]

In reality, St. Mary's, even in its heyday, "had a shifting population, the fairly small numbers of pirates who had settled there permanently, resting between voyages or waiting for a passage home, being increased dramatically when one or more of the pirate ships came in from a cruise."[51] In Robert C. Ritchie's words, "the pirate settlement on the island was by all accounts a ramshackle affair. It consisted of a few houses, a low palisade, and a couple of cannon."[52] Nonetheless, some authors on pirate history, most notably Frank Sherry, continue the Madagascar romanticism deep into the 20th century. Sherry declares that "in the late seventeenth and early eighteenth centuries, there was only one true democracy on earth: the pirate brotherhood forged in Madagascar."[53] He also calls the community a "maritime state" with "formed fleets"[54] and something "new in the experience of the world: international in scope, well financed, numerous, independent, and apparently powerful."[55]

Powerful, maybe. But in what way? If the Madagascan pirates' documented involvement in the slave trade alone does not clear the romantic mist surrounding them, then perhaps the following lengthy passage from the *General History* in which Captain Johnson describes the life of these "sovereign princes among the inhabitants" thus:[56]

> When our pirates first settled amongst them, their alliance was
> much courted by [the local] princes, so they sometimes joined one,
> sometimes another. But wheresoever they sided, they were sure to
> be victorious; for the negroes here had no firearms, nor did they
> understand their use. So that at length these pirates became so
> terrible to the negroes, that if two or three of them were only seen on

one side, when they were going to engage, the opposite side would fly without striking a blow. By these means they not only became feared, but powerful; all the prisoners of war, they took to be their slaves; they married the most beautiful of the negro women, not one or two, but as many as they liked, so that every one of them has as great a seraglio as the Grand Seignior at Constantinople. Their slaves they employed in planting rice, in fishing, and hunting, etc.; besides which, they had abundance of others, who lived, as it were, under their protection, and to be secure from the disturbances or attacks of their powerful neighbours; these seemed to pay them a willing homage. Now they began to divide from one another, each living with his own wives, slaves and dependents, like a separate prince; and as power and plenty naturally beget contention, they sometimes quarrelled with one another and attacked each other at the head of their several armies; and in these civil wars, many of them were killed…. If power and command be the thing which distinguish a prince, these ruffians had all the marks of royalty about them, nay more, they had the very fears which commonly disturb tyrants, as may be seen by the extreme caution they took in fortifying the places where they dwelt.[57]

If Johnson can be trusted here, these lines must resoundingly shatter any romantic image of a true democracy, even for those turning a blind eye to the slave trade. It should also render it of little surprise that Baldridge's post was eventually razed by an attack of Madagascan natives. It was soon replaced by a new post under the administration of one Edward Welsh—it became neither as successful nor as legendary as Baldridge's.[58]

The following description of the daily routine on St. Mary's probably describes whatever freedom the pirates had on the island much better than any talk about democracies and republics: "Life in this exotic pirate settlement appears to have been pleasant enough with, sad to say, slaves to wait on the freedom-loving pirates, plenty of women, locally produced beef and rice to eat, and drink from the slavers' store or from the natives who fermented honey and sugar to produce a powerful form of mead called *toke*."[59]

The significance of Madagascar as a pirate haunt waned with the overall recess in piracy caused by the privateering boom during the Spanish War of Secession (1701–1714). Cordingly and Falconer summarize:

When the English privateer Woodes Rogers was at the Cape in
1711 he was told by two ex-pirates who had spent some years in
Madagascar that only 60 to 70 pirates remained, and that they, far
from reigning as kings in tropical paradise, lived in squalor and
distress, 'most of them very poor and despicable, even to the natives.'
In 1719 the East Indiaman *St George* visited St. Mary's, and found the
dispirited remnants of the pirate John Halsey's company, some 17
men worn down by the tedium of exile, who 'wanted but one hit more
and then to go home, for they were aweary of their course of life.'[60]

Around 1720, as a belated consequence of the new rise of piracy in the
Caribbean, the defeat of New Providence as a pirate headquarters, and the
overall increasing persecution of piracy in the West Indies, Madagascar once
again became a center of the trade. It was during this time that James Plantain
founded his "kingdom" at the infamously named "Ranter Bay" (not far from
St. Mary's Island). However, this second boom was over within a few years,
and Madagascar never regained the reputation as a pirate paradise that it had
held in the 1690s.

West Africa

The west coast of Africa was the last addition to the list of prominent golden
age pirate hunting grounds, mainly due to the lucrative slave trade that
evolved along its shores.

Despite rumors about their alleged existence, no known pirate settlement
akin to New Providence or St. Mary's was ever established in West Africa.
Pirates had safe havens but those appear to have been small illegal trading
posts that never had more than a dozen permanent inhabitants and a maximum of two or three pirate ships visiting at the same time. Compared to the
Caribbean and the Indian Ocean, relatively few pirates operated here, and
they did so usually en route between the Caribbean and Madagascar. Only
Bartholomew Roberts's crew seemed to enjoy a longer stint in the region in
1721/22, before being captured off modern-day Gabon.

The most important of the mentioned trading posts was the one at the
mouth of the Sierra Leone River. It is also the one usually serving as the
only example for alleged West African pirate settlements. The forthright
description of the post as "a tiny outlaw colony of European smugglers and

interlopers, who were not adverse to trading with pirates"[61] seems more convincing, however, than the claim that it constituted a "pirate stronghold" in which the pirates' "communitarian urge … took landed form."[62]

If it is true that, as Peter Lamborn Wilson argues, "pirates' activities on land (pirate utopias or temporary autonomous zones) should be considered just as significant as their activities at sea,"[63] then Heiner Treinen's judgment is not too encouraging:

> The history of the parasitic radical democracy of the Caribbean ends with the pirates leaving their ships. No case of a successful community established by pirates on land has ever been known. This is not self-explanatory. Attempts have been made. … However, the purpose of these has hardly ever been to establish anarchist communities; usually, the on-land pirate communities were founded because pirates could not return to their home countries. The one thing that all the attempts shared was that they all dissolved very quickly—if they were able to avoid violent internal conflict. Even though little outside pressure was put on these communities, they were never able to turn into functioning anarchic societies.[64]

Treinen's perspective will definitely sound too negative for those who insist that pirates were—at least on occasion—able to "carry over … the democratic organization to which they had become accustomed aboard ship."[65] Be that as it may, what appears hard to challenge in Treinen's analysis is that we know of no on-land pirate settlement that prevailed.

4.10. "Piratical Imperialism," Hypocrisy, and the Merchants' Wrath: Piracy and Capitalism

Turning into a dominant force in world history in the 17th century, capitalism, along with its demands and its logic, played a decisive part in the rise and fall of golden age piracy. Neville Williams sees piracy "interwoven—like rogue's yarn in a dockyard hawser—with … commercial interests."[1] Franklin

W. Knight sums up the role of the buccaneer communities by stating that they "represented a stage in the transition from pioneering colonialism to organized imperialism."[2] Other authors speak of a "piratical imperialism," a policy according to which "many governments supported or at least condoned piracy committed by their own subjects, seeing it as a cheap and effective way of advancing trade and empire."[3] Chris Land describes the role of the privateering buccaneers in detail:

> Privateers were generally commissioned by a head of state to disrupt the trade of hostile nations and seek plunder and wealth for the crown. They were agents of a form of primitive accumulation … based upon the monarchic state. As Jacques Gélinas … has noted, this period was crucial to the monetization of the European economy and the end of barter, particularly the exploitation of Aztec and Inca gold and silver from South America. Without monetization the commodity form could not have become generalized and industrial capitalism as we know it could not have developed. The privateers were indispensable to the eventual development of industrial capitalism in England.[4]

This was not only true for England and its European rivals, but for the Americas and the Caribbean, too. The buccaneers proved essential in a two-step infiltration of the region by European powers competing with the Spanish. First, the buccaneers "destabilized the Spanish colonial system and made it possible for other nations to gain a foothold in the Western Hemisphere."[5] Second, once these powers were established, they facilitated "a crude form of imperial revenue-sharing."[6] Colonies struggling to get a strong legal economy off the ground welcomed the sea robber's trade deep into the golden age. "The two colonies which had perhaps the worst reputation for favoring pirates were Carolina and Rhode Island. Once, when a prisoner was actually foolish enough to plead guilty to piracy, a Rhode Island jury assured that they must of course have misheard him, and acquitted nonetheless."[7] John Franklin Jameson states that the privateers' and pirates' "activities had an important influence on the development of American commerce" and calls privateering "one of the leading American industries" during certain periods (for example the American Revolution).[8]

Once the Spanish dominance over the Americas was broken and other colonial powers and their colonies' economies were well established, the buccaneers turned from a useful mercenary force to a nuisance and potential danger. According to Janice E. Thomson, "colonial support for piracy began to erode in mid-1699" because "by that time there were so many pirates off the southeast coast of the United States that there was not enough 'glamorous plunder' for all, and they began seizing colonial commodities, like tobacco."[9] Angus Konstam concludes that "when piracy began to hinder the economic development of the American colonies and cut into the profit margins of European merchants and investors, the climate changed."[10] For Peter Earle, "this change reflected a growing belief in mercantile and shipping circles that piratical imperialism had served its purpose and that it should henceforth be the duty of the government and the navy to eradicate piracy and so make the seas safe for trade and shipping."[11]

As Peter Earle also points out, "the colonists would still have liked to buy cheap pirated goods, but their governors increasingly would not let them do so."[12] Even though there were exceptions to this rule—most notably North Carolina governor Charles Eden who remained friendly with the pirates till the late 1710s—Earle's observation would also indicate that the golden age pirates had indeed sympathizers among the "common folk" in the Caribbean and the Americas and that those most afraid of them where the ones who had riches to protect. It was certainly the rich who now went after them most fervently, after having profited from sea robbery in the Caribbean and the Americas for nearly a century.

Various authors on piracy have shared their version of the situation. Robert C. Ritchie: "Infant economies everywhere on the peripheries of empire eagerly sought easy money. When they eventually became established, the colonial merchants found the rough ways of the pirates too high a price to pay and turned against the buccaneers, but for nearly a century they provided sanctuary."[13] David F. Marley: "Around the globe, Europe's colonies were growing increasingly stable and prosperous, and no longer dependent upon privateers for their security. Instead they now regarded these as an impediment to good trade, and so gradually eradicated them."[14] Franklin W. Knight: "Individual, uncontrolled marauding became politically counterproductive to the genesis of exploitation societies based on slave-operated plantations and organized international commerce."[15] Stephen Snelders: "When merchant capitalism grew more settled in the Caribbean, pirates became a kind of aberration, a reminder of the earlier times of original accumulation that was no longer welcome."[16] Chris Land: "As mercantile capitalism and a more open form of trade became the dominant form of accumulation, piracy became more and more of a hindrance to the effective development of world trade and the pirates ceased to be politically or economically useful. As France, England and Spain entered a period of relative peace and sought to secure accumulation through more open trade, piracy became a problem that needed to be 'exterminated.'"[17]

This is reminiscent of the fate of social bandits, as explained by Hobsbawm: "With economic development the rich and powerful are increasingly likely to see bandits as threats to property to be stamped out, rather than as one factor among others in the power-game. Under such circumstances bandits become permanent outcasts."[18] Paul Galvin summarizes the corresponding consequences for the buccaneers: "When their benefactors consolidated sufficient power and territory on their own, the buccaneers had outlived their usefulness. Those who could not conform to the new colonial establishment—and they were many—either removed to the outer frontier, perhaps trying their hand at the logwood trade, or struck out on their own account as freebooters."[19]

The War of the Spanish Succession caused a last delay in the common effort of the colonial powers to erase golden age piracy as it "quickly devolved into a global contest of commercial interceptions and blockades."[20] Privateers were needed, and, as always, the borders to "out-and-out piracy" were blurred. Once the war was over and the need for privateers had ceased, the authorities of all nations united in their now uncompromising campaign against sea robbery that, to them, had turned into "the terror of the trading part of the world."[21]

The golden age pirates' effectiveness in disrupting some of the world's main trade routes seems confirmed by Jamaican governor Nicholas Lowes who wrote to the English authorities in 1718: "There is hardly any ship or vessel coming in or out going out of this island that is not plundered."[22] According to Marcus Rediker, the golden age pirates "practiced indirect terror against the owners of mercantile property"[23] and "Anglo-American pirates created an imperial crisis with their relentless and successful attacks upon merchants' property and international commerce between 1716 and 1726."[24] David F. Marley asserts that Bartholomew Roberts's crew alone had "by the spring of 1721 ... nearly brought Antillean commerce to a standstill."[25] The seriousness of these actions seems confirmed by Captain Johnson who quotes a court speech directed at the members of Bartholomew Roberts's crew during their trial at Cape Coast Castle: "To a trading nation nothing can be so destructive as piracy, or call for more exemplary punishment; besides, the national reflection it infers. It cuts off the returns of industry and those plentiful importations that alone can make an island flourishing; and it is your aggravation that ye have been the chiefs and rulers in these licentious and lawless practices."[26]

The pirates not only robbed—they also destroyed. The eyewitness report of an attack on a merchant ship by Roberts's crew, published in the *Boston News-Letter* in 1720, reads like this:

> The next thing they did was, with madness and rage to tore up the
> hatches, enter the hold like a parcel of furies, where with axes, cut-
> lasses, etc., they cut, tore and broke open trunks, boxes, cases and
> bales, and when any of the goods came upon deck which they did not
> like to carry with them aboard their ship, instead of tossing them into
> the hold again they threw them overboard into the sea.[27]

Peter Earle believes that "perhaps above all, pirates liked to burn ships for the sheer joy of seeing these mercantile symbols of the world they had left behind go up in flames, such entertainment being explained by one captured pirate when asked why he burned ships which turn'd to no advantage among 'em. The prisoner laughed and replied 'twas for fun."[28]

Once again, this is reminiscent of social bandits:

> Primitive ... insurgents have no positive programme, only the negative
> programme of getting rid of the superstructure which prevents men
> from living well and dealing fairly, as in the good old days. To kill,
> to slash, to burn away everything that is not necessary and useful
> to the man at the plough or with the herdsman's crook, is to abolish
> corruption and leave only what is good, pure and natural. Thus the
> brigand-guerrillas of the Italian South destroyed not only their
> enemies and the legal documents of bondage, but unnecessary riches.
> Their social justice was destruction.[29]

It is not surprising that the authorities soon employed all means to destroy the golden age pirates' "counterculture to the civilization of Atlantic capitalism."[30] Peter Earle describes the situation thus:

Henceforth, English governments would be committed to what has been called by one historian mercantile imperialism, 'a grand marine empire,' in which trade, shipping and the empire itself would be promoted, protected and controlled for the benefit of merchants and government alike. The state would provide protection for trade and, in return, would receive a flow of revenue from increased wealth and customs duties and a pool of trained sailors to fight in its naval wars. There was to be no place for pirates in this new world, no place for individualist marauders on the periphery of empire. The state would have a monopoly of violence at sea, through its navy at all times and through privateers properly commissioned and policed in times of war. Pirates were to be destroyed, not just as enemies of mankind but as enemies of capitalism and commercial expansion, a nice turn-around from the position only a little earlier in English history when piracy had been condoned as a promoter of the expansion of trade.[31]

In the succinct summary of the authors of "Pirate Utopias," "the pirates' war on trade had become too successful to be tolerated."[32] In response, the state unleashed its own war—a war that seemed to confirm Deleuze and Guattari's theory that "the factors that make State war total war are closely connected to capitalism."[33] Indeed, it seems that right down to its end, this war was fueled by merchants' interests. Marcus Rediker tells us that "when two groups of merchants petitioned Parliament for relief in early 1722, at the very peak of Roberts's depredations, the House of Commons ordered an immediate drafting of another bill for the suppression of piracy, which, with Robert Walpole's assistance, was quickly passed."[34] Rediker adds that "pirates now had to be exterminated in order for the new trade to flourish."[35]

The pirates' odds were terrible: "Unlike their buccaneer forebears, they enjoyed no cloak of legitimacy from any government ... and were therefore doomed to swift eradication."[36] The grizzly story of the "extermination campaign" that brought golden age piracy to its end has been told earlier.[37] The outcome was that in the 1720s, "the long war of attrition against smugglers and pirates was finally won, and the seas were left free for English merchants to make profits in."[38] Once again it is to Rediker that we owe a splendid summary—this time of capitalism's role in eliminating what had turned from a tactical ally for expansion into one of its worst enemies:

If the plantation capital of the Caribbean, allied with the merchant capital of the metropolis, killed the first generation of pirates— the buccaneers of the 1670s—and if the capital of the East India Company killed the pirates of the 1690s, when the company's ships were hothouses of mutiny and rebellion, it was the African slave-trading capital that killed the pirates of the early eighteenth century. Pirates had ruptured the Middle Passage, and this would not be tolerated. By 1726 the maritime state had removed a major obstacle to the accumulation of capital in its ever-growing Atlantic system.[39]

The hypocrisy of the authorities throughout the history of Caribbean buccaneering and pirating has been pointed out by both contemporary victims and 20th-century commentators. Pirate John Quelch, hanged in Boston in 1704, stated before his execution that "they should also take care how they brought money into New-England, to be hanged for it!"[40] His fellow pirate Erasmus Peterson evoked the eternal fate of the underdog when he stated— against the backdrop of the riches made by the criminals in office—that "it is very hard for so many men's lives to be taken away for a little gold."[41] As far as the double standards involved in the official responses to Caribbean sea robbery go, historian David F. Marley states with respect to Bartholomew Roberts that "half a century earlier his intelligence, charisma and courage might have earned him a knighthood."[42]

Golden age piracy might have marked the biggest threat to international maritime trade ever and remains a powerful "symbolic focus for anti-Capital's desire."[43] As David Cordingly and John Falconer state: "Individual piratical acts continued to occur for the rest of the [18th] century and beyond, but with declining frequency and without the previously devastating effects on trade and the commerce in the area."[44]

4.11. Victims of Circumstance or Bloodthirsty Sadists? Piracy and Violence

One of many startling passages in Friedrich Nietzsche's *The Genealogy of Morals* reads as follows: "When man wanted to create a memory for himself, this could never be done without blood, pain, sacrifice; the most gruesome gifts and sacrifices ... the most appalling mutilations ... all this finds its origin in the instinct which understands that pain is the strongest mnemonic tool."[1]

With respect to the Caribbean buccaneers and pirates, this would suggest that without their legendary violence they would have never entered the popular legacy of the Western world in the way they did. Indeed, the violence of the Caribbean sea robber is, as Hans Turley puts it, "part of his mystique."[2] While Exquemelin's account of the buccaneers excels in "bloodthirsty stories,"[3] Captain Johnson tells that "in the commonwealth of the pirates, he who goes the greatest length or wickedness is looked upon with a kind of envy amongst them, as a person of a more extraordinary gallantry, and is thereby entitled to be distinguished by some post, and if such a one has but courage, he must certainly be a great man."[4] As if to illustrate his point, Johnson peppers his accounts of pirate captains with comments like: "[He, Edward Low] took a fishing boat off of Block Island, but did not perpetrate so much cruelty to her, contenting himself with only cutting off the master's head."[5]

Following is a list of ten famed examples of buccaneer and pirate atrocities. Almost all are based on Exquemelin and Johnson. A couple of early ones relate to Francis l'Ollonais, in the words of Philip Gosse, "a monster of cruelty, who would, had he lived to-day, have been confined in an asylum for lunatics."[6]

1. The buccaneers allegedly punished members of their own community by cutting off their noses and ears.
2. L'Ollonais is said to have hacked torture victims who would not provide information instantly to pieces with his cutlass, "licking the blood from the blade with his tongue."
3. L'Ollonais is also said to have cut out the heart of a prisoner and forced another to eat it.
4. Rock Braziliano was allegedly prone to spitting prisoners on wooden stakes and roasting them, "like killing a pig."
5. Mountbars the Exterminator apparently opened the abdomen of a prisoner, nailed his intestines to a post and chased the prisoner with a torch.
6. Captain Nicolo, after taking a merchantman, reportedly cut off the master's head and the hand of each seaman.
7. Edward Low allegedly cut off the lips of a Portuguese prisoner and broiled them before his face.
8. There apparently existed a common practice of wrapping a rope around a prisoner's head and slowly twisting it tighter to make his eyeballs pop out.

9. Another practice consisted of "tying men back to back and throwing them into the sea."
10. Finally, the practice of *sweating* is reported in which the victim was stripped naked, pierced with sail needles and thrown into a barrel with cockroaches.

These and similar stories have led authors to fanciful descriptions. John Masefield, for example, tells us of the buccaneers: "They discovered that the cutting out of prisoners' hearts, and eating of them raw without salt, as had been the custom of one of the most famous buccaneers, was far less profitable than the priming of a prisoner with his own acqua-vitae."[7] Yet the references to the buccaneers' and pirates' random cruelty are too common to simply disregard them. In fact, the suggestion that one buccaneer captain whipped a crew member to death "for no apparent reason" appears not inconceivable.[8] Sometimes, the cruelty seems to have caught up with the buccaneers and pirates themselves. Angus Konstam wryly comments on Francis l'Ollonais's death: "L'Ollonais was killed and probably eaten; an appropriate end for such a vicious man."[9]

There has been plenty of debate among contemporary pirate scholars as to how violent the buccaneers and pirates really were. Opinions seem to differ much according to political orientation. While Stephen Snelders, for example, formulates somewhat defensively that "there should be no doubt that buccaneers and flibustiers were very dangerous cutthroats, with a salting of desperate and even sadistic elements,"[10] David Cordingly seems less inhibited in his judgment when stating that "the real world of the pirates was often closer to some of today's horror movies than anything which appeared in contemporary books or plays."[11] Overall, however, historians seem to agree that the reports on the buccaneers' and pirates' violence were exaggerated. As far as the accounts of Exquemelin and Johnson go, we ought not forget that they meant to sell copies, and that gory sensationalism probably proved as effective for that purpose at the time as it does today. As far as the buccaneers' and pirates' enemies are concerned, we can image that the more gruesome the former's reputation was, the easier it became to justify their persecution. Finally, the buccaneers and pirates themselves might have had an interest in grooming such a reputation. It might have made their looting easier as it prompted their victims to abstain from resistance in fear of terrible retribution.

Douglas Botting has called the pirates "masters of psychology"[12] and their cultivated image a "basic weapon"[13] in their raiding efforts. According to the records, the tactic seemed effective. It appears as if golden age pirates hardly ever had to use actual violence to take a merchantman—hoisting the Jolly Roger and firing a couple of warning shots usually sufficed.

Many authors have made efforts to see the violence of the buccaneers and pirates in its historical frame. Marcus Rediker suggests that the reason for their gruesome acts was that they could neither "resolve the contradictions of their times"[14] nor "escape the system of which they were a part."[15] Stephen Snelders argued the importance of viewing the pirates' actions in perspective,[16] stating "we must realize that in the seventeenth century the use of torture in no way deviated from 'normal' conduct in society," and that "torture and other forms of physical violence were very much the standard in all kinds of social activities."[17] B.R. Burg suggests that "buccaneers lived in an age when the infliction of pain was an art form,"[18] and even David Cordingly and John Falconer concede that the "numerous ... acts of violence and cruelty committed by the buccaneers [should be] set in the context of their time."[19] Many buccaneer and pirate sympathizers would certainly subscribe to Stephen Snelders assertion that "when we address the problem of 'cruelty' the point is not whether the buccaneers were cruel (they often were), but whether they were worse than their enemies and contemporaries—and whether there were reasons for their cruelty and bloodlust."[20]

To a certain extent, this is true. It is important to understand the reasons for the violence of the buccaneers and pirates, and it is important to consider the historical circumstances under which it occurred. It seems probable that their violence was no worse (and possibly less) than the violence of merchant and navy captains or of the colonial authorities. It seems also probable that the violence of the latter contributed to the violence of the pirates. This is as much expressed in Robert I. Burns's succinct statement that "every generation gets the pirates it deserves,"[21] as in the pirate John Philps's accusation levied against one of his former officers that "it was such dogs as he that put men on pirating."[22] Likewise, it is probably true that "the harsh conditions of indenture produced physically tough and spiritually callous individuals, capable of surviving the exacting and hazardous conditions of international piracy,"[23] and that "the mistreatment of captive masters and officers was a passionate discharge of the rancor that the sea outlaws felt toward a detested and feared civilization as personified by a cruel ship's captain."[24] At the same time, this does not resolve the problem of how people today can relate to this violence. The above declarations turn the golden age pirate into a role model for contemporary political struggle. Despite all the inspiration that can be drawn from the golden age pirate experiment, it hardly seems appropriate to brush aside the unpleasant parts with the simple explanation that they happened in a different age. No slave-trading community, for example, ought to become an unqualified reference point for political radicals. Whether it existed 30 or 300 years ago matters little. Stephen Snelders may be right when he says that the ambiguities inherent in the golden age pirates' communities "need not be resolved."[25] Yet radicals today need to resolve their own ambiguities—also with respect to violence. An uncritical embrace of the violence of the Caribbean buccaneers and pirates will do little to advance the cause. What seems mandatory is to strengthen theory and praxis by accepting contradictions in the radical past to improve the radical future.

During the last phase of the golden age, the pirates were caught in a downward spiral. Violence and cruelty increased dramatically. Marcus Rediker writes: "In its final phase, the war turned savage. As naval captains and executioners killed more and more pirates, those who remained at large became more enraged, more desperate, more violent, and more cruel. The dialectic of terror … reached a climax in carnage."[26] In Frank Sherry's words, "a handful of pirate captains carried on a last-ditch combat on the sea-lanes against the forces of law and order. As happens with most lost causes, these … fought with special fury and cruelty."[27]

This should not surprise us. It seems to be a common pattern among "criminal" as well as "revolutionary" outlaws that once defeat seems certain and they feel the full force of the "law," their desperation and hence their violence increases, which causes even more counter-violence, etc. As the authors of "Pirate Utopias" point out, in the case of the golden age pirates "there developed a deadly spiral of increasing violence as state attacks were met with revenge from the pirates leading to greater state terror."[28] With respect to banditry, Hobsbawm describes the phenomenon thus:

> Banditry, we have seen, grows and becomes epidemic in times of
> social tension and upheaval. These are also the times when the

conditions for such explosions of cruelty are most favorable. They do
not belong to the central image of brigandage, except insofar as the
bandit is at all times an avenger of the poor. But at such times they will
no doubt occur more frequently and systematically. Nowhere more so
than in those ... insurrections and rebellions which have failed to turn
into social revolutions, and whose militants are forced to fall back into
the life of outlaws and robbers: hungry, embittered, and resentful even
against the poor who have left them to fight alone.[29]

According to Marcus Rediker, the Caribbean buccaneers and pirates
employed violence for three reasons: "to avoid fighting; to force disclosure of
information about where booty was hidden; and to punish ship captains."[30]
The third reason is at the heart of the following section.

4.12. Vengeance as Justice: Pirate Ethics

Is there such a thing as "pirate ethics"?[1] The golden age pirates undoubtedly
sailed with certain principles—their articles being only the most tangible
expression of this. In a very basic sense, principles alone can constitute an
ethics, especially when they relate to a particular understanding of justice.
The principles of the golden age pirates clearly did this, stressing fair distribution of property, equal influence on decision-making processes, and honesty
and loyalty as important values within their community. Marcus Rediker
even calls the golden age pirates' notion of justice "the foundation of their
enterprise."[2] As far as the interior workings of the golden age pirate communities are concerned, an ethics would thus be defined.

Things become more complicated, however, if our definition of ethics
implies a universal application of one's principals—an extension of one's own
values to the "outside world." Arguably, this was not the case with the golden
age pirates. In general, their ethical world seemed reduced to the confines
of their own exclusive social realm. Beyond that, one was hardly bound by
principles at all. Still, there was one feature—ever more pronounced the closer
golden age piracy drew to its end—that would suggest a principle's universal
application: meting out justice against those who have done wrong. No matter
how rudimentary the concept, and no matter how vague the understanding
of "justice" and of "doing wrong," as the avenger described by Hobsbawm,

the golden age pirate becomes an ethical figure by all standards—someone who designs an *ethics of vengeance* by employing a negative notion of justice: justice is done by avenging what is perceived as *injustice*, namely the arbitrary violence and domination exercised by those with "authority." In the context of many pirates' lives, this meant first and foremost the cruel and sadistic captain of the merchant ship who would become the focus of their ethics of vengeance—an ethics that is perhaps best expressed in the famed *Pirate Song* of unknown origins: "'Tis to drink to our victory—one cup of red wine. / Some fight, 'tis for riches—some fight, 'tis for fame: / The first I despise, and the last is a name. / I fight, 'tis for vengeance! I love to see flow, / At the strike of my sabre, the life of my foe."

An emphasis on vengeance among sea robbers was no invention of the golden age—we might recall the famous buccaneer Montbars the Exterminator. However, among the golden age pirates vengeance as a guiding principle became ever more pronounced. Frank Sherry calls "the chance to take vengeance on the cruel and unjust society that most pirates had left behind" one of the age's most important reasons to turn pirate.[3] Similarly, Chris Land states that "one of the main motivators for a pirate was not profit but revenge."[4] The account of William Snelgrave, whose ship was taken by Howell Davis's crew off the West African coast, confirms this. Snelgrave was apparently told by one of the pirates that "their reasons for going a pirating were to revenge themselves on base Merchants, and cruel commanders of ships."[5]

In this sense, "numerous sailors, once they became pirates, seized their new and unusual circumstances to settle old scores in vengeful ways."[6] David F. Marley confirms that this was particularly pronounced during the golden age's final phase: "Unlike their precursors from the 1690s, this generation was noticeably not motivated by a lack of potential prizes in the New World, but rather by an excess of official retaliation."[7]

Among the last of the golden age pirate captains, this retaliation seems to have reached an organized level. Captain Johnson tells us in his account of Captain John Evan's crew: "Upon seizing of this ship, the pirates began to take upon themselves the distribution of justice, examining the men concerning their master's usage of them, *according to the custom of other pirates*."[8] Peter Earle adds an interesting observation concerning the composition of the pirate crews of that period:

This business of judging and punishing merchant captains is unique
in the history of piracy and reflects the radical, 'world-turned-upside-
down' nature of the golden age of piracy. How sailors must have
loved to see the powerful brought low and the oppressor oppressed.
Such vengeance also reflects the make-up of the pirate crews, for
never before had these been drawn predominantly from the more
disgruntled members of the crews of merchant ships. Few buccaneers
had served on long journeys in merchant ships and they could not
care less how the Spanish captains of their prizes treated their crews,
though they might kill them simply because they were Spaniards.
But large numbers of the pirates of the years 1715–25 had served
on transatlantic or West African voyages or in the Newfoundland
fishery where the effects of harsh captains would have been most
severely felt. And for them such cruel revenge must have been very
sweet.[9]

Earle also cites a dispatch that illustrates the scope that the pirates'
vengeance could reach: "Erring captains might have their nose and ears cut
off, 'for but correcting his own sailors,' wrote the Governor of Virginia in a
letter begging for a naval vessel to carry him home to England lest he suffer
the same fate."[10]

The flipside of this was, of course, that merchant captains who had treated
their sailors well could expect mercy. We find a famous story about such an
event in Captain Johnson's account of Captain Edward England, when a "fellow with a terrible pair of whiskers, and a wooden leg" (already encountered
in the section on piracy and disability) saves the captured Captain Mackra by
stating that he had "formerly sail'd with him" and that he was "an honest fellow." A similar picture reaches us of captain William Snelgrave, held prisoner
by pirates off the West African coast: he was saved from pirate retaliation
because no one of his crew had any complaints about him.[11] Rediker believes
that by demonstrating leniency to those who had proven good or honest,
"pirates hoped to show these merchants that good fortunes befell good captains."[12] The fact that Marcus Rediker calls the case of William Snelgrave "the
best description of pirates' notions of justice" demonstrates once more the
ethical ambiguity that haunts golden age pirate society: after all, the "good
captain" Snelgrave was also a slave trader.

Within their own communities, the golden age pirates usually summoned councils to deal with matters of justice related to their principles and articles. The cases at hand were discussed and brought to a conclusion communally. Sometimes these councils could take on the forms of quasi-courts. Captain Johnson's *General History of the Pirates* includes a remarkable passage lauding the advantages of the pirate courts:

> Here was the form of justice kept up, which is as much as can be said of several other courts that have more lawful commissions for what they do. Here was no seeing of council, and bribing of witnesses was a custom not known among them; no packing of juries, no torturing and wresting the sense of the law, for by ends and purposes, no puzzling or perplexing the cause with unintelligible canting terms, and useless distinctions; nor was their sessions burdened with numberless officers, the ministers of rapine and extortion, with ill-boding aspects, enough to fright *Astrea* from the court.[13]

This serves as a powerful reminder of the concrete notions of justice that can be exercised in small ("primitive") communities whose social forums allow for an equal participation of all. Adding to the "primitive" comparison, it might also be noted that the harshest punishment the golden age pirates commonly executed against their own, namely marooning, bears a striking resemblance to the ostracism that is known as one of the harshest punishments among many so-called primitive societies.[14] It confirms the fact that in tight-knit communities, exclusion from the social body has always equaled symbolic death.

In conclusion, the pirate understanding and execution of justice, in its immediacy and concreteness, must have at least lacked the systematic arbitrariness inherent in every system of formal law, especially in a class society. Let us, for example, recall the sorrow of the convicted members of Bartholomew Roberts's crew who said that they were "hanged, while others, no less guilty in another way, escaped."[15]

In a Nietzschean sense the most important—and maybe for radicals the most inspiring—aspect of pirate justice was that the pirates went beyond dominant moral conventions and created their own moral principles and codes. As Snelders writes: "Since they lived outside the bounds of what was normally defined as good and evil, pirates behaved as they liked within the confines of their own customs."[16] In fact, the connections between a Nietzschean philosophy and the life of the golden age pirates are striking in many ways.

4.13. Dionysus in the West Indies: A Nietzschean Look at Golden Age Piracy

While it is difficult to define golden age piracy politically, the possibilities for radical adaptations remain wide open, since at the core of golden age pirate life lies an unrestrained existential vitality, or, in Nietzsche's terms, a *Dionysian philosophy*—an incredibly strong and powerful anti-authoritarian and liberatory force that knows no restriction by social considerations, ethical principles, or political ideals. It is a force that can therefore turn into anything: an ally in the fight for freedom or justice, or a dreadful fascist enemy.

Dionysus, the Greek god of wine, ecstasy, festivity, and, according to some, "inspired madness," plays a principal role in Nietzsche's philosophy since his first published work, *The Birth of Tragedy* (1872). In this essay, Nietzsche analyzes Greek tragedy as an art that blends both "Apollonian" and "Dionysian" elements—the latter often being neglected in our lives and finally totally abandoned by the "Socratic tendency."[1] Nietzsche, however, urges us to "believe in the Dionysian life"[2] and, to his last texts, declares himself the defender of the "Dionysian spell."[3] In one of his best-known works, *Beyond Good and Evil* (1886), he calls himself "the last disciple and initiate of the god Dionysus."[4] So what does the Dionysian moment stand for?

It is, according to Nietzsche, "a fundamental counter-doctrine and counter-evaluation of life, purely artistic, purely *anti-Christian*."[5] Its desires are characterized by "initiative, audacity, revenge, cleverness, rapacity, lust for power,"[6] its values by "a vigorous physicality, a blooming, rich, abundant health, and by everything this depends on: war, adventure, hunting, dance, fighting, and everything that implies strong, free, joyful activity."[7] In the words of Gilles Deleuze, arguably the most sophisticated representative of what has been dubbed a *left Nietzscheanism*, "it is Dionysus' task to make us graceful, to teach us to dance, to give us the instinct of play."[8]

It would be wrong to suggest that golden age pirates represented a Dionysian community in Nietzsche's eyes. Given his cultural elitism, Nietzsche would have probably seen the festive excesses of pirate crews as the expression of a "grotesque and vulgar" Dionysianism, which he criticizes in the *Birth of Tragedy*.[9] Nonetheless, disregarding Nietzsche's own possible objections, it is certainly revealing to analyze the golden age pirates' social experiment from a Dionysian perspective.

Affirmation

"Dionysian art wants to persuade us of the eternal joy of being," writes Nietzsche in *The Birth of Tragedy*,[10] and this "affirmation of life," "the Dionysian yes"[11] remains a crucial theme throughout his work. Against the perceived "decadence" and "nihilism" of his era, Nietzsche uses the figure of Dionysus to champion an uncompromising embrace of life in all its dimensions, not inhibited by bourgeois values and limitations. Dionysus "is the god for whom life does not have to be justified, for whom life is essentially just."[12]

Golden age pirates seem to have shared this sentiment. Philip Gosse relates that Captain William Jennings explained that he was a pirate "for the love of the life,"[13] while one George Bendall is quoted by Peter Earle as saying that "he wished he had begun the life sooner for he thought it was a very pleasant one, meaning the piratical way.'"[14] In the same vein, Captain Johnson tells us of two pirates, Phineas Bunce and Dennis Macarty, who, soon after they had accepted a royal pardon, "began to rattle and talk with great pleasure and much boasting of their former exploits when they had been pirates, crying up a pirate's life to be the only life for a man of spirit."[15]

All this seems to confirm Stephen Snelders conclusion that buccaneering "was not simply a way to make a living, but a way of life."[16] A decisive factor—confirming the *affirmation* so important in Nietzsche's thought—is that the lives of the buccaneers and pirates were created by themselves; they had seized their lives by their own motivation and activity. Nietzsche would have rejoiced at the observation of Marcus Rediker that the pirate Walter Kennedy "like the others, was not merely escaping oppressive circumstances. He was escaping *to* something new, a different reality ... "[17]

Liberty

Nietzsche writes in *The Gay Science*:

> Indeed, we philosophers and 'free spirits' feel as if a new dawn shines on us when we hear that the 'old God is dead'; our heart overflows with gratitude, awe, intuition, expectation—finally, the horizon is

free again ... and we can finally board our ships and sail into whatever danger we will encounter. Those eager to know can be daring again; the sea, our sea, has been opened once more; in fact, maybe there has never been a sea that 'open'![18]

"There is another world to discover—and more than just one! Onto the ships, philosophers!"[19]

The allegories might be random, but the notion of liberty associated with them echoes those of the golden age pirates. Various authors concur that the thirst for liberty was a decisive factor in motivating seamen to *go on the account*. Peter Lamborn Wilson writes that "looking at the whole picture, rather than individual careers, we get the impression that desire for total liberty constituted perhaps the deepest motive for classical piracy";[20] for Stephen Snelders the pirates were "maximizing the liberty of seamen";[21] Frank Sherry calls "the chance that piracy offered to ordinary sailors to live as free men [piracy's] real lure";[22] Chris Land believes that "for many pirates the self conscious pursuit of liberty and autonomy became the main reason for their choice of life";[23] and Marcus Rediker observes that "in the popular mind, the pirate was not 'the common enemy of mankind' but rather the freest of mankind."[24]

Nietzsche adds an important distinction between "free-thinkers" and "free-doers": "The free-doers are at a disadvantage to the free-thinkers, since action makes humans suffer much more than thought."[25]

Defiance

The notion of liberty combined with Nietzsche's demand for a "transvaluation of values"[26] (the creation of new, self-determined moralities) and a "twilight of the idols"[27] (the rejection of everything we are taught to revere) corresponds markedly to the golden age pirates' anti-authoritarianism: "Pirates constructed a culture of masterless men. They were as far removed from the traditional authority as any men could be in the early eighteenth century. Beyond the church, beyond the family, beyond disciplinary labor, and using the sea to distance themselves from the powers of the state, they carried out a strange experiment."[28] "Indeed, there was 'so little Government and Subordination' among pirates that 'they are, on Occasion, all Captains, all Leaders.'"[29]

Self-Determination

In direct relation to the above, Nietzsche declares: "It is only for the few to be independent—it is only for those who are strong. Those who assert their independence—with every right but without being forced—prove that they are not only strong but fearless and audacious. They leap into a labyrinth and multiply the dangers of life by a thousand."[30]

This sense of independence, or, as we might more aptly say, self-determination, is echoed in some depictions of the golden age pirates' life. In order to illustrate what he conceives as a "kind of proto-individualist-anarchist attitude," Peter Lamborn Wilson relates the following anecdote: "At one time, Eston was told that James I of England had offered him a pardon. 'Why should I obey a king's orders,' he asked, 'when I am a kind of king myself?'"[31] Marcus Rediker elaborates on the imagery: "Perhaps this illuminates Daniel Defoe's description of pirates, where every man was 'in his own Imagination a Captain, a Prince, or a King.' Such positions of authority may not have been so bad as long as everyone could claim a title."[32] Accordingly, the traditional authorities were regarded with little respect. Bartholomew Roberts's crew allegedly told the captain of the raided merchantman *Samuel*: "We shall accept no Act of Grace, may the King and Parliament be damned with their Act of Grace for us"[33] Rediker deduces that "the pirate was someone with whom 'no Faith, Promise, nor Oath is to be observed.'"[34] Stephen Snelders, pondering why we enjoy the pirates' stories despite the early "moral judgment" they received, comes to the conclusion that it is "because a pirate takes his life in his own hands." Claes G. Compaen, for example, a Dutch buccaneer portrayed by Snelders, "played his own game. And for three years he got away with it, which is much longer than most of us will ever even try."[35] Paraphrasing the Situationists' "Theses on the Paris Commune," Snelders later notes that "the pirates had become masters of their own history, not so much on the level of 'governmental' politics as on the level of their everyday life."[36] Finally, it is worth quoting once more the famous outburst that Captain Johnson ascribes to Saul Bellamy, directed at the captain of a recently taken merchantman after his refusal to join Bellamy's crew:

> You are a devilish conscientious rascal, d-n ye, replied Bellamy. *I am a*
> *free prince, and I have as much authority to make war on the whole world*
> *as he who has a hundred sail of ships at sea, and an army of 100,000 men*

in the field, and this my conscience tells me. But there is no arguing with
such snivelling puppies, who allow superiors to kick them about deck at
pleasure and pin their faith upon a pimp of a parson, a squab, who neither
practices not believes what he puts upon the chuckle-headed fools he
preaches to.[37]

Merit

The notions of liberty, defiance and self-determination imply another defining aspect of golden age pirate life, namely the possibility for individuals to
find a place within the community based on merit alone. While Robert C.
Ritchie remarks on Captain Every that "like so many of the pirates, his life is
a blank until he emerged from the ranks of faceless sailors to captain a pirate
ship,"[38] Stephen Snelders writes with respect to Jan Erasmus Reyning, that
"his life is an example of how the Brotherhood could take a sailor with no
prospects and offer him new opportunities, roving on the account in a life
that was continuously adventurous and dangerous."[39]

According to Maurice Besson, in the world of the Caribbean buccaneers
and pirates, "courage alone conferred distinction."[40] A notion that echoes all
of Nietzsche's ideals of the *masters*—an aristocracy not defined by birth but
by standing the test of life itself.[41]

Festival

Being the god of wine, Dionysus is inextricably linked to festival and celebration. Nietzsche speaks of "Dionysian delights,"[42] "the ecstatic aspects of the
Dionysian festival,"[43] "the Dionysian celebration."[44] Deleuze evokes the "trin-
ity of dance, play and laughter."[45] It seems apt that Stephen Snelders would
call a book chapter dedicated to the buccaneer and pirate lifestyle "Joie de
Vivre: An Eternal Festival."[46] The authors of "Pirate Utopias" comment casu-
ally: "The pirates certainly seem to have had more fun than their poor suffering counterparts on naval or merchant vessels. They sure had some pretty
wild parties."[47]

According to Marcus Rediker, the pirates "made merry. Indeed, 'merry' is
the word most commonly used to describe the mood and spirit of life aboard
the pirate ship."[48] Rediker further explains: "Not surprisingly, many observers
of pirate life noted the carnivalesque quality of pirate occasions—the eating,
drinking, fiddling, dancing, and merriment—and some considered such

'infinite Disorders' inimical to good discipline at sea."[49] The special role of
the musicians on pirate ships ought not surprise then. According to Frank
Sherry, they were "by far the most popular members of any pirate crew, men
who could coax a song out of a pipe or a horn, and who were often excused
from the most onerous duties in recognition of their tuneful talent."[50]

Chance

The festive character of pirate life implied that the moment of chance was
a decisive one. The life of the golden age pirates has been described as "a
life insecure in the extreme—one could not know what might happen even
within the next few hours."[51] This corresponds to Nietzsche's conviction that
the "true philosopher ... lives 'unphilosophically' and 'unwisely,' especially
unreasonably, and feels the call and duty to engage in hundreds of experiments and temptations of life—he risks himself all the time, he plays the evil
game."[52] He belongs to those who "love danger, war, and adventure."[53]

The golden age pirates' life was a life that depended on moments of *intensity*,
philosophically embraced in (post)modern times by Jean-François Lyotard
and others.[54] In Stephen Snelders's words: "Nothing happened for whole days
except the flowing of the seas and the passing of fish and birds. Then everything happened at once, danger and excitement soared, and a moment could
make them rich or dead."[55] When Snelders proceeds to speak of a "veritable
feast on the Wheel of Fortune,"[56] we cannot help but recall Nietzsche asking:
"Shall we not roll the dice only because we might lose?"[57] The metaphor seems
particularly apt with respect to the pirates' well-documented obsession with
gambling. According to Maurice Besson, what the Caribbean buccaneers and
pirates needed "were combat and assault, and when they returned, orgies and
the gambling board."[58]

Flux

Intrinsically linked to the notion of chance is the fact that golden age pirate
life was characterized by instability and insecurity, permanent change, and
flux. Daniel Botting writes: "Pirate crews were ..., in every sense, a floating
population, in a constant state of flux, never the same size or composition
from one month to another, owing allegiance to nothing and no one, neither
ship, nor captain, nor cause."[59] Marcus Rediker adds: "Occasionally upon
election of a new captain, men who favored other leadership drew up new

articles and sailed away from their former mates. ... Those who had experienced the claustrophobic and authoritarian world of the merchant ship cherished the freedom to separate."[60]

An interesting detail to consider in relation to this aspect of Caribbean pirate culture is that the buccaneers apparently gave up their names when joining the community of the *Brethren of the Coast*. In the words of Maurice Besson, the buccaneer's "past was forgotten; he became a unit in a troop ceaselessly decimated and as ceaselessly renewed."[61] If this is true, then the *proto-individualism* of the buccaneers and pirates depicted by Peter Lamborn Wilson would have met with a *rejection of the subject* that should have poststructuralist theorists rejoice with delight, and that, in any case, reminds us of Nietzsche's assertion that "the ban of individuation is shattered by Dionysus' jubilant howl."[62]

Fear

Nietzsche never denies that a life of insecurity and chance does include cruelty and fear. In fact, it is a crucial aspect of his philosophy that he demands these aspects of life to be embraced as part of embracing life itself. In *The Gay Science*, Nietzsche defines *being heroic* as "simultaneously heading towards one's most severe suffering and one's highest hopes."[63] In simple words: it is worth being afraid if this means that we can live exciting lives, and no life can be exciting without danger; fear then simply becomes the inevitable supplement. In the words of Gilles Deleuze: "'Those who affirm the superabundance of life' make suffering an affirmation in the same way as they make intoxication an activity."[64] Nietzsche himself states: "Who would not prefer to fear when he can admire at the same time; rather than not fear but be condemned to watch ill-bred, weakened, degenerated, poisoned men only? ... We suffer of man, there is no doubt. But not because we fear him. Rather because there is nothing in him to fear anymore. He has turned into a worm."[65]

Death

Nietzsche not only embraces fear as a part of life, but death as well. In *Thus Spoke Zarathustra*, he notes: "Many die too late, and some die too early. ... Die at the right time! Thus spoke Zarathustra. Then again: He who never lives at the right time, how shall he die at the right time?"[66]

The lives of many golden age pirates seemed to reflect this sentiment. The possibility of death was always near—and became a reality for many. Marcus Rediker relates that "premature death was ... the pirate's lot" and that "at least one in four died or was killed."[67] In an entry in *The Pirates' Who's Who*, Philip Gosse mentions that one Thomas Hazel, hanged at the age of fifty, "is one of the longest lived pirates we have been able to hear of."[68]

Still, the possibility of death seemed to be no deterrent for most pirates to pursue their trade. There are probably some psycho-sociological explanations for this, like the one by David Cordingly: "Despite the great risk of being captured and executed for your deeds, piracy was an attractive alternative to dying of starvation, becoming a beggar or thief on land, or serving in appalling conditions on a ship with no chance of substantial financial reward."[69] This is confirmed by one Robert Sparks, seaman of the *Abington*, who is quoted by Marcus Rediker as saying "that their ship 'would make a good Pirate Ship, for,' he insisted, 'they had better be dead than live in Misery.'"[70] This conviction even translated into belittling the prospects of execution: "As more and more pirates were hanged, and as the likelihood of death for anyone who went 'upon the account' increased, pirates responded by intensifying their commitment to each other, 'one and all.' And they did so with a laugh."[71]

The golden age pirates' attitude towards death (and life) was most famously captured in a quote that Captain Johnson ascribes to the famed pirate captain Bartholomew Roberts: "'In an honest service,' says he, 'there is thin commons, low wages, and hard labour; in this, plenty and satiety, pleasure and ease, liberty and power; and who would not balance creditor on this side, when all the hazard that is run for it, at worst is only a sour look or two at choking. No, a merry life and a short one, shall be my motto.'"[72] Indifference towards the likely prospect of death was also a main feature of many variations of the Jolly Roger: "Some records of pirate flags show dancing skeletons, meaning dancing a jig with death, synonymously playing with death, or not caring about fate. This was also the symbolism behind raised drinking glasses, the image referring to a toast to death in store—those flying this flag didn't care about their fate."[73] Rediker suggests that "a defiance of death" was not only the meaning of the pirate flag, but perhaps "of piracy altogether."[74] In another famous quote related by Johnson, Mary Read says "that as to hanging, she thought it no great hardship, for were it not for that, every cowardly fellow would turn pirate, and so infest the seas that men of courage must starve."[75]

Even if hanging was thus accepted as deterrence, it is only fitting that many pirates, in their self-determined ways, were set on denying the authorities the gratification of executing them even when they were ready to die. Men of Bartholomew Roberts's crew allegedly told passengers on one of the vessels they took that they would not "go to Hope Point to be hanged a-sun-drying," but that, "if it should chance that they should be attacked by any superiour power or force, which they could not master, they would immediately put fire with one of their pistols to their powder, and go all merrily to hell together!"[76] According to Marcus Rediker, "indeed, many crews pledged to each other that 'They would blow up rather than be taken.'"[77]

Together with their defiance of death, many pirates seemed to forsake heaven too. William Snelgrave reports that members of pirate captain Thomas Cocklyn's crew affirmed that they were on a "voyage to hell."[78] Once again, it is a quote from Captain Johnson's *General History* that sums up the sentiment best. When Tho. Sutton, one of the captured pirates of Bartholomew Roberts's crew, asks a fellow praying prisoner, "What he proposed by so much noise and devotion," and receives, "Heaven, I hope," as an answer, he declares: "Heaven, you fool ... Did you ever hear of any pirates going thither? Give me h-ll, it's a merrier place; I'll give Roberts a salute of 13 guns at entrance."[79]

Destruction

The associations between golden age piracy, raiding, and cruelty pose no problem in the context of Nietzsche's philosophy. In fact, Nietzsche sees direct links between destructive activity and existential advance. An often-quoted passage from *Beyond Good and Evil* inevitably reminds of the golden age pirates' endeavors:

> Let us clarify without reservations how each higher form of culture
> began that the earth has known: Men who were still in touch with
> their natural selves, barbarians in each terrible sense of the word,
> raiders who still had unconstrained will and a desire for power,
> attacked weaker, more civilized, more peaceful races—maybe traders
> or pastoralists representing old and weary cultures in which the last
> glimpses of life have disappeared behind the overwhelming charades
> of reason and ruin. The most noble caste was originally always the

barbarian caste: their dominance was not primarily physical but spiritual—they were *more complete* human beings.[80]

Gilles Deleuze ties the meaning of destruction to the Dionysian moment in Nietzsche's thought:

> Destruction becomes active to the extent that the negative is transmuted
> and converted into affirmative power: the 'eternal joy of becoming'
> which is avowed in an instant, the 'joy of annihilation,' the *affirmation* of
> annihilation and destruction' ... This is the 'decisive point' of Dionysian
> philosophy: the point at which negation expresses an affirmation of life,
> destroys reactive forces and restores the rights of activity. The negative
> becomes the thunderbolt and lightning of a power of affirming.[81]

It is not surprising then that Nietzsche states that "the active, attacking, importunate human is in any case a hundred steps closer to justice than the reactive,"[82] and that he would praise a "justice of punishment,"[83] reminiscent of the core of the golden age pirates' ethics.

Intoxication

Dionysus being the god of wine and, in Nietzsche's words, the "artist of intoxication,"[84] it seems impossible not to mention the significance of drink within the pirate community. Stephen Snelders contents himself to point out that "alcohol was a binding element among the pirates."[85] Other commentators, however, are more bold: while Marcus Rediker suggests that "for one man (and probably a great many more) who joined the pirates, drink was more important than the wealth that he might gain,"[86] Frank Sherry writes that "it was the freedom to drink as much and as often as he liked that the ordinary sea outlaw prized above all others."[87] Indeed, while Exquemelin suggests that the buccaneers drink brandy "as liberally as the Spaniards do clear fountain water,"[88] Captain Johnson relates that "nay, sobriety brought a man under a suspicion of being in a plot against the commonwealth, and in their sense, he was looked upon to be villain that would not be drunk."[89] Another entertaining passage from the *General History* confirms the esteem that alcohol was held in by the pirates: When planters from Mauritius visited a food-poisoned pirate crew aboard their ship, "they advised their drinking plentifully of strong liquors, which was the only way to expel the poison ... [The pirates] readily followed this advice, as the prescription was agreeable."[90]

Nietzsche would have probably not approved of the golden age pirates' drinking orgies. In fact, in *The Dawn* he criticizes those who "perceive intoxication as their true life, as their actual self" and who believe in "intoxication as the life within life."[91] Nonetheless, he declares in *The Birth of Tragedy* that "the essence of the *Dionysian* principle becomes most comprehensible for us through the analogy of *intoxication*."[92]

Maybe the West Indies really were a welcoming place for Friedrich Nietzsche—or, in any case, for the god of wine, Dionysus. In the *Genealogy of Morals* Nietzsche writes:

> It seems like the moralists hate the jungle and the tropics; it seems that they have to discredit the 'tropical human' by all means—be it that they call him a disease or a degenerated being, be it that they suggest him living in hell, a sort of earthly purgatory. But why? To defend the 'temperate zones'?[93]

The political ambiguities that we have encountered throughout this book cannot be resolved by arguments over the 'right' interpretations. This will only lead us into ideological dead ends. The said ambiguities can only be resolved by adaptation instead. It is too late for both Nietzsche and the golden age pirates to do this. It is not too late for us.

5. Conclusion:
The Golden Age Pirates' Political Legacy

THE HISTORY OF RADICAL adaptations of the pirate theme is long. The authors of "Pirate Utopias" mention that "the Paris Commune ... had a daily paper called *Le Pirate*."[1] One of the widest and most dedicated resistance movements to the Nazi regime in Germany was called *Edelweißpiraten (Edelweiss Pirates)*. Today, Ramor Ryan writes a "pirate journal,"[2] the website of the anarchist CrimethInc. project is adorned by a CrimethInc.-characteristic Jolly Roger spin-off,[3] a Capt'n Mayhem explains in a pamphlet entitled *Long Live Mutiny!* how "pirate tactics" can inspire radical organizing,[4] and a radical fan culture with global appeal has formed around the pirate flag of the St. Pauli soccer club supporters.[5] We even have a group of folks sailing the oceans as Pirates for Peace [6]—a misnomer so apparent that it is bound to arouse interest. Even academics use the skull and crossbones to add some extra radical credibility to their oeuvres, as anyone who visits the *Constituent Imagination* website can testify to.[7] In fact, there are at least two popular books by radical intellectuals whose titles include a pirate reference even though they are not about pirates at all: Noam Chomsky's *Pirates and Emperors* (a book about US imperialism in the Middle East), and Tariq Ali's *Pirates of the Caribbean* (a book about new leftist movements in Latin America).

Of course the Jolly Roger not only adorns radical websites but also—in much higher numbers—baby socks, plastic plates, beer can coolers, corporate toys, video games, and records by really bad bands—not to even mention the ubiquitous Oakland Raiders paraphernalia. To many radicals this is a major source of irritation since (another) one of "their" symbols has become commercialized. There seems to be no reason to despair, however. The

173

ambiguity of the golden age pirates' politics has been one of the main topics of this book. Radical and revolutionary elements did exist within golden age pirate culture—"something menacing ... that even Hollywood can't erase," as the editors of *No Quarter: An Anarchist Zine about Pirates* preciously state.[8] At the same time, the golden age pirates can hardly be unconditionally embraced as radicals and revolutionaries. This means that radicals find themselves on shaky ground if they cry foul every time they see pirate symbols in a context they do not like. Actually, it seems likely that many pirates of the golden age would derive more satisfaction from the multi-billion-dollar movies that are based on their lives than from finding their insignia on the walls of some run-down squat. Besides, making money off the pirate glory is no new invention. Historians tell of "a sailmaker's widow in a hovel in Nassau [who] made a precarious living" by stitching Jolly Rogers.[9]

In short, the golden age pirates are not "ours"—but their legacy is ours to take. The radical and revolutionary aspects of golden age piracy have to be teased out and applied to contemporary radical and revolutionary politics. Such an approach seems liberating in fact. By not claiming ownership or "true representation" of the golden age pirates, quite a few rather trite—and in the end often pointless—arguments can be avoided: whether they were more violent than merchant captains, whether the Africans on their ships were crew members or slaves, whether they had an anti-capitalist conscious-ness or not, etc. Instead, we can focus our energies on proving the radical and revolutionary aspects of golden age piracy by bringing them alive in our poli-tics. And this too would probably satisfy at least some of the pirates who, we can safely assume, would rather continue to provide sparks of freedom than survive as mere objects of history.

Unconditionally embracing the golden age pirates as role models for radi-cal politics has repeatedly been questioned in this book. The reasons might be summed up by focusing on the two most central problems:

1. *The golden age pirates lacked a wider ethical and political perspective.* Pirates were, in the end, mainly concerned with their own well-being. They failed, as Chris Land puts it, "to offer a ... vision of a new political-economic order."[10] This of course leads us back to century-old discussions about "individualism vs. collectivism/socialism." There seems little point in revisiting these dis-cussions here. However, abandoning any commitment to making life better *for all* seems hard to accept for a radical political movement. Individualist

theories of liberation stressing the need to *liberate yourself (and the rest will follow)* build on a strict dichotomy between the individual and society that, in the end, only serves capitalism and the state, as it undermines the collective effort necessary to bring about the fundamental social change needed to free us all. The individual cannot exist without society nor can society exist without the individual. Neither form of liberation—individual or collective—is superior to the other. They are one and the same. Trying to separate them will doom our struggle to failure. In fact, the golden age pirates might be a case in point.

2. *The golden age pirates lacked a level of coordination that could have allowed for establishing a sustainable counterculture and an effective communal defense against their enemies.* The golden age pirates did share a common culture that implied solidarity and feelings of collective identity but this never translated into the kind of concrete network that would have been necessary to sustain their nomadic, libertarian and independent lifestyle in the face of the powers that came after them. It is worth quoting two historians at length whose observations sum this up very convincingly. Kenneth J. Kinkor writes:

> Unable to mobilize their own full strength, as well as the potential support of other oppressed segments of the society they had rejected, the eighteenth-century pirates were, at their strongest, a tenuous collection of loosely linked, amorphous, floating commonwealths surviving only by predation on the very societies from which they had divorced themselves. 'Inability to disengage themselves fully from their enemy was the Achilles heel of maroon societies throughout the Americas.' While discipline and centralized authority helped land-based maroon societies survive, and even flourish, the central feature and paramount attraction of piracy was its libertarian character. It is a profound irony that it was, in part, the pirates' own thirst for freedom which doomed them in an 'aimless rebellion [which] ended by suppressing itself.'[11]

In the same vein, Marcus Rediker explains:

> Pirates themselves unwittingly took a hand in their own destruction. From the outset, theirs had been a fragile social world. They produced nothing and had no secure place in the economic order. They had no

nation, no home; they were widely dispersed; their community had virtually no geographic boundaries. Try as they might, they were unable to create reliable mechanisms through which they could either replenish their ranks or mobilize their collective strength. These deficiencies of social organization made them, in the long run, relatively easy prey.[12]

It is enlightening to return once more to the theorists of guerrilla warfare in this context. Let us compare the following observations of Che Guevara and Mao Zedong with the analyses above. Guevara writes:

> The guerrilla army comprises all the people of a region or a country. That is the reason for its strength and for its eventual victory over whatsoever power tries to crush it; that is, the base and grounding of the guerrilla is the people. One cannot imagine small armed groups, no matter how mobile and familiar with the terrain, surviving the organized persecution of a well-equipped army without this powerful assistance. The test is that all bandits, all brigand gangs, eventually succumb to the central power.[13]

Mao states:

> Ability to fight a war without a rear is a fundamental characteristic of guerrilla action, but this does not mean that guerrillas can exist and function over a long period of time without the development of base areas. History shows us many examples of … revolts that were unsuccessful, and it is fanciful to believe that such movements, characterized by banditry and brigandage, could succeed in [an] era of improved communications and military equipment.[14]

It is not only the lack of social organization that has been named as a reason for the pirates' inability to resist the authorities' attack. Edward Lucie-Smith is but one who has argued that "what mitigated against the long continuation of piracy on the grand scale was not so much the success of the authorities in dealing with it as the inherent weakness of pirate society. Perhaps more pirates died of drink and disease than were ever imprisoned or hanged. … Many ships were wrecked, rather than sunk or captured."[15] Some passages from Captain Johnson's volumes seem to confirm this. One pirate crew is described as having lost "their captain and thirty men, by the distemper they contracted,"[16] while another "lost 70 men by their excesses; having been long without fresh provision, the eating immoderately, drinking *toke* (a liquor made of honey) to excess and being too free with the women, they fell into violent fevers which carried them off."[17]

Marcus Rediker has pointed to another aspect that helps explain the golden age pirates' failure to generate a long-lasting community. It seems trivial yet persuasive: "By limiting the role of women aboard their ships, pirates may have made it more difficult to reproduce themselves as a community and hence easier for the state to wage its deadly assault upon them."[18] The observation reflects Hobsbawm's verdict on the haiduks: "Haiduks were always free men, but in the typical case of the Balkan haiduks they were not free *communities*. For the *četa* or band, being essentially a voluntary union of individuals who cut themselves off from their kin, was automatically an abnormal social unit, since it lacked wives, children and land."[19]

Finally, there is the question of economic sustainability which the golden age pirates had no provisions for. In Chris Land's words: "The pirates of the golden age appear to have had no vision of an alternative political economy and their uprising would have failed had it brought an end to the Atlantic trade."[20] In the final analysis, this rendered their "anti-capitalist" activities ineffective: "The pirates did little to overthrow the power of the European, colonial states or the global flows of capitalist accumulation."[21]

However, as has been argued consistently throughout this volume, the impossibility of embracing golden age pirates as radical role models does not render them insignificant for contemporary radical politics. In fact, the ways in which golden age pirates can inform these are multifold:

1. The golden age pirates are sources of inspiration.

When Eric Hobsbawm writes that the "tragedy" of the bandits was that their "contribution to modern revolutions was ... ambiguous, doubtful and short [because] as bandits they could at best, like Moses, discern the promised land,"[22] the assumption that this was a tragedy may be challenged. It does not necessarily seem tragic to "discern the promised land." In fact, it might rather be a remarkable achievement. As Marcus Rediker succinctly puts it, the pirates "dared to imagine a different life, and they dared to try to live it."[23] If there is no inspirational momentum in such a venture, where can inspirational momentum come from? Frank Sherry's conclusion seems apt: "Clearly the brigands of Madagascar and New Providence still speak to us. They tell us, even across the centuries, that if men are denied the chance to live in freedom, they will make their own freedom, even if the specific shape of that freedom may not be beautiful or idealistic."[24] We ought also consider Anton Gill's insightful interpretation of William Dampier's attraction to the logwood cutters in the Bay of Campeche: "They were free men, and it was the freedom of their way of living, not the way they lived, that appealed to Dampier."[25]

2. The golden age pirates' forms of social organizing imply potential for revolutionary organizing.
Eric Hobsbawm concedes that there are "two things" that can turn the "modest, if violent, social objective of bandits ... into genuine revolutionary movements":[26] one, to become "a symbol, even the spearhead, of resistance";[27] and two, to evoke the "human life dream of ... a world of equality, brotherhood and freedom, a totally *new* world without evil."[28]

The golden age pirates became such a symbol and they evoked such a dream—and it is this momentum that contemporary radicals have to invigorate.

The three most concrete aspects in which such momentum manifested itself during the golden age were: One, *anti-authoritarianism*, or the above-mentioned "proto-individualist-anarchist attitude" with which "a pirate entered the political spheres of anarchist organization and festival."[29] Two, *defiance*, which seems best illustrated by yet another comparison to Hobsbawm's social bandit: "He is an outsider and a rebel, a poor man who refuses to accept the normal roles of poverty, and establishes his freedom by means of the only resources within reach of the poor, strength, bravery, cunning and determination. This draws him close to the poor: he is one of them."[30] And three, *internal democracy and egalitarianism*, which created "an alternative to the appalling conditions under which ordinary seamen had to live."[31] Rediker summarizes this as follows:

> The early-eighteenth-century pirate ship was a 'world turned upside down,' made so by the articles of agreement that established the rules and customs of the pirates' social order. ... Pirates distributed justice,

elected officers, divided loot equally, and established a different discipline. They limited the authority of the captain, resisted many of the
practices of the capitalist merchant shipping industry, and maintained
a multicultural, multiracial, multinational social order. They sought
to prove that ships did not have to be run in the brutal and oppressive
ways of the merchant service and the Royal Navy.[32]

That all three of these aspects had a high political significance cannot only
be deduced from Hobsbawm's concession that a bandit "forms a nucleus of
armed strength, and therefore a political force,"[33] but also from the authorities' reactions at the time. Even if the defense of commercial interests was a
prime motivation for embarking on their crusade against the pirates, there
was more to it. The golden age pirates did pose a political threat as well. Partly
due to the inherently political character of commerce which rendered the
pirates' attacks on merchant ships, as Janice E. Thomson puts it, "a protest
against the obvious use of state institutions to defend property and discipline
labor,"[34] but partly also because the golden age pirates brought to mind the
realistic possibility of an alternative way of life. As Marcus Rediker states,
"the more that pirates built and enjoyed the merry, autonomous existence the
more determined the authorities grew to destroy them."[35]

*3. There is a libidinal dimension to the golden age pirates' revolt that has proven
essential in liberatory politics throughout the ages.*
This dimension of the pirate protest is closely tied to Nietzsche's vitalism and
Dionysian philosophy. It is one that no subversive movement wanting to sustain itself and attract new comrades can forgo. Stephen Snelders says it well:
"The social rebellion involved in piracy resembles the instinctive and violent
social rebellion of Bonnie and Clyde: as much concerned with having a good
time as with shooting down the enemy."[36]

*4. The golden age pirates, their actions, their lore and their imagery form the
backdrop to various effective radical interventions in contemporary politics.*
Chris Land's essay "Flying the Black Flag" does a wonderful job relating
golden age piracy to current political activism—and distinguishing these
relations from commercial ones. As Land points out: "So long as people keep
consuming piracy—rather than practicing it—then capitalism won't have a

problem. But if people started actually engaging in piracy, Disney would be one of the first up in arms."[37] There are a number of examples in which the "more oppositional and insurgent figure of piracy"[38] and its "subversive tradition"[39] shows itself today and proves that "the pirates' political legacy has been long lasting and has made a significant contribution to the development of the contemporary culture of radical, anti-capitalist and anarchist dissent."[40]

a) There is the strong tradition of the *Temporary Autonomous Zone* that the golden age pirates—among many others—have been part of.[41] This tradition manifests itself today from underground social centers to squats, radical neighborhoods, open cyberspaces, intentional communities, self-controlled workshops, independent indigenous communities, free festivals, or roaming groups of wanderers and travelers. All of them, as much as the golden age pirates, confirm that, at least temporarily, a life of "freedom, equality, harmony, and abundance"[42] through practical experiment is possible. They "make some part of the myth real, if only for a short time."[43]

b) Anti-capitalist protesters around the world rightfully adopt pirate emblems to indicate their unwillingness to participate in a system of exploitation, oppression, and economic injustice. At the 2005 anti-G8 protests in Gleneagles, for example, the Jolly Roger was highly visible in various forms, turning into a sort of unofficial symbol for the organizing network Dissent!.[44]

c) Copyright violation is not incidentally called pirating. (Also the term *bootlegging* has long been used in reference to pirates—Philip Gosse, for example, calls the original rum-running bootleggers of the early 20th century "worthy descendants of the pirates."[45]) The copyright violators expropriate and redistribute wealth the way the golden age pirates did. Chris Land points to the irony that "those in the entertainment industry who are so busy commodifying the pirates of the Caribbean are also those most vociferously opposed to its current practice."[46] Unfortunately, a lot of copyright violation is egotistically and commercially motivated and lacks political consciousness, and it would be hard to make an argument for it having per se revolutionary momentum. At the same time, politically conscious copyright violation does, without doubt, give the pirate label radical credibility in this context. Pioneering groups include Sweden's Piratbyrån and its offshoot, The Pirate Bay.[47] The threat that such initiatives pose is reflected in the ever-increasing efforts to implement legal as well as technological barriers. The persecution of the Swedish activists, initiated by the corporate entertainment industry (well known for its "Piracy, It's a Crime" trailers), has been depicted in the documentary *Steal this Film (Part 1)*. It has not stopped popular sympathy. In June 2009, Swedish voters sent the Pirate Party, the liberal wing of the country's file sharing movement, to the European Parliament in Brussels. The party received a convincing 7.1 percent of the popular vote.

d) The copyright pirates are only one group of current activists that warrant comparisons to the golden age pirates regarding questions of economy. The so-called freegan movement advocates turning capitalism's excess into a source of sustainability rather than contributing to its cycle of production and consumption.[48] Similar sentiments can be found among sympathizers of the CrimethInc. project, an open network of anarchists stressing the revolutionary potential of interventions in everyday life.[49] *Evasion*, an anonymous travel diary published by CrimethInc. and relating the exploits of an anti-consumerist young male traveling the US by means of trainhopping and hitchhiking, has become a defining book for many who embrace what the author calls "militant unemployment." Both freegans and CrimethInc. adherents have had to deal with the critique of being "parasitic" rather than "revolutionary" for a long time. While such a distinction might make sense at face value, the revolutionary potential of radical adaptations of a "parasitic economy" ought not be disregarded too quickly. If embedded in political consciousness, it can be a practical—and ethically sound—survival technique within a wider revolutionary struggle. For those who can afford such a lifestyle, it promises to free time and energy both to weaken this very system and build alternatives in the process. Besides, it creates many possibilities for fusing fun and revolution (which does not necessarily mean mistaking one for the other)—we might say a very pirate way to go about things. The problems of a parasitic existence are obvious: self-indulgence, exclusivity, stagnation. But to categorically discredit dumpster diving, shoplifting or anti-corporate scams—cornerstones of a more militant freegan lifestyle (though many freegans do not engage in illegal activities)—as "irrelevant" in the fight against capitalism, would render the golden age pirates' attacks on merchantmen irrelevant too. The impact of our actions alone (which was certainly bigger in the case of golden age piracy) should not lead to a difference in judgment.

e) There are several examples for "pirate" interventions in social semiotics and public space. The best known of these may be the pirate radio. In the introduction to *Seizing the Airwaves: A Free Radio Handbook*, Ron Sakolsky, commenting on "the controversy that surrounds the term 'pirate' in micropower radio circles," explains the aptness of the pirate label in this context convincingly:

> Personally, I have never objected to the term pirate. ... Since I do not
> believe that the money that has been privately accumulated by banks
> is any more the result of an equitable distribution of wealth than that
> the oligopoly over the airwaves that presently reigns is a fair distribu-
> tion of a public resource, I would contend that the term radio pirate
> as it is commonly used is a positive poetic metaphor relating to the
> redistribution of resources between the haves and have nots.[50]

The question of space has always been significant for piracy. The example of the golden age pirates demonstrates how important it is to defend space as a means to freedom. This, of course, means airspace too. Defying the attempts to control it, radio pirates, no doubt, make important contributions to radical politics. Equally effective "pirate tactics" in reclaiming and appropriating space are employed by graffiti writers, or, more generally, street artists—see, for example, Josh MacPhee's superb collection *Stencil Pirates*.

These examples are only the latest expressions of a legacy. As Chris Land states, the golden age pirates' "ever-present insurrectionary potential ... has actualized itself in diverse settings throughout the last 300 years."[51] Marcus Rediker illustrates this contention:

> The sailors' hydrarchy was defeated in the 1720s, the hydra beheaded.
> But it would not die. The volatile, serpentine tradition of maritime
> radicalism would appear again and again in the decades to come, slith-
> ering quietly below decks, across the docks, and onto the shore, bid-
> ing its time, then rearing its heads unexpectedly in mutinies, strikes,
> riots, urban insurrections, slave revolts, and revolutions.[52]

Despite all the bourgeois and commercial exploitation of the golden age pirates, radicals can still fly the Jolly Roger proudly—all they have to do is earn the right.

6. Notes on Pirate Literature

FOR RADICALS INTERESTED IN the history of golden age piracy, the definitive work is Marcus Rediker's *Villains of All Nations: Atlantic Pirates in the Golden Age* (2005). The book contains—in slight alterations—most of Rediker's previous work on piracy, including the pirate chapters from *Between the Devil and the Deep Blue Sea: Merchant Seamen, Pirates, and the Anglo-American Maritime World, 1700–1750* (1987), and *The Many-Headed Hydra: Sailors, Slaves, Commoners, and the Hidden History of the Revolutionary Atlantic* (with Peter Linebaugh, 2000), as well as articles from various anthologies. Both *Between the Devil and the Deep Blue Sea* and *The Many-Headed Hydra* are immensely valuable sources for understanding and analyzing golden age piracy in a wider context: the maritime culture of the 17th and 18th century (*Between the Devil...*) and alternative forms of communities resisting the colonial-capitalist paradigm of the Caribbean and the Americas (*Many-Headed Hydra*).

Out of the non-radical history books on piracy with important sections on the golden age, I find three particularly noteworthy: Robert C. Ritchie—albeit mainly focusing on Captain William Kidd—provides plenty of eye-opening analysis in *Captain Kidd and the War against the Pirates* (1986). David Cordingly analyzes the popular legacy of golden age piracy meticulously in *Life Among the Pirates: The Romance and the Reality* (1995). And Peter Earle adds a lot of valuable material, found mainly in the Admiralty records, in *The Pirate Wars* (2003). The literary nucleus of all golden age piracy research remains of course Captain Charles Johnson's *General History of the Robberies and Murders of the Most Notorious Pirates* (1724–1726).

There exist several well researched and lavishly illustrated coffee table books on piracy. The most distinguished are perhaps Daniel Botting's *The*

Pirates (1979), David Cordingly and John Falconer's *Pirates: Fact & Fiction* (1992), David F. Marley's *Pirates: Adventurers of the High Seas* (1995), and two volumes by Angus Konstam, *The History of Pirates* (1999; republished in 2007 as *Pirates: Predators of the Seas*) and *Scourge of the Seas: Buccaneers, Pirates and Privateers* (2007).

Several pirate anthologies include important essays on the golden age. Particularly useful for this book proved *Pirates: An Illustrated History of Privateers, Buccaneers, and Pirates from the Sixteenth Century to the Present* (US edition: *Pirates: Terror on the High Seas from the Caribbean to the South China Sea*) and *Bandits at Sea: A Pirates Reader*, edited by C.R. Pennell (2001). The latter includes essays of special interest to radical readers, most notably Anne Pérotin-Dumon's "The Pirate and the Emperor: Power and the Law on the Seas, 1450–1850," John L. Anderson's "Piracy and World History: An Economic Perspective on Maritime Predation," and Kenneth J. Kinkor's "Black Men under the Black Flag." C.R. Pennell's "Introduction: Brought to Book: Reading about Pirates" provides a very comprehensive overview of English pirate literature. Another recommended essay by Anne Pérotin-Dumon is "French, English and Dutch in the Lesser Antilles: from privateering to planting, c. 1550–c. 1650," which appeared in the second volume of *General History of the Caribbean*.

Philip Gosse's volumes *The Pirates' Who's Who* (1924) and *The History of Piracy* (1932) provide a good impression of research on piracy in the early 20th century (and include many delightful turns of phrase). Neville Williams's *Captains Outrageous: Seven Centuries of Piracy* (1961) serves as a good example for the pirate historiography of his period.

The volume *Privateering and Piracy in the Colonial Period: Illustrative Documents*, edited by John Franklin Jameson (1923), contains many important historical documents for the study of piracy's history, such as court transcripts and newspaper articles.

For anyone interested in the history of the pirate legend, it is probably worth looking into Howard Pyle's *Book of Pirates: Fiction, Fact and Fancy Concerning the Buccaneers and Marooners of the Spanish Main*, compiled by Merle Johnson (1921). Pyle's work remains one of the most influential sources for the pirate image of the 20th century.

Out of the many popular books written on golden age pirate history—those whose "quality depends on the literary skill of the authors rather than on content"[1]—I particularly enjoyed Frank Sherry's *Raiders & Rebels: The Golden Age of Piracy* (1986). Despite a definite exaggeration of the significance of the Madagascan pirate community, questionable political terminology, and a sometimes melodramatic prose, the book is well researched and a very engaging read. I would also recommend Edward Lucie-Smith's *Outcasts of the Sea: Pirates and Piracy* (1978); much less sensationalist than Sherry's in approach and very sophisticated in presentation, it contains a number of interesting musings on the pirate phenomenon. The recent *The Republic of Pirates* by Colin Woodard (2007) also contains valuable details, especially concerning the role of New Providence as a major pirate haunt from 1716 to 1718.

As far as the history of the Caribbean buccaneers is concerned, I believe that there is little substitute for the original sources. Very little has come to light about the lives of the buccaneers since and—even more so than with Captain Johnson's work and the history of golden age piracy—almost all histories draw on Exquemelin's *The Buccaneers of America*, and, to a lesser degree, on the accounts of William Dampier, Basil Ringstone, and Raveneau de Lussan. Probably the best summary is C.H. Haring's *The Buccaneers in the West Indies in the XVII Century* (1910), even though the more compact P.K. Kemp and Christopher Lloyd's *The Brethren of the Coast: Buccaneers of the South Seas* (1961) is very instructive as well. For a short yet comprehensive introduction, Angus Konstam's *Buccaneers* (2000) is highly recommended. For those particularly interested in Dutch privateers and buccaneers, Virginia W. Lunsford presents an amazing collection of material in *Piracy and Privateering in the Golden Age Netherlands* (2005); this book will mainly appeal to academics, however.

For special interest areas, R.B. Burg's *Sodomy and the Pirate Tradition: English Sea Rovers in the Seventeenth-Century Caribbean* (1983), though highly contested, remains an interesting read. Hans Turley's *Rum, Sodomy and the Lash: Piracy, Sexuality & Masculine Identity* (1999) is a much more complex (and arguably more interesting) study but is laden with academic jargon. Paul Galvin's *Patterns of Pillage: A Geography of Caribbean-based Piracy in Spanish America, 1536–1718* (1999) seems to be one of the most underrated books on piracy, although it contains a lot of valuable information for even the most well-read students of Caribbean sea robbery. Janice E. Thomson's *Mercenaries, Pirates and Sovereigns: State-Building and Extraterritorial Violence in Early Modern Europe* (1994) includes a careful analysis of the connections between piracy, commerce, and the state. With respect to women pirates, Ulrike Klausmann and Monika Meinzerin's *Women Pirates* (1997) remains a pioneering and provocative study. Also noteworthy—albeit not focused on the golden age—is John C. Appleby's essay "Women and Piracy in Ireland: From Gráinne O'Malley to Anne Bonny," published in *Bandits at Sea*.

As far as the field of "radical piratology" is concerned, the must-reads—apart from Rediker's work—are Christopher Hill's essay "Radical Pirates?" (1984) (there are also important remarks on piracy in Hill's *Liberty Against the Law: Some Seventeenth-Century Controversies*, 1996); Peter Lamborn Wilson's *Pirate Utopias: Moorish Corsairs & European Renegadoes* (1995) (even though it focuses on piracy along the North African Barbary Coast, the book includes much thought-provoking commentary on the pirate phenomenon in general and golden age piracy in particular); Stephen Snelders's *The Devil's Anarchy* (2005) (which also includes valuable firsthand accounts of Dutch privateers and buccaneers); and the essays "Pirate Utopias: Under the Banner of King Death" in the anarchist *Do or Die* journal (no. 8, 1999), and Chris Land's "Flying the black flag: Revolt, revolution and the social organization of piracy in the 'golden age'" (*Management & Organizational History* 2, no. 2, 2007), which draws many inspiring comparisons between Golden Age piracy and contemporary radical movements. Another much-referenced essay among radical scholars is J.S. Bromley's "Outlaws at Sea, 1660–1720: Liberty, Equality and Fraternity among the Caribbean Freebooters," which I, admittedly, find a bit tedious. The work by German authors Heiner Treinen and Rüdiger Haude was highly valuable for this volume but is unfortunately not available in English. William S. Burroughs's *Ghost of Chance* (1991) and Kathy Acker's *Pussy, King of the Pirates* (1996) are both enticing literary adaptations of the pirate theme. Finally, a DIY treat for all radical pirate fans is the *No Quarter* zine hailing from Calgary, Canada.

APPENDIX

Interview with *Darkmatter*

Published in *Darkmatter: In the Ruins of Imperial Culture* no. 5, December 20, 2009.

For those not too familiar with pirate history: what is the golden age?
The golden age refers to the heyday of the pirate era that emerged in the Caribbean in the late seventeenth century before spreading to the Indian Ocean and eventually to the west coast of Africa. Basically all of the popular Euro-American pirate images derive from this era, whether we encounter them in Robert Louis Stevenson's *Treasure Island* or in Disney's *Pirates of the Caribbean*. The Jolly Roger, the most powerful of all pirate symbols, stems from the golden age too. Historians give the era different frames, but we are roughly looking at the period from 1690 to 1725.

Why did piracy become so strong then?
Sea robbery had occurred in the Caribbean for more than a hundred years prior to the golden age. In the sixteenth century, when the run for the colonies in the Caribbean and the Americas began, European powers sent sea robbers as a sort of unofficial mercenary force to the region to plunder ships of their colonial rivals. As legend has it, Francis Drake was called "my pirate" by Queen Elizabeth.

In the seventeenth century, an outlaw hunting community gathered on the island of Hispaniola, today divided into Haiti and the Dominican Republic. The community consisted of marooned or shipwrecked sailors, runaway servants and slaves, adventurers and dropouts. They were called "buccaneers" after a meat-smoking practice they adopted from the indigenous Carib Indians. When they took to sea robbery to supplement their income, they began serving a similar role to the likes of Drake, being issued with a "letter of marque" by one colonial power and attacking ships of another. Eventually, some buccaneer expeditions gained military-like dimensions, the successful 1671 attack on Spanish-ruled Panama under Henry Morgan serving as the most famous example.

By the end of the seventeenth century, colonial policies had changed enough to render the buccaneers' services increasingly less important. This left many of them without an income. As a consequence, they continued their attacks on merchant ships indiscriminately and turned, in the words of some historians, into "pirates proper": a community of sea robbers who would no longer serve a particular master but who "waged war on the whole world," as Captain Charles Johnson's *General History of the Pirates* famously puts it. This was the beginning of the golden age.

For three decades, the golden age pirates were surprisingly successful. Then they were crushed by combined efforts of the powers that had created them. It's a scenario very similar to many we see today: governments equip men to fight in their interests—and then criminalize and persecute them when they are no longer useful.

So golden age piracy is directly bound to colonialism?
Most certainly. Without European colonization there wouldn't have been a golden age of piracy. And not only because Europeans wouldn't have traveled to the Caribbean or to the Indian Ocean, but also because golden age piracy was a direct result of activities that were financed and encouraged by colonial powers.

The relations between the golden age pirates and the colonial era are complicated, because once pirates started to prey on ships of all nations they began to pose a threat to the economic profitability of the colonies and therefore to the colonial enterprise itself. However, this doesn't change the fact that they are an inherent part of the colonial legacy. To portray golden age pirates as some kind of anti-colonial force seems misleading. Many of the pirate strongholds of the golden age—in the Caribbean, in Madagascar, and along the West African coast—functioned as renegade colonial outposts. True, they were not established under the flag of any European nation-state, but they still reinforced the control of Europeans over native populations.

Can you elaborate on this? Some historians have claimed that pirate crews overcame the racial prejudices of their times?

Whenever we talk about what golden age pirate crews did or did not do, we are facing a serious problem, namely a lack of reliable sources. We have no log-books, diaries, letters—not a single document that would provide an "authentic" image of what life was like on their ships. All we have is what in a court of law would be considered "circumstantial" evidence: newspaper articles, court transcripts, governmental records.

This leaves the role that non-Europeans played on golden age pirate ships very unclear. On the one hand, there are indications that some Caribbean Indians and Africans who sailed on pirate ships were full crew members, sometimes very respected ones. On the other hand, there are many indications that Indians and Africans were used as laborers or servants. It is interesting to note that when the British Navy hunted down the most notorious of all golden age pirate captains, Bartholomew Roberts, basically all of his nearly two hundred European crew members were brought to trial, while the seventy-five Africans were sold into slavery. This might just reflect the attitudes of the British officials at the time, but it might also indicate the status these men really had.

I think it is true that pirate crews offered a chance for non-Europeans to live relatively free lives when this was practically impossible anywhere else within European society. It must also be true that the lure of freedom that drew Europeans to piracy drew runaway slaves to piracy too. So I'm not denying that there has been an element of transgressing racial limitations in the pirate experience. However, to portray golden age pirate communities sweepingly as "multiracial" or "postracial" seems too daring to me.

Can you say something about the relations between the golden age pirates and the slave trade?

Again, it's not a clear-cut issue. It seems well documented that some of the golden age pirates' strongholds doubled as slave trading posts, especially in Madagascar and West Africa. According to the records, it also seems likely that slaves were mostly considered cargo like any other when pirates took a slave ship and that they were sold at the next good opportunity.

At the same time, it is unlikely that all golden age pirates were involved in the slave trade. There were Africans sailing as full crew members on pirate ships, which makes it appear improbable that slaves would have been treated as mere commodities. Then again, freeing some slaves didn't end slavery in the South of the United States either—we simply don't know.

Some historians have suggested a strong anti-slavery moment among golden age pirates because they disrupted the slave trade that developed in West Africa. This is a questionable conclusion. It is true that the pirates' activities disrupted the slave trade and that this was one of the reasons why the authorities became ever more determined to hunt them down. However, we are not talking about an interference based on enlightened moral values. The pirates interfered with the slave trade in the same way that organized crime interferes with alcohol or tobacco sales: the pirates hurt the official slave trading industry by claiming a share of its profits, not by challenging the trade per se.

It has also been suggested that some golden age pirates attacked slave ships to free all Africans on board. Even if this is true—and the stories don't seem very convincing to me—such events must have been exceptional.

Golden age pirates have been described as communities transcending national boundaries too. Would you agree?
The concept of the nation is a difficult one to deal with. If we speak of nation-states, yes, the golden age pirates defied this concept and all that goes with it: citizenship, borders, administrative rule. The Jolly Roger remains a powerful symbol in this sense alone. Did the golden age pirates lose all sense of national identity, though, as in: all sense of belonging to a particular group of people united by language, geography, heritage, or whatever else can be used to construe a nation? Hardly so.

It is true that in certain ways golden age pirates overcame the national boundaries that were still characteristic of the buccaneer communities. In the golden age, Anglo-American, French, and Dutch pirates fought together rather than against one another. However, most other nationalities remain conspicuously absent from golden age pirate ships, most notably the Spanish. The main colonial rivalry of the Americas was hence still reflected in the makeup of the pirate crews.

In general, the multinational melting pots that golden age pirate crews are sometimes made out to be seem overrated. The overwhelming majority of golden age pirates were Anglo-American. There were significant numbers of French and Dutch pirates, but only a smattering of pirates from other European nations, and some Indians and Africans. Arguably, the population of most colonies at the time was more diverse than golden age pirate crews. True, national identity among the pirates might have been more flexible, horizontal, and egalitarian, but prejudices and conflicts certainly remained.

In short, given the absence of a nation-state as an authoritarian unifying concept, there was definitely an anti-national streak in golden age piracy, and the political significance of this must not be underestimated. Yet, to imagine a utopian paradise where national allegiances of all sorts had evaporated oversimplifies matters.

It appears, though, that this anti-national streak was a very characteristic feature of golden age piracy—also one that would distinguish the golden age from other pirate eras.
It is at least related to what I would call the most distinguishing feature of golden age piracy, namely its nomadism. This aspect is missing in all other great eras of piracy, whether we are talking about piracy off the North African coast in the sixteenth century, piracy in the South China Sea in the 1800s, or piracy along the Somali coast today. Golden age pirates had no home, no permanent land base, no community they were part of, could retreat to, and disappear in. When asked where they came from, they famously replied, "From the Sea." They had safe havens, allies, and business partners on land, but these ties were merely pragmatic and very fleeting.

The nomadic aspect of golden age piracy is very unique—and very fascinating, in many ways. It is the reason why all of our popular pirate images relate to this era: the golden age pirate, more so than any other pirate, is the ultimate outlaw, one who has cut off all ties with the conventions of a bourgeois life: home, security, stability. No surprise then that he's been such a common object of projection: both by the bourgeoisie that sees secret desires fulfilled, and by radicals who find their dreams of liberation materialized.

The final part of your book discusses the political legacy of golden age pirates and whether they can inform contemporary radicals. Can they?
Well, they obviously do. Look at how present the Jolly Roger is in radical circles: it adorns autonomous spaces, appears in anti-globalization rallies, and is a favorite in any radical art show. The question is whether this is mere

romanticism or whether there is any substance to back up such adaptation. I think this is an important distinction to make. Nothing against romanticism, but when it becomes a dominant force in politics it can prevent both complex analysis and convincing vision.

I do believe that there is substance behind the radical embrace of golden age pirates. Certain characteristics must appeal to any radical endeavor: 1) an uncompromising defiance of authority; 2) risking one's life for freedom rather than spending one's life in chains; and 3) setting a remarkable example of direct democracy, as the egalitarian organization of pirate crews is not disputed even by the most conservative historians.

However, golden age pirates were no model revolutionaries, no principled socialists, no perpetrators of a class war. I think that we can learn much more from golden age pirates if we take their shortcomings into account rather than making unsupported claims. The most important shortcomings seem to be: 1) a lack of moral perspective beyond an immediate group of peers; 2) a lack of social organization beyond the confines of one's own ship; 3) a lack of long-term political vision; 4) an economic dependency on one's enemies. In short, the golden age pirate communities were not sustainable. They had no inherent mechanisms for reproduction, preservation, and progression. It is telling that they lasted but one generation.

Your book covers a lot of ground—we have talked about colonialism, nationality, race, radical politics, and there are chapters on gender, sexuality, disability, Friedrich Nietzsche etc. How do all these parts tie together?
By reflecting upon golden age piracy from many angles, I've been trying to add new perspectives. Due to the mentioned lack of firsthand sources, the study of golden age piracy involves endless speculation. Of course certain theories are much more plausible than others, and spouting random nonsense is as meaningless, boring, and offensive as claiming a truth that isn't there. But the inevitability of speculation is part of the pirate mystique and an important factor for our never-ending fascination with the subject.

Interview with *Junge Welt*

Published in *Junge Welt*, June 10, 2015.

The Caribbean pirates of the eighteenth century fascinate people to this day. Is the romantic notion of freedom and adventure a literary invention?
The notion was already groomed during the golden age. In England, theater plays portraying the supposedly jolly lives of the pirates were staged for captivated audiences. Pirates have always aroused the longing for freedom so deeply rooted in bourgeois society. This is also the reason for their ongoing popularity. The romantic notion is therefore rather a literary "representation" than a literary invention. The pirates did indeed live in relative freedom. Yet the pirate life was no paradise.

But it was apparently attractive enough for thousands of men to risk their lives.
At the peak of golden age piracy, about two hundred pirates sailed on twenty to twenty-five pirate ships. Their lives were certainly freer than those of most people at the time. But they were also riddled with dangers. The life expectancy of a pirate was but a few years. Pirates died of diseases, in shipwrecks, during battle, or on the gallows. But they took that risk in order to live independent lives, free from the domination and oppression of the state and its henchmen. This was an impressive gesture of resistance.

What was wrong with the European societies where the pirates came from?

The pirates of the golden age had different backgrounds. They included former seamen and soldiers, but also escaped prisoners, forced laborers, and
slaves. The pirates were rebels because they refused to enact the social roles
expected from them, taking their lives into their own hands.

The problems of European societies at the time were essentially the same
they have today: there was no social justice and massive inequality and poverty. For many of the poor, a life in the navy or on merchant ships was the only
way to make a living. But the discipline and the overall living conditions on
board were brutal. Mutiny and joining the pirates were ways out.

How were the crews composed ethnically and nationally?
On pirate ships, people from different backgrounds came together. That is
why they were often referred to as "men without fatherland." The majority of
pirates, however, came from countries colonizing the Caribbean: England,
France, and the Netherlands. We can add to this political prisoners from
Ireland and Scotland, adventurers from various European countries, slaves
from Africa, and members of indigenous communities of the Americas.

Were pirates and seamen opponents of slavery?
That is certainly not a general truth. There were pirates who were actively
involved in the slave trade. But many pirates also felt a strong solidarity
with victims of oppression and exploitation as well as a basic respect for
those who rebelled against injustice. That was more important than ethnic
or national backgrounds. In that sense, the pirate communities were indeed
very progressive.

**In the seventeenth century, there were rebellions against the English
crown. Did the ideas of the English Revolution influence the pirates?**
The pirates cannot really be compared to the rebels of the English Revolution.
The pirates had no political agenda. But there was a connection through political prisoners of the English Revolution being exiled to the Caribbean. Their
ideas might have had an impact on piracy.

There was a strong sense of solidarity among the pirates. But golden age
piracy was no political movement, and it would be wrong to claim that the
pirates tried to establish a different political system; this would exaggerate
the ideological aspect. Pirates collaborated with corrupt authorities whenever

it was convenient, and their booty was spent on booze and gambling rather than being redistributed among the poor. They were not maritime Robin Hoods. Yet the antiauthoritarian impulse was strong, and the pirates longed for the "good life." This had political relevance, set an example, and enthused many people, even if it the pirates were primarily concerned with their own "good life" and not necessarily that of others.

The pirates had experienced oppression and made a conscious decision to escape it, no matter the price. They organized their own communities in egalitarian ways, which was, without doubt, one of the most progressive aspects of their lives. While we must not exaggerate the pirates' political vision, we must not underestimate their moral principles either. There was a pirate ethos, and the egalitarian organization of their communities belonged to the idea of the "good life," prevented internal strife, and strengthened social cohesion.

Can you call the settlements the pirates created "republics"?
It depends on what we mean by "republics." Pirate settlements did not replicate the monarchies of the time. In that sense, they had republican traits. But there were no constitutions warranting a republican system. The pirate settlements were too anarchic.

Pirate settlements were also short-lived. In the golden age, none existed for more than a couple of years; this was true for the settlements established both in the Caribbean and in Madagascar, which were created after the pirates had advanced all the way to the Indian Ocean.

Especially the Madagascan settlements had little to do with modern republicanism. They were characterized by internal hierarchies and the oppression of indigenous peoples. The reality was far from the story we hear about the utopian pirate community of Libertalia, which reflects ideals and hopes that European republicans projected onto pirate communities. But that projection wasn't entirely random. There were republican tendencies among the pirates, but they were part of a very complicated and ambiguous reality.

Were the pirates influenced by indigenous peoples?
We can assume that. There is little evidence, but forced laborers and slaves who escaped their masters in the Caribbean and became pirates often received help from indigenous peoples. Indigenous people also sailed on pirate ships.

There must have been some mutual influence, even if the indigenous contributions are often overlooked in European history books.

Could the pirate settlements have provided an alternative to European colonialism, both for European sailors and the indigenous people?
As I hinted at before, the pirate settlements did not really serve as a political model. They were almost exclusively composed of men, and the economy was purely parasitic. Pirates didn't produce anything; their entire economy was based on robbery. This is also why terms such as "maritime proletariat" are problematic.

But for those who like thought experiments: yes, possibly the pirates could have undermined the colonial order to a degree where other political possibilities could have opened up for the population. But this did not happen.

Yet it is still fascinating that a couple of thousand people on two dozen ships could have such significance.
Golden age piracy was a real threat to early colonial trade. The pirates threatened not only the trade itself but also the related political system, since they showed that a different kind of life was possible. There were also direct attacks on representatives of the system. Sometimes, the pirates made an example of despotic captains and officers, punishing them in front of their crews. This made them appear even more fearsome in the European imagination than what they actually were. It is true: the traces that the pirates of the golden age have left in the collective memory of humankind are remarkable given their numbers.

Eventually, the golden age pirates were eradicated after concerted efforts by the colonial powers.
That's not surprising. They were relatively few men on few ships. Being almost exclusively male, pirate society could not reproduce itself. The pirates were not only dependent on successful heists but also on new recruits. When repression increased and both heists and recruitment became increasingly difficult, their society quickly unraveled. Some pirates managed to start new lives, if they managed to hide and had some plunder left. Others accepted amnesty offers and were pardoned. But most of them died during the final

confrontations with state power. Mass executions, in which up to fifty pirates lost their lives, characterized the last years of golden age piracy.

Why has the maritime perspective, which is so important for both colonialism and modernity, been neglected by historians?
Maybe there is a lack of research in the German-speaking world, I don't know. Internationally, there has been much research during the last decades, also by progressive historians. The work by Marcus Rediker, including the book *The Many-Headed Hydra: Sailors, Slaves, Commoners, and the Hidden History of the Revolutionary Atlantic*, coauthored with Peter Linebaugh, was groundbreaking.

What were the main differences between the European pirates and the Barbary Coast pirates who operated in the Mediterranean around the same time?
The Barbary Coast pirates were coastal dwellers of North Africa who, because of certain political and economic circumstances, integrated sea robbery into their economy. The pirates of the golden age had no safe hinterland. They were an international and nomadic community whose settlements were never more than temporary retreats. Their home was the ship they sailed on. This is what makes them unique in the history of piracy and turned them into pirate prototypes, almost single-handedly responsible for the fascination that pirates inspire to this day.

Have the pirates left a legacy?
Of course. We only need to go watch a St. Pauli football game.
    The St. Pauli example also shows how reality and wishful thinking—but also rebellion and commerce—intertwine. It is yet another reason why the golden age is so fascinating.

Do you see parallels to today's piracy?
There is sea robbery today, and poor social conditions are a major reason for it. But the parallels don't reach much further. Piracy in Southeast Asia or along the coasts of Nigeria and Somalia is—much like in the case of the Barbary Coast—geographically much more contained than golden age piracy was. It is not about a "different form of life." Today's pirates are rooted in the societies

they come from and live their daily lives there. We might be able to interpret them as social rebels, but not as nomadic outsiders who "declared war on the whole world," as was said about the pirates of the golden age.

How would you summarize the message of your book?
It is legitimate to evoke the rebellious heritage of golden age pirates in political contexts, as long as it happens without idealization and a dose of self-irony.

Interview with *No Quarter*

Published in *No Quarter* no. 5, March 2010.

How and when did you first get interested in pirates and the golden age of piracy?
As a child, like so many others. I was always fascinated by the outlaw image of pirates, had pirate toys, dressed up as a pirate, etc. Incorporating that fascination into my work later on just seemed like a natural step.

I first encountered your writing when I read "Life Under the Death's Head: Anarchism and Piracy," in the book *Women Pirates and the Politics of the Jolly Roger* by Ulrike Klausmann, Marion Meinzerin and yourself (published by Black Rose in 1997). What's the relationship between that essay and the new book?
I think there are clear similarities in how I try to look at golden age piracy through social, political, and cultural theory. The big difference is that I now know much more about piracy than when I wrote that essay. This has changed my outlook in several ways. In the essay I used golden age piracy mainly as a historical backdrop onto which I projected a few general ideas about radical politics. Doing justice to the actual history of golden age pirates was much less important than propagating political beliefs. At the end of the essay I say something like, "I know I will be accused of romanticism, but I don't care." A very flippant remark, of course, but, well, it gives you an idea of the background of that essay.

This book takes a different angle. It tries to tie certain political ideas—which are very similar to the ones in the essay, not much has changed there—much more to what the golden age pirates' reality might have actually been like. So the assessment of their politics—rather than the projection of ours as contemporary radicals—plays a more important role. One consequence of this was that most of the romanticism went out the door . . .

Let me pick up on this. I think that perhaps the most important thing about *Life Under the Jolly Roger* is the way you engage with works of radical piratology critically. I feel like you are very quick to acknowledge the strengths of the works, but also argue very strongly against what you feel they got wrong. These are often very important differences (the interpretation of the story of Captain Mission and Libertalia, and the relationship between pirates and slavery being just two examples out of many). Why is it so important to correct these idealizations? Why is it so easy to make these kinds of mistakes?
Well, personally, I wouldn't even speak of mistakes. I think one of the aspects that make work on golden age piracy so difficult—and so intriguing—is the lack of firsthand sources. We have no letters, diaries, or logbooks of pirates, no accounts of people who traveled with them or who studied them at close hand. In short, apart from the traceable material facts (approximate numbers, areas of operation, ships used, etc.), there is very little certainty when it comes to the life of golden age pirates, their motives, their social relations, their political and ethical beliefs, etc. All we can do is read the "circumstantial evidence" (newspaper clippings, court transcripts, navy records), relate it to what we know of the era's general history, add our perception of how humans behave under certain circumstances, and then come up with a picture that seems convincing and believable to us. Now, different scholars will come up with different pictures, but that only makes everything more interesting.

But to answer your question about idealizations and why I find it important to correct them: I think mainly because I want a radical political movement to be a credible movement; a movement that has to be taken seriously by its opponents on an intellectual and theoretical level. Now don't get me wrong, there is a place for romanticism: romanticism inspires, motivates, and reassures, and that's all great. But I also think that there is a place for serious examination where we take a step back, take a breath, and say, "Okay, let us look at what things might have really been like." And on this level, I think the ability to be self-critical is tremendously important. It makes for better discussion among ourselves as radicals, and for a more productive exchange with people whose politics differ.

Are you worried that people will get offended by your critiques—either the writers themselves or radicals who hold some of these idealized notions about golden age piracy very dearly?
I am a little worried that some of the writers might misinterpret my intentions, because I'm really not out to disrespect anybody's work. I wouldn't even say that I'm criticizing much, at least not in the sense of saying that someone is "wrong" on this point or another. The work by Marcus Rediker, Peter Lamborn Wilson, and Stephen Snelders is fantastic, there is absolutely no doubt about that, and my work builds almost entirely on theirs. Most importantly, I see them as authors who share similar political ideals, and this is much more significant to me than whether we share the same view on the ethics or ideals of Blackbeard or Bartholomew Roberts.

For me, when I differ from their interpretations, it's just about different perspectives, and about a lively, constructive debate. This is what I believe takes us further as radicals interested in historical analysis and political theory. Let us take Marcus Rediker's *Villains of All Nations* as an example. It is without any doubt the most accomplished book written on golden age piracy, particularly from a radical angle. Of course we could just be like, "All right, Marcus Rediker has said it all, and that's that on golden age pirates." But I think that'd be rather boring, and I can't see Rediker wishing for that either. Radical discussion needs new takes and new thoughts, and I hope I've been able to formulate some in this book. Whether they'll make sense to readers and will be considered contributions to a valuable debate is for them to decide, but I think it's necessary to try. Radical discussion must never stop or it stops being radical.

Am I worried that I might offend some readers? To be honest, I haven't given that much thought. I guess I assumed that it's clear enough that I'm writing from a radical perspective and that I'm raising questions as a comrade and not as a foe. If people don't agree with me and think that I am too negative in my view of golden age pirates, that's perfectly fine. I'm glad that there are different positions. I just wish for respect and solidarity.

You wrote: "Perhaps there was neither anarchist nor revolutionary consciousness among pirates of the golden age—but they certainly carried anarchist and revolutionary momentum" (75). Could you elaborate on what you mean by that?

I just think that it'd be hard to make a convincing case that golden age pirates were very much concerned with universal values of equality and justice or with creating a better world for all. All considered, it just doesn't seem plausible to me. Their motivating factors rather appeared to be an individual escape from oppressive social structures and the pursuit of a joyful life. However, this does not mean that there was nothing revolutionary about them. "Lack of consciousness" has probably been overrated as a dividing line between people who deserve the revolutionary attribute and those who don't. To me, there does lie a revolutionary—and anarchist—element or potential in the rejection of oppressive structures and the pursuit of a joyful life, no matter how "individualistic" it is. No one can take this away from the golden age pirates, and I think it's what inspires radicals to this day. So even if golden age piracy probably cannot be called a "liberation movement" based on revolutionary "consciousness," it carries what I would call a revolutionary element, potential, or, well, "momentum."

You use the work of a number of people that might not be obvious when examining the golden age of piracy—Deleuze and Guattari, Pierre Clastres, and Nietzsche, for instance. Why did you use this approach?

The answer is pretty simple: I studied philosophy and always enjoyed reading theory. At the same time, I've always wanted to tie theory to issues that seemed relevant politically, instead of ending up in very isolated academic dialogue. My relationship with academia was always complicated, and I have had very little to do with it since finishing my university studies almost fifteen years ago. If you will, this book is an example of trying to make theory meaningful not only to academics but also to people who share common interests—in this case, an interest in pirates and/or radical politics—but never had the time or motivation to read much theory. Among the nicest compliments I can get is someone telling me, "This is the first time Foucault (or whoever) really grabbed my attention."

Ultimately what lessons do you think radicals can draw from the golden age of piracy?

I lay this out in more detail in the last chapter of the book, but the core aspects are: 1) The rejection of authority and of dominant social norms. This seems an essential aspect of any radical engagement. 2) The golden age pirates' internal social structure that stands as an extraordinary experiment in egalitarianism and direct democracy. It's not to be idealized as it was exclusive, i.e., the guiding principles were only shared among crew members and did not extend to others, but it is nonetheless a shining and inspiring example of radical self-determination. 3) The "libidinal" dimension of golden age pirate life, which I consider indispensable for making radical politics attractive. You gotta have fun being a radical. A boring society is hardly worth fighting for, and it will not endure either. It's like that famous quote attributed to Emma Goldman, "If I can't dance, I don't want to be part of your revolution." I think the golden age pirates were always up for a good dance.

Besides these central points, there are a few other aspects: For example, the "Temporary Autonomous Zones" that the pirates created in the sense of Hakim Bey. Then their challenge to the control of space which renders terms like "pirate radio" very apt. And a number of important economic aspects, like the rejection of both the wage labor system and capitalist production (which allows to draw interesting parallels to modern-day dumpster divers, freegans, etc.), or the undermining of ownership rights (which today continues in the form of piracy as "copyright violation").

There are a lot of lessons to draw from golden age pirates for contemporary radicals, no doubt. As I argue in the book, though, the decisive question is how we can turn these lessons into effective political work today. The golden age pirates provide no model for a free and just society for all, due to ever-changing historical circumstances, their own contradictions, and also their special relationship to the sea. They carry the said revolutionary "momentum," but today this has to be brought to life by those who want to defend their legacy. In this context, what's crucial is not whether the golden age pirates were revolutionary, but how we and future generations can keep their legacy a revolutionary one. This has no longer to do with projection; it is rather a matter of adaptation.

What do you think about contemporary piracy, especially off the coast of Somalia?
My knowledge is limited. I don't think it has much to do with what I'm studying in the book, because for me the central feature of the golden age pirates

is their lack of home, their "nomadism." All that the golden age pirates really had were their ships. They came indeed, as the traditional pirate greeting indicates, "from the sea." This distinguishes them from all other famous pirate communities, including those of North African corsairs in the sixteenth century, the nineteenth-century pirate syndicates of the South China Sea, or contemporary pirates along the Horn of Africa.

To me, the approach of studying the latter wouldn't differ much from the general study of bandit groups with strong roots and acceptance in local communities. Personally, I think that the work of Eric Hobsbawm remains unsurpassed here. Of course, there are tactical and strategic differences between bandits operating in the desert, in the forest, or on the sea, but the overall social dimensions of their actions are very similar. It is the nomadic character of the golden age pirates that makes them a unique social phenomenon and demands specific analysis.

But to give you an answer to Somali piracy based on the little I do know, I would say that it is a consequence of three overlapping factors, namely a dire social situation, war, and imperialism. Somalis wouldn't turn to piracy in the same numbers if it wasn't an economic necessity; they wouldn't have the weapons and the military know-how if they hadn't been surrounded by war for nearly two decades; and they had less justification for their actions if there wasn't a sense that international maritime trade was plundering their resources. Whether this creates a social movement with promising political dimensions, I'm not sure. There are certainly anti-imperialist and anticolonial aspects, and there is a sense of self-determination, but I don't know whether we're looking at any attempt here to actually alter the structure of Somali society. It is certainly an interesting development to observe for anyone interested in piracy, and we will see where it is headed.

Interview with Radio Dreyeckland

Broadcast by Radio Dreyeckland on April 4, 2012.

How did you start working on piracy?
I first worked on pirates in the early 1990s while I was a student at the University of Innsbruck. I belonged to a small group of philosophy students who wanted to engage with topics that weren't part of the regular curriculum. Like many others, we were intrigued by pirates and looked into the topic more closely. Out of this came a text that was published as a pamphlet by Monte Verità, an anarchist publisher in Vienna. The text was later translated into English and became part of the book *Women Pirates and the Politics of the Jolly Roger*, published by Black Rose. After that, I didn't work on piracy for years. It was PM Press that asked me if I didn't want to give it another shot; they had just been founded and were building their catalog. I said yes, because I still found the topic intriguing. *Life Under the Jolly Roger* was the result.

I'd like to read you a quote by Jann M. Witt, who authored a German book about the history of piracy. He says: "The pirates were no maritime Robin Hoods; they robbed and plundered not for noble reasons but because of greed. The true history of sea robbery is an endless stream of murder, pillage, and rape." What is your response?
This is a very good example for one school of pirate historians, which we might call the "classical," "conventional," or "conservative" school. But, in the past twenty years, another one emerged, composed of historians who look at piracy from a social-revolutionary perspective. Today, this polarization

characterizes pirate research: pirates are seen either as cutthroats and criminals or as social rebels and revolutionaries. What I have tried to do in the book
was to develop a perspective that doesn't fit into the tradition represented by
the quote you just read, but that doesn't end up romanticizing either.

**The history of piracy is a long one. Already the Romans fought pirate
wars, and today there is much talk about the situation in Somalia. You
have looked at the golden age. What was it?**
It was the era of piracy originating in the Caribbean, stretching roughly from
1690 to 1725. Piracy in the Caribbean developed in the context of the region's
colonization and the fight between colonial powers. Eventually, it extended
all the way to the Indian Ocean, with Madagascar becoming the center.
During the final years, pirates operated mainly along the west coast of Africa
in connection with the slave trade.

What makes the golden age special in European cultural history—and
what gives it the name "golden age"—is that the majority of golden age pirates
were European and that the colonial powers played a central role in piracy's
development. "Exotic places" such as the Caribbean islands and Madagascar
allowed Europeans to project many things onto pirate communities, both
good and bad.

Golden age piracy determines the popular imagination of piracy in Europe,
based on dozens of pirate films. Other eras of piracy lasted longer and were
more successful, for example in the South China Sea during the nineteenth
century, but they are hardly known.

A particularly interesting aspect of golden age piracy from a research
angle is its nomadic character. During all other peaks of piracy, also today in
Somalia, pirates had a home in coastal areas and were integrated into local
communities. They would go to sea and attack ships, then retreat. This wasn't
possible for golden age pirates. They had no communities they could retreat
to; their homes were their ships. This makes the romantic appeal very strong.

**You mentioned the popular imagination of piracy, which includes eye
patches, bandannas, cutlasses, and so on. How much of that is reality and
how much of it is myth?**
Separating fact from fiction is very difficult when working with golden
age piracy. This also makes it particularly intriguing. There are no letters,

logbooks, photographs, or the like from life on board the pirate ships, so it becomes very difficult to say what is true and what the result of fancy. But if we look at the research that has been done, we can assume that there is a kernel of truth in the images of eye pads, peg legs, and extravagant clothing. The latter has often been described as a pirate parody of English aristocracy. But pirates probably only dressed up like that when they went ashore. On the ships, they were dressed like ordinary seamen.

As far as their social organization is concerned, it was very democratic for the era. Yet it is naive to portray pirate communities as the nuclei of liberated, direct-democratic communities. There were internal power structures, and democratic principles that were accepted within the community weren't accepted outside of it. Golden age pirates did not just attack rich merchant ships and hand the booty to the poor. All sorts of ships were attacked, and the most common victims were ordinary fishers rather than rich traders. There are some examples of spectacular heists and staggering booty, but those are the exceptions.

Libertalia often appears in radical literature on the golden age, a pirate haven hailed as an early anarchist utopia. What is your take?
Libertalia most probably never existed. The story comes from Captain Charles Johnson's *General History of the Pirates*, a book that is tremendously valuable for pirate research but is also known to include fabricated parts. The chapter on Libertalia is most likely one of them. What I find particularly interesting, though, is that if you look at how Libertalia was described by Johnson, it was far from an anarchist or communist ideal. It had a liberal foundation, with property rights protected by the state. It reminds us mainly of social contract theory and the ideas of John Locke or Thomas Hobbes. Those ideas were progressive for their time, and Captain Charles Johnson probably invented Libertalia to propagate them, but Libertalia is not a radical utopian society. This understanding seems to have been lost at some point during the controversies between conservative and left-leaning pirate historians: Libertalia turned into a symbol that people quarreled about without bothering to actually read up on it. At least that's my impression.

You mentioned that the last phase of golden age piracy overlapped with the emergence of the slave trade. What was the pirates' role? Did escaped slaves join them or were the pirates complicit in selling slaves?

Both. Once again, the sources aren't easy to interpret, but things played out in different ways. On the one hand, the colonial order was undermined in pirate communities, which had an antiauthoritarian impulse. This meant, among other things, that some escaped slaves did join pirate crews and became full members. But most Africans on pirate ships weren't full crew members and had to do the hardest labor, sometimes under slave-like conditions. And when slave ships were successfully attacked, the slaves were usually treated as part of the booty and sold at the next good opportunity. In Madagascar, there was much collaboration between pirates and slave traders.

There is also a misunderstanding that concerns piracy along the coast of West Africa. Pirates did attack slave ships, yes, but to profit, not because they were against the trade per se. It's like selling pirated porn: it might cut into the profits of the big players of the industry, but it's not an attack on the industry as such.

Final question: Pirate imagery still appears regularly in radical left and subcultural contexts. The Jolly Roger is hoisted on squats and so on. At the same time, pirates are at the center of the cultural industry—Johnny Depp as Captain Jack Sparrow is just one example. Is there really a subversive potential in the image of the pirate as a countercultural, rebellious figure?
I think that dimension exists. As I said, I think it's unfortunate when we have to choose between only two pirate images on offer: either that of a cutthroat or that of a revolutionary. Pirate life was more complex. But part of that complexity were elements that can inspire progressive and radical movements to this day. We have already mentioned a strong antiauthoritarian impulse and democratic structures. But let us think of something like "pirate radio." It makes sense to use that term, as it is reminiscent of people applying unoccupied space to their own needs and challenging total control of those in power. There was also an element in golden age piracy that we find propagated in certain anarchist circles today: the idea that you can challenge capitalism by removing yourself completely from the production process. This is controversial, but golden age pirates are legitimate reference points if you believe in it. So, it is neither surprising nor inappropriate for pirate imagery to appear in radical circles. From an analytical perspective, it is of course most interesting to ask ourselves which aspects of pirate life can indeed inform radical politics today and which can't. Romanticization can inspire and provoke, but it can also make you lose credibility and, in the worst case, look foolish.

Interview with Radio Obskura

Broadcasted by Radio Obskura, August 24, 2011.

Can you tell us about the golden age pirates' political, social, and economic background?
Social inequality, poverty, and the authoritarian structures both on merchant ships and the Caribbean colonies. These were the circumstances that made certain men feel that joining the pirates would make their lives better. They could live in relative equality, make a living without being worked to death, and, if they were lucky, get rich very quickly.

Some pirates also were former seafaring mercenaries employed by the colonial powers. They were out of a job when the English, French, and Dutch signed peace treaties in the late seventeenth century, and they continued with their exploits, now targeting all merchant ships indiscriminately.

What do you mean by living in relative equality?
Some pirates had privileges in pirate communities, too, especially the captains, but these privileges were rather limited compared to those of the ruling classes. Pirate crews always agreed communally on the rules that would guide life on their ships, the division of labor, and the distribution of booty. And the privileged captains also had special duties, for example to support the crew when supplies were drying up, and so on. Important decisions on the ship were also made communally as well. Captains only really had authority during times of battle.

But how much evidence is there for this? Marcus Rediker and Peter Linebaugh even make the pirates part of an early world proletariat not divided by racism. Do you agree?

It is difficult to talk about evidence. We have no logbooks, diaries, or letters from golden age pirates, and no firsthand accounts by people who sailed with them. Much of what we know is based on Captain Charles Johnson's *The General History of the Pirates*, a book known to include fabricated parts. But the documents we do have, for example navy records or trustworthy newspaper articles, confirm the egalitarianism on pirate ships. This isn't doubted even by conservative historians. But how far do you want to take the radical interpretations? Like, does it really make sense to include the pirates into a world proletariat, even though they didn't produce anything and operated entirely outside established labor relations? In a very broad sense, possibly, but I'm not sure about the analytical value.

But you speak of them as "social rebels," referencing Eric Hobsbawm.

For Hobsbawm, social banditry is a form of rebellion against the dominant political and economic forces that resonates with large parts of the population, especially underprivileged groups. At the same time, it lacks the political consciousness that Hobsbawm, as a Marxist, deems necessary for a true change of social structures. This applies to golden age piracy in the sense that there was a strong rebellious element, which was also appreciated by many people, but no ability to create a better society, and perhaps no will either. Golden age pirates left important reference points for radicals to this day— the rejection of state power, the interruption of capitalist trade, and so on— but they didn't provide a model for an egalitarian world beyond their own confines.

Why is the outlaw appeal of piracy so strong?

People dream of individual freedom—especially in bourgeois societies, where individual freedom is praised as a principle but limited by many norms and rules. Bourgeois folks want to be free but don't dare to be. Projecting their longing onto pirates—or, for that matter, bandits of all kinds—helps to deal with that. And the further away the object of your projection is—both in time and space—the less dangerous this is politically; you don't have to draw any consequences in your personal life because the object of your projection is so far removed from it. How many people who idolize the heroes of historical pirate films idolize the pirates of Somalia? It just doesn't work the same way. Somali piracy is way too close, maybe not geographically, but it happens today, the targets are modern cargo ships and oil tankers, and we have trials of Somali pirates in North America and Europe. It's much harder to project your secret longings onto any of that.

When we compare the golden age with contemporary piracy, what are the continuities and what the ruptures?
The ruptures are obvious. There have been enormous technological changes, which affect piracy in many ways: the boats, the weapons, the navigation systems, and so on. The tactics have also changed. Today, it is mainly about hijackings and ransoms, which weren't a feature of golden age piracy at all. Yet the biggest difference between golden age piracy and all other pirate eras concerns the golden age's nomadic character: Somali pirates go out at sea, attack, and then retreat back into their coastal communities. The golden age pirates couldn't do this; they only had self-established, temporary retreats, and perhaps havens with people who were friendly toward them, at least for a while. In general, they were just floating around, which added to their romantic aura.

What are the continuities? The motivations are still similar: people react to social injustice, poverty, and specific political circumstances. Somalia, for example, has a coastline of over two thousand miles that is no longer protected by the state since the state has basically collapsed. That's why some Somali pirates refer to themselves as Somalia's new coast guard. Now, does that justify what they do, or is it just an excuse for crime? These questions are very similar to questions we can ask about the pirates of the golden age.

Email Exchange with Anna Vo

At the very first presentation of *Life Under the Jolly Roger*, in Sydney, Australia, in December 2009, I was asked a question that challenged the romanticization of pirates among radicals as being characteristically Western. A decade later, I got in touch with Anna Vo, who had asked that question, in an entirely different context (hardcore punk and straight edge) and used the opportunity to discuss it once more. Anna Vo kindly agreed to have the exchange included in this edition of the book. It took place in October 2018.

Anna Vo is a zine maker, artist, and educator living in Portland, Oregon.

Gabriel: When I presented *Life Under the Jolly Roger* in Sydney in 2009, you asked a question about ethnocentric images of pirates and the anticolonial impression of a particular type of white pirate. As I understand it, this was also related to firsthand experiences with real-life pirates of family and friends. Now that we've got the chance, I'd like to revisit that discussion. To begin with: was this a fair representation of your question?

Anna Vo: Hmm, I think I was interrogating the idea and dominant narrative that pirates are only a specific type of aesthetic/pirate, and the question was to clarify which type/s your book was addressing. Additionally, I was critiquing the romanticization (which is still current!) of a concept that has specifically caused much kidnapping, rape, and murder in my culture and family's history.

Gabriel: What's the specific type that's dominant in common representations of pirates? And what type is missing?

Anna Vo: The swashbuckling white "yarrharrharr" type around the time of the East India Tea Company made popular by the image of Johnny Depp and his fair maiden Keira Knightley at the time of that conversation. One thing that is missing is the portrayal or inclusion of the atrocities that those (and any "war heroes" or colonialists) were involved in, which were extreme misogyny, brutality, assault, and killing that went along with their pillaging.

Gabriel: You also said that these experiences were part of your culture and family's history. Can you say more about that?

Anna Vo: It was a common story during the time after the Vietnam war was won by the North/HCM that family members would risk leaving via boat and they would go missing. When people went missing it was either witnessed or understood that it was because of pirates. And more often than not, there were stories from witnesses where pirates would grab kids and young women from boats, and no one would see them again. It was understood that the young girls and young women were assaulted and then murdered, their bodies thrown into the sea.

    When my parents tried to escape Vietnam, it was with the understanding that there would be a large chance that they would not survive due to pirates. For that reason my dad did not tell his parents that he was leaving, because he didn't want them to stop him or to fear for his life. He left one day on a boat and did not have contact with them again for another ten years. He was twenty-one. On the boat that my parents were on, they encountered pirates, however the pirates decided to invade and loot the boat next to them instead of my parents' boat. They heard the sounds of that invasion. My mother felt that she and her boat had the luck and protection of our ancestors on that journey, because if things had been slightly different, she would definitely have been kidnapped. Their boat was able to steer away while the pirates were busy. She was twenty at the time and one of the few girls on her boat. It was a common story when I was a kid, one that I would hear every few nights: the sounds of the pirates approaching, and the fears of my mum's family and their attempts to hide her in case they were about to get hijacked.

Gabriel: If one wanted to defend positive references to piracy in radical circles, I guess the explanation would have to be that some pirates have always been out there to prey on others, while some pirates tried to establish egalitarian communities and only targeted the rich and powerful. I don't think it's a very good explanation, though, because I don't think those boundaries were ever clearly drawn. Considering the horrific stories of your family: do you have any understanding for pirate references and symbols among radicals, or is this just plain cynicism?

Anna Vo: Maybe I could ask a question back: Where is the distinction or evidence that those colonial Anglo-Celtic pirates were absolutely not engaged in preying on others for personal gain? Was there intentional delineation from looting noncolonialist ships? Was there active, structured redistribution of wealth? If there was no delineation or redistribution, then, yes, I think it's naive to put a rose-colored Robin Hood anarcho-communist spin on it. Anarcho-capitalist? Sure, why not.

A modern example/comparison could be an anarcho-punk shoplifting thousands of dollars' worth of Apple merch, stating that it's in the interest of "bringing down giant corporations," but then profiting from selling it on Craigslist and hoarding the profits without sharing those resources with the community or those in more need. And then when the same punk steals from another individual (like a housemate instead of a huge company) for personal gain, what then? Can they justify it by saying they are unemployed/spending through their income/need new Doc Martens, so they are attempting to create a more egalitarian microcommunity in that household through the act?

Forgive me if there are accounts of said pirates funding uprisings and antimonarchy movements with their loot instead of hoarding it.

Gabriel: There is no evidence that the colonial Anglo-Celtic pirates of the so-called golden refrained from preying on others for personal gain. Some might have intentionally refrained from looting noncolonialist ships, but, at best, there'd be circumstantial evidence.

There is more concrete evidence—if records of the era can be trusted—that suggest active redistribution of wealth. Certainly within the pirate community, possibly also beyond it. The modern-day anarcho-punk you're describing would probably not have survived on a golden age pirate ship had they been caught stealing from others. They would have also been expected to share the profits made from the Apple merch.

Regardless, I'm no supporter of the anarcho-communist spin. Golden age pirate communities were riddled with contradictions. To my knowledge, they did not fund any social or political uprisings. They didn't hoard their loot either; they just spent it for personal pleasure. The attraction among radicals can, I believe, only be justified on a symbolic level: here were folks trying to escape the yoke of both the state and rich businessmen (capitalists), experimenting with a (very exclusive) model of democracy. But: 1) This symbolism probably only works if you haven't had firsthand encounters with real-life pirates. 2) It is nothing particularly radical; everyone in Western culture loves pirates and uses them to imagine a bad-ass life beyond the confines of a mundane bourgeois existence.

I'm rephrasing my question: Do you understand that symbolic attraction, or is it just cynical given the pirate reality?

Anna Vo: Understood. The exclusive part of that idealism is where I feel is a political contradiction, e.g. in current times when folks reproduce the trappings of the bourgeoisie under the guise of working as a proletariat. But alas, that becomes a separate book . . .

In terms of symbolism, like any signifier it can get separated from origin and meaning, and like any logo it can be co-opted and/or reappropriated by popular culture. (Yes, I'm proposing punk and radicalism and some aspects of DIY as popular consumer culture and, yes, I would say the Jolly Roger has become a logo.) Similarly, I've seen the hammer and sickle used to sell beer, the Black Lives Matter movement to sell soda, and Native American ceremonial practices to promote sports teams.

So to answer your question, I understand all listed symbolism in the same manner: with an acknowledgment of the thing it is a reference to via popular culture, or the aesthetic it seeks to communicate, while keeping in mind its historical context tied with its cultural ramifications, within the limits of my own knowledge.

Gabriel: Okay. Are you saying that under certain circumstances it's all right to romanticize a certain kind of pirate?

Anna Vo: I'm not labeling things good or bad or all right, but any romanticization or co-optation of a symbol without historical understanding makes me uncomfortable.

Gabriel: So if there is historical understanding, you feel comfortable with it? I guess what I'm trying to get at is this: if people conditioned by Western culture find that golden age pirates—albeit having been deeply conditioned by that culture, too—cracked things open a little bit, because at least they rebelled against some of that culture's most loathsome expressions (class divisions, the tyranny of the rich and powerful, a very regulated life), then maybe that inspires these people to find some more cracks or even make their own. And since I tend to label things to be good or bad or all right, I would say that's not a bad thing. What would you say?

Anna Vo: I think history holds a lot of lessons, good and bad, that people either learn from or they keep repeating. Any gateway to radicalization or analysis or critique or dismantling systems is valuable, yes.

Gabriel: Yes, we need the gateways. But they can come at a price. Like, you create your gateway but by means that piss off or offend others. It's a delicate balance. To be honest, I'm not sure how the pirate gateway fares. Any last words?

Anna Vo: Pick your battles, actions, and community well!

NOTES

0. Introduction

1   Chris Land, "Flying the Black Flag: Revolt, Revolution and the Social Organization of Piracy in the 'Golden Age,'"*Management & Organizational History* 2 (2007): 170.

2   Edward Lucie-Smith, *Outcasts of the Sea: Pirates and Piracy* (New York: Paddington Press, 1978), 7.

3   Jenifer G. Marx, "The Brethren of the Coast" in *Pirates: An Illustrated History of Privateers, Buccaneers, and Pirates from the Sixteenth Century to the Present*, ed. David Cordingly (London: Little, Brown and Company, 1995), 37.

4   Douglas Botting, *The Pirates* (Amsterdam: Time-Life Books, 1979), 177.

5   David Cordingly, *Life Among the Pirates: The Romance and the Reality* (London: Little, Brown and Company, 1995), 282.

6   Ibid., 3.

7   Marcus Rediker, *Villains of All Nations: Atlantic Pirates in the Golden Age* (London & New York: Verso, 2004), 176.

8   Peter Earle, *Sailors: English Merchant Seamen 1650–1775* (London: Methuen, 1998), 181. Similarly, Philip Gosse has stated: "The picturesque swashbuckler, with pistols stuck in his belt and curses pouring from his mouth, makes a very good subject for a story, but ... the genuine article was on the whole a coward and a cut-throat" (*The History of Piracy*, New York: Tudor Publishing Company, 1932; Glorieta, NM: The Rio Grande Press, 1990, 298).

9   Rediker, *Villains of All Nations*, 176.

10 Angus Konstam, *The History of Pirates* (New York: The Lyons Press, 1999), 189.

11 Philip Gosse, *The Pirates' Who's Who: Giving Particulars of the Lives & Deaths of the Pirates & Buccaneers* (London: Dulau and Company, 1924; Glorieta, NM: The Rio Grande Press, n.d.), 21.

12 John Exquemelin's *The Buccaneers of America*, first published in Dutch in 1678, is by far the most influential. Exquemelin spent several years living among the buccaneers. Raveneau de Lussan tells of the two years he spent among French buccaneers (1685/86) in his *Memoirs*. The account of Jan Erasmus Reyning—transcribed by a physician friend—covers the period from 1668 to 1671, was published

in Amsterdam in 1691, and has only recently been related in English thanks to the work of Stephen Snelders (*The Devil's Anarchy*). William Dampier traveled several years with privateers and spent some time among the logwood cutters in the Bay of Campeche. His accounts were published as *Dampier's Voyages* between 1697 and 1699. Basil Ringrose's *The Dangerous Voyage*, first published in 1685, tells about a buccaneer excursion under Captain Bartholomew Sharp.

13   The identity of Captain Johnson remains disputed. In the 1930s, literary historian John Robert Moore announced that Captain Charles Johnson was a nom de plume for the famed novelist Daniel Defoe. He supported his thesis so convincingly in the book *Defoe in the Pillory and Other Studies* (1939) that some editions of *A General History* even began to carry Defoe's name. However, in 1988, P.N. Furbank and W.R. Owens published *The Canonisation of Daniel Defoe* and profoundly challenged Moore's assumptions, insisting that there was "not a single piece of external evidence to support, and quite a few pieces of such evidence to argue (apparently) against" Defoe's authorship (102). For those interested in the details of the debate, the references in Marcus Rediker's *Villains of All Nations*, 179–80, are a good starting point. In recent years, German scholar Arne Bialuschewski has identified journalist and newspaper editor Nathaniel Mist as a likely author of the *General History* (Woodard, *The Republic of Pirates*, 325).

14   C.R. Pennell, ed., *Bandits at Sea: A Pirates Reader* (New York: New York University Press, 2001), 9.

15   Peter Earle, *Pirate Wars* (London: Methuen, 203), 129.

16   Profane Existence, "Anarchy, Punk, and Utopia," *Profane Existence Catalog* 12 (1995): 29.

17   Lucie-Smith, 9.

18   Maurice Besson, ed., *The Scourge of the Indies: Buccaneers, Corsairs and Filibusters* (London: George Routledge & Sons, 1929), xf.

19   Konstam, *History of Pirates*, 188.

20   Hans Turley, *Rum, Sodomy and the Lash: Piracy, Sexuality & Masculine Identity* (New York: New York University Press, 1999), 7.

21   Ibid.

22   Konstam, *History of Pirates*, 189.

23   A note on referencing Marcus Rediker: Rediker has regularly used revised versions of previously published texts for subsequent publications. I have done my best to quote and reference the latest published versions only but cannot guarantee that I have done so in each and every case.

24   Peter Earle states in *Pirate Wars*: "I was brought up to admire the navy and my instincts are on the side of law and order, so that the navy rather than the pirates has my support" (12).

25   Marcus Rediker, "Hydrarchy and Libertalia: The Utopian Dimensions of Atlantic Piracy in the Early Eighteenth Century" in David J. Starkey, et al., *Pirates and Privateers: New Perspectives on the War on Trade in the Eighteenth and Nineteenth Centuries* (Exeter: University of Exeter Press, 1997), 81.

26 Pennell, *Bandits at Sea*, 9.
27 "Life Under the Death's Head" was never intended to be a scholarly
    contribution to pirate history. I tried to tie the little I knew about piracy to
    certain theories I deemed subversive. The idea was to stimulate radical thought
    and politics. While the intention of this book is very similar, it rests on much
    more solid historical study and hopes to have left behind the original essay's
    pretentiousness.

1. BACKGROUND

1.1. Privateers, Buccaneers, Pirates: Matters of Terminology

1   Gosse, *The Pirates' Who's Who*, 14.
2   Cordingly, *Life Among the Pirates*, 6.
3   Treinen, "Parasitäre Anarchie: Die karibische Piraterie im 17 Jahrhundert," *Unter
    dem Pflaster liegt der Strand* 9 (1981): 11.
4   Turley, *Rum, Sodomy and the Lash*, 29.
5   See Janice E. Thomson, *Mercenaries, Pirates and Sovereigns: State-Building and
    Extraterritorial Violence in Early Modern Europe* (Princeton, NJ: Princeton
    University Press, 1994), 107.
6   Ulrike Klausmann, Gabriel Kuhn and Marion Meinzerin, *Women Pirates and the
    Politics of the Jolly Roger* (Montreal: Black Rose, 1997), 166–67.
7   Used by the Romans as a legal definition for sea robbers, the phrase was
    resurrected in golden age piracy trials. (Rediker, *Villains of All Nations*, 174.)
8   See Marcus Rediker's book of the same name.
9   Klausmann et al., 166–67.
10 See Thomson, 107.
11 Earle, *The Pirate Wars*, 108.
12 Ibid., 101.
13 Peter T. Leeson, "An-*arrgh*-chy: The Law and Economics of Pirate Organization,"
    Journal of Political Economy 15, no. 6 (2007): 1052.
14 Konstam, *History of Pirates*, 10.
15 "The Tryal, Examination and Condemnation, of Captain Green 1705" in Turley,
    44.
16 Robert C. Ritchie, *Captain Kidd and the War against the Pirates* (Cambridge:
    Harvard University Press, 1986), v.
17 For an overview of these pirate communities consult any of the general pirate
    histories recommended in the "Notes on Pirate Literature."
18 Ritchie, 19.
19 Anonymous, "Pirate Utopias: Under the Banner of King Death," *Do or Die*, no. 8
    (1999).
20 Charles Johnson, *A General History of the Robberies and Murders of the Most
    Notorious Pirates*, ed. Arthur L. Hayward, 4th ed. (London: T. Woodward, 1726;
    George Routledge & Sons, 1926), 560.

21 Konstam, *History of Pirates,* 11.
22 Marx, "The Brethren of the Coast," 38.
23 Thomson, 54.
24 Konstam, *History of Pirates,* 11.

1.2. What "Golden Age"? A Little History

1   Ibid., 126.
2   Neville Williams, *Captains Outrageous: Seven Centuries of Piracy* (London: Barrie and Rockliff, 1961), x.
3   Earle, *The Pirate Wars,* 93–94.
4   Jan Rogoziński, *A Brief History of the Caribbean:From the Arawak and Carib to the Present* (New York: Facts on File, 1999), 77.
5   Ibid., 63.
6   Peter R. Galvin, *Patterns of Pillage: A Geography of Caribbean-based Piracy in Spanish America, 1536–1718* (New York: Peter Lang, 1999), 110.
7   Basil Fuller and Ronald Leslie-Melville, *Pirate Harbours and Their Secrets* (London: Stanley Paul & Co.: 1935), 69.
8   Anne Pérotin-Dumon, "French, English and Dutch in the Lesser Antilles: from privateering to planting, c. 1550–c. 1650" in *General History of the Caribbean,* ed. P.C. Emmer (London and Basingstoke: UNESCO Publishing, 1999), 2:149.
9   C.H. Haring, *The Buccaneers in the West Indies in the XVII Century* (London: Methuen & Co., 1910), 59.
10 Apart from boars and cattle, there were also wild dogs and horses on Hispaniola. Exquemelin was not too fond of them, however: "They are but low of stature, short-bodied, with great heads, long necks, and big or thick legs. In a word, they have nothing that is handsome in all their shape" (John Exquemelin [Esquemeling], *The Buccaneers of America,* London: Swan Sonnenschein & Co. / New York: Charles Scribner's Sons, 1893, 37).
11 John Masefield, *On the Spanish Main* (London: Methuen & Co., 1906), 120.
12 Gosse, *The Pirates' Who's Who,* 12.
13 Konstam, *History of Pirates,* 74.
14 Stephen Snelders, *The Devil's Anarchy: The Sea Robberies of the Most Famous Pirate Claes G. Compaen & The Very Remarkable Travels of Jan Erasmus Reyning, Buccaneer* (New York: Autonomedia, 2005), 67.
15 Marx, "The Brethren of the Coast," 38.
16 Besson, 6–7.
17 Marx, "The Brethren of the Coast," 38.
18 Fuller and Leslie-Melville, 74.
19 Ritchie, 22.
20 Haring, 58.
21 Galvin, 110.
22 J.H. Parry and P.M. Sherlock, *A Short History of the West Indies* (London: Macmillan & New York: St. Martin's Press, 1957), 82.
23 Fuller and Leslie-Melville, 169.

24 Peter Wood, *The Spanish Main* (Amsterdam: Time-Life Books, 1980), 104.
25 Snelders, 94.
26 Carl Bridenbaugh and Roberta Bridenbaugh, *No Peace Beyond the Line: The English in the Caribbean 1624–1690* (New York: Oxford University Press, 1972), 176.
27 Angus Konstam, *Buccaneers* (Oxford: Osprey, 2000), 10.
28 Lucie-Smith, 158.
29 Konstam, *Buccaneers*, 52.
30 Marx, "The Brethren of the Coast," 38.
31 Ritchie, 22.
32 Franklin W. Knight, *The Caribbean: The Genesis of a Fragmented Socialism* (New York: Oxford University Press, 1990), 97–98.
33 Earle, *Pirate Wars*, 92–93.
34 Christopher Hill, "Radical Pirates?" in *Collected Essays: People and Ideas in 17th Century England* (Brighton: Harvester Press, 1986), 174.
35 Parry and Sherlock, 93.
36 Snelders, 168.
37 David F. Marley, *Pirates: Adventurers of the High Seas* (London: Arms and Armour Press, 1997), 119.
38 Earle, *Pirate Wars*, 149.
39 Rediker, *Villains of All Nations*, 168.
40 Cordingly, *Life Among the Pirates*, 236.
41 Earle, *Pirate Wars*, 155.
42 Ritchie, 234.
43 Earle, *Pirate Wars*, 192.
44 Anonymous, "Pirate Utopias: Under the Banner of King Death."
45 Galvin, 66–67.
46 Ibid., 67.
47 Cordingly, *Life Among the Pirates*, 234–35.
48 Konstam, *History of Pirates*, 96.
49 Rediker, *Villains of All Nations*, 170.
50 Earle, *Pirate Wars*, 198. Earle goes on to quote John Atkins, the surgeon of the *Swallow*, responsible for the death of Roberts and the arrest of his crew: "Discipline is an excellent path to victory; and courage, like a trade, is gained by an apprenticeship, when strictly kept up to rules and exercise. The pirates though singly fellows of courage, yet wanting such a tie of order and some director to unite that force, were a contemptible enemy. They neither killed or wounded a man in the taking; which ever must be the fate of such rabble" (198).
51 Ibid., 203–4.
52 Rediker, *Villains of All Nations*, 37.
53 Earle, *Pirate Wars*, 204.
54 Ibid., 166–67. Robert C. Ritchie even suggests that "if ordinary mariners refused to join a pirate crew, they were abused, tortured, and even killed" (234).
55 James Burney, *History of the Buccaneers of America*, quoted in Lucie-Smith, *Outcasts of the Sea*, 176.

56   Marcus Rediker, *Between the Devil and the Deep Blue Sea: Merchant Seamen, Pirates and the Anglo-American Maritime World, 1700–1750* (Cambridge, MA: Cambridge University Press, 1987), 283.

57   Cordingly, *Life Among the Pirates*, 236.

58   Earle, *Pirate Wars*, 206.

59   Johnson, 416.

60   Gosse, *The Pirates' Who's Who*, 43.

61   Ibid., 47.

62   Lucie-Smith, 197.

63   Johnson, 57.

64   Ibid., 302.

2. "Enemy of his own civilization": An ethnography of Golden Age Piracy

1   Snelders, 187.

2   Ibid., 205.

3   Ibid., 3.

4   Ibid., 173.

5   Ibid., 205.

6   Anonymous, "Pirate Utopias: Under the Banner of King Death."

7   Treinen, 18.

8   Rüdiger Haude, "Frei-Beuter: Charakter und Herkunft piratischer Demokratie im frühen 18. Jahrhundert," *Zeitschrift für Geschichtswissenschaft* 7/8 (2008): 607.

9   Frank Sherry, *Raiders & Rebels: The Golden Age of Piracy* (New York: Quill, 1986), 20.

10   Ibid., 95.

11   Peter Lamborn Wilson, *Pirate Utopias: Moorish Corsairs & European Renegadoes*, 2nd rev. ed. (New York: Autonomedia, 1995 & 2003), 22.

12   Rediker, *Villains of All Nations*, 168

13   Ibid., 85

14   Ibid., 16.

15   Rediker, *Between the Devil and the Deep Blue Sea*, 285.

16   Peter Linebaugh and Marcus Rediker, *The Many-Headed Hydra: Sailors, Slaves, Commoners and the Hidden History of the Revolutionary Atlantic* (Boston: Beacon Press, 2000), 156.

17   See also Earle, *Pirate Wars*, 101.

18   David Graeber, *Fragments of an Anarchist Anthropology* (Chicago: Prickly Paradigm Press, 2004), 11–12.

2.1. "From the Sea": Maritime Nomads

1   A.M. Khazanov, *Nomads and The Outside World*, trans. Julia Crookenden (Cambridge: Cambridge University Press, 1984), 15–16.

2   Ibid., 15.

3   Snelders, 198.
4   See, for example, Johnson, 536.
5   David Cordingly and John Falconer, *Pirates: Fact & Fiction* (London: Collins and Brown, 1992), 32.
6   Cordingly, *Life Among the Pirates*, 110.
7   Elman R. Service, *The Hunters*, 2nd ed. (Englewood Cliffs, NJ: Prentice-Hall, Inc., 1966 & 1979), 4.
8   Khazanov, 3.
9   Knight, 90.
10   Rediker, *Between the Devil and the Deep Blue Sea*, 248.
11   David E. Sopher, *The Sea Nomads: A Study Based on the Literature of the Maritime Boat People of Southeast Asia*, Memoirs of the National Museum 5 (Singapore, 1965), 46.
12   Sopher, 253.
13   Khazanov, 1.
14   Ibid., 1–2.

2.2. "Smooth" vs. "Striated": The Question of Space

1   Gilles Deleuze and Félix Guattari, *Nomadology: The War Machine* (New York: Semiotext(e), 1986), 73.
2   Bridenbaugh and Bridenbaugh, 62.
3   Marley, *Pirates*, 7.
4   Haude, 598.
5   Rediker, *Villains of All Nations*, 25.
6   Lucie-Smith, 177.
7   Deleuze and Guattari, *Nomadology*, 61.
8   Ibid., 34.
9   Marshall D. Sahlins, *Tribesmen* (Englewood Cliffs, NJ: Prentice-Hall, 1968), 36.
10   Johnson, 6.
11   Gilles Deleuze and Félix Guattari, *A Thousand Plateaus* (London: Continuum, 2004), 13–14.
12   Anonymous, "Pirate Utopias: Under the Banner of King Death."
13   Haring, 76.
14   Cordingly, *Life Among the Pirates*, 241.
15   Gosse, *The History of Piracy*, 1. New York: Tudor Publishing Company, 1932.
16   See also "The Geographical Backdrop to Piracy," in Pennell, *Bandits at Sea*, 62–64.
17   Deleuze and Guattari, *Nomadology*, 61–62.
18   Earle, *Pirate Wars*, 150.
19   Snelders, 172.
20   Cordingly, *Life Among the Pirates*, 258.
21   Marley, *Pirates*, 152.
22   Lucie-Smith, 245.
23   Ritchie, 238.

2.3. Pirate Captains and Indian Chiefs: Remembering Pierre Clastres

1   Clastres mainly studied Indian societies of the Amazon but claims that his analysis applies to most American Indian cultures. See *Society Against the State*, trans. Robert Hurley (New York: Zone Books, 1987), 28.

2   Clastres, 27–47.

3   Ibid., 28.

4   David Cordingly, introduction to *The History of Pirates* by Angus Konstam (New York: The Lyons Press, 1999), 6.

5   Johnson, 167–68.

6   Gosse, *The Pirates' Who's Who*, 18.

7   Basil Ringrose, "The Dangerous Voyage and Bold Assaults of Captain Bartholomew Sharp and Others, Performed in the South Sea, for the Space of Two Years, etc." in Exquemelin, 399.

8   Sherry, 128.

9   Snelders, 187.

10   Deleuze and Guattari, *Nomadology*, 11.

11   Johnson, 544.

12   Clastres, 30.

13   Johnson, 185.

14   Sahlins, *Tribesmen,* 78. Sahlins also lists several pages worth of examples for this practice in *Stone Age Economics* (London: Tavistock Publications, 1974), 246–64.

15   Sahlins, *Tribesmen,* 79.

16   Clastres, 30.

17   Ibid., 31.

18   Johnson, 108.

19   Clastres, 30.

20   Treinen, 31.

21   Clastres, 207.

22   Johnson, 185.

23   Clastres, 209.

24   Rediker, *Villains of All Nations,* 65.

25   Clastres, 29.

26   Deleuze and Guattari, *Nomadology,* 11.

27   Similar parallels can be drawn to the description of nomadic chiefdoms. "Where there was a supreme chief his functions frequently were partially similar to those of a chief in a sedentary society, for legal procedure, ceremonial and external relations. However, no less, if not more important were his other functions, for mediation in internal conflicts and military leadership. ... In normal circumstances absences of a legitimate and coercive power to enforce decisions is even more characteristic of nomadic leaderships than it is of the leaderships of a sedentary chiefdom ... the chiefdoms themselves to a certain extent may be called *dispositional.* It is for this reason that nomadic chiefdoms are usually extremely unstable, that their leadership is diffuse and decentralized and their composition fluid and impermanent" (Khazanov, 166–69).

28   Clastres, 206.

29   Ibid., 207.
30   Ibid., 209.
31   Johnson, 56.
32   Snelders, 181.
33   Johnson, 543.
34   Cordingly, *Life Among the Pirates*, 132.
35   Johnson, 168.
36   Ibid., 230.

2.4. Potlatches, Zero-Production, and Parasitism: Pirate Economy

1   Sherry, 131.
2   Earle, *Pirate Wars*, 11.
3   Cordingly, *Life Among the Pirates*, 111.
4   J.S. Bromley, "Outlaws at Sea, 1660–1720: Liberty, Equality and Fraternity among
     the Caribbean Freebooters," in *History from Below: Studies in Popular Protest
     and Popular Ideology in Honour of George Rudé*, ed. Frederick Krantz (Montréal:
     Concordia University, 1985), 309.
5   Snelders, 96.
6   Clastres, 193.
7   Ibid., 196.
8   Sahlins, *Tribesmen*, 79.
9   Snelders, 108.
10   Sahlins, *Stone Age Economics*, 35.
11   Botting, 45.
12   Sahlins, *Stone Age Economics*, 1.
13   Snelders, 205.
14   Clastres, 197.
15   Clastres, 195.
16   Besson, 197.
17   Sahlins, *Stone Age Economies*, 1–2. On the "original affluent society" specifically,
     see the chapter of the same name, 1–39.
18   Exquemelin, 40.
19   Ibid., 72.
20   Ibid.
21   Cordingly and Falconer, *Pirates*, 114.
22   Ibid.
23   Besson, 14.
24   Klausmann et al., 165 & 169.
25   Land, 178.
26   Snelders, 10.
27   Service, 16.
28   Gustavo Martin-Fragachan, "Intellectual, Artistic and Ideological Aspects of
     Cultures in the New World," in *General History of the Caribbean,* ed. P.C. Emmer
     (London and Basingstoke: UNESCO Publishing, 1999), 2:274.

29   Anonymous, "Pirate Utopias: Under the Banner of King Death."

30   Kathy Acker, *Pussy, King of the Pirates* (New York: Grove Press, 1996), 276.

31   Service, 74–75.

32   Sahlins, *Tribesmen*, 80.

33   Sherry, 122.

34   Friedrich Engels, *Der Ursprung der Familie, des Privateigentums und des Staats*, in Karl Marx and Friedrich Engels, *Werke*, Band 21, 5. Auflage (Hottingen-Zürich: Schweizerische Genossenschaftsdruckerei, 1884; Berlin: Dietz, 1975), 155.

35   Service, 16–17. For Sahlins's description see *Tribesmen*, 82–95, and the chapter "On Sociology of Primitive Exchange" in *Stone Age Economics*, 185–275, with many practical examples relevant for the pirate comparison on pages 263.

36   Anonymous, "Pirate Utopias: Under the Banner of King Death."

37   Ringrose, 500–501.

38   Earle, *The Pirate Wars*, 130.

39   As far as land bandits are concerned, see "Social Bandits" which includes a number of comparisons. For wreckers, see the work of Trevor Bark, for example "Victory of the Wreckers," *Mayday: Magazine for Anarchist/Libertarian Ideas and Action* 1 (2007/2008).

40   Sahlins, *Stone Age Economics*, 41–99.

41   Sahlins, *Tribesmen*, 41.

42   On pirate fashion see "Fashion, Food, Fun, Lingo" in the next chapter.

43   See in particular the account of William Dampier, *Dampier's Voyages*, ed., John Masefield (London: E. Grant Richards, 1906). Original texts published between 1697 and 1729.

44   P.K. Kemp and Christopher Lloyd, *Brethren of the Coast: Buccaneers of the South Seas* (New York: St. Martin's Press, 1961), 5.

45   Cordingly and Falconer, 70.

46   Cordingly, *Life Among the Pirates*, 130.

47   Earle, *Pirate Wars*, 176–77.

48   Konstam, *History of Pirates*, 96.

49   Anne Pérotin-Dumon, "The Pirate and the Emperor: Power and Law on the Seas, 1450–1850," in *Bandits at Sea: A Pirates Reader*, ed. C.R. Pennell (New York: New York University Press, 2001), 40.

50   Khazanov, 122.

51   Snelders, 6.

52   Charles Grey, *Pirates of the Eastern Seas (1618–1723): A Lurid Page of History* (London: Sampson Low, Marston & Co., n.d.), 16.

53   Gosse, *The Pirates' Who's Who*, 10–11.

54   Sahlins, *Tribesmen*, 36.

55   Knight, 101.

56   Eric Hobsbawm, *Bandits* (London: Weidenfeld and Nicholson, 1969), 73–74.

2.5. No State, No Accumulation, No History: Pirates as "Primitives"?

1   Clastres, 200.

2   Ibid., 205.
3   Rediker, *Villains of All Nations*, 176. Compare also the definition of piracy in *The Tryal, Examination and Condemnation, of Captain Green* 1705, already quoted in "Matters of Terminology": "A pirate is in a perpetual war with every individual, and every state, Christian or infidel. Pirates properly have no country, but by the nature of their guilt, separate themselves, and renounce on this matter, the benefit of all lawful societies" (Turley, 44).
4   Sahlins, *Tribesmen*, 6.
5   Service, 5.
6   Ibid., 2.
7   Clastres, 13.
8   Johnson, 36.
9   Clastres, 200.
10   Ibid., 213.
11   Parallels also exist with respect to Southeast Asia's sea nomads, at least if we believe David E. Sopher's claim that "the loose organization of the sea nomads in small groups is characteristic of forest primitives" (266).
12   Sahlins, *Tribesmen*, viii & 21.
13   Ibid., 21.
14   Ibid., 23.

2.6. "Cultural Contact": Pirates and the Non-European People of the Caribbean

1   See "Revolutionary, Radical, and Proletarian Pirates?" in Chapter Four for an extended discussion.
2   Julian Granberry, *The Americas that Might Have Been: Native American Social Systems Through Time* (Tuscaloosa: University of Alabama Press, 2005), 127–28.
3   Irving Rouse, "The West Indies," in *Handbook of South American Indians* vol. 4, ed. Julian H. Steward (Washington: United States Government Printing Office, 1948).
4   See for example David Watts, "The Caribbean Environment and Early Settlement," in *General History of the Caribbean*, ed. P.C. Emmer (London and Basingstoke: UNESCO Publishing, 1999), 2:33–34.
5   Knight, 14.
6   Granberry, 137.
7   Knight, 10.
8   See the description of William Dampier's time spent among the logwood cutters in *Dampier's Voyages*.
9   Snelders, 71.
10   See Jack Weatherford, *Indian Givers: How the Indians of the Americas Transformed the World* (New York: Ballantine Books, 1988).
11   David B. Stout, "The Cuna," in *Handbook of South American Indians*, ed. Julian H. Steward (Washington: United States Government Printing Office, 1948), 4: 261.
12   Clastres, 28.
13   Rouse, "The West Indies," 496.
14   Exquemelin, 104.

15 Irving Rouse, *The Tainos: Rise and Decline of the People Who Greeted Columbus* (New Haven, CT: Yale University Press, 1992), 22.

16 Rouse, "The West Indies," 555.

17 For a short overview of contemporaneous reports on the relations between Mosquito Indians and buccaneers, see Baron Pineda, *Shipwrecked Identities: Navigating Race on Nicaragua's Mosquito Coast* (New Brunswick, NJ: Rutgers University Press, 2006), 35–38.

18 See Paul Kirchhoff, "The Caribbean Lowland Tribes," in *Handbook of South American Indians,* ed. Julian H. Steward (Washington: United States Government Printing Office, 1948) 4: 224–25.

19 See the relevant section in Chapter Four.

3. "SOCIAL ORIGINS," OR THE EUROPEAN LEGACY: GOLDEN AGE PIRACY AND CULTURAL STUDIES

1 Knight, 100.

2 Chris Jenks, *Subculture: The Fragmentation of the Social* (London: Sage, 2005), 129.

3 Ibid.

3.1. Fashion, Food, Fun, Lingo: Circumscribing the Pirate Subculture

1 Cordingly, *Life Among the Pirates,* 56.

2 Rediker, *Villains of All Nations,* 63.

3 Gosse, *The History of Piracy,* 3.

4 Ibid., 194.

5 Cordingly, *Life Among the Pirates,* 26.

6 Margo DeMello, *Bodies of Inscription: A Cultural History of the Modern Tattoo Community* (Durham, NC: Duke University Press, 2000), 44–70.

7 Juliet Fleming, "The Renaissance Tattoo," in *Written on the Body: The Tattoo in European and American History,* ed. Jane Caplan (London: Reaktion, 2000), 61–81.

8 Maarten Hesselt van Dinter, *The World of Tattoos: An Illustrated History* (Amsterdam: KIT, 2005), 215–16.

9 Dampier, 494–503.

10 Ritchie, 114.

11 Snelders, 194–95.

12 Konstam, *History of Pirates,* 184.

13 See Ritchie, 114–15.

14 Angus Konstam, with Roger Michael Kean, *Pirates: Predators of the Seas* (New York: Skyhorse Publishing, 2007), 233.

15 Cordingly, *Life Among the Pirates,* 7.

16 Jan Rogoziński, *Pirates! An A–Z Encyclopedia: Brigands, Buccaneers, and Privateers in Fact, Fiction and Legend* (New York: Da Capo Press, 1996), 302–3.

17 Anton Gill, *The Devil's Mariner: A Life of William Dampier, Pirate and Explorer, 1651–1715* (London: Michael Joseph, 1997), 78. The author's emphasis.

18 Lucie-Smith, 207.

19 Jenifer G. Marx, "The Golden Age of Piracy," in *Pirates: An Illustrated History of Privateers, Buccaneers, and Pirates from the Sixteenth Century to the Present* (London: Salamander, 1996), 109.

20 Cruz Apestegui, *Pirates in the Caribbean: Buccaneers, Privateers, Freebooters and Filibusters 1493–1720* (London: Conway Maritime Press, 2002), 169.

21 Ibid., 169.

22 Marx, "The Golden Age of Piracy," 109.

23 Gosse, *The History of Piracy*, 182.

24 Johnson, 230.

25 Neville Williams, *Captains Outrageous: Seven Centuries of Piracy* (London: Barrie and Rockliff, 1961), 153.

26 Johnson, 259.

27 Ibid.

28 Wilson, *Pirate Utopias*, 49.

29 Gosse, *The History of Piracy*, 201.

30 Sherry, 95–96.

31 *Boston News-Letter,* August 22, 1720, quoted in John Franklin Jameson, ed., *Privateering and Piracy in the Colonial Period: Illustrative Documents* (New York: Macmillan, 1923), 315.

32 Johnson, 492.

3.2. "Villains of All Nations?": Piracy and (Trans)Nationality

1   Snelders, 198.

2   Rediker, *Villains of All Nations*, 53.

3   See Sherry, *Raiders & Rebels*, 85–100.

4   Anonymous, "Pirate Utopias: Under the Banner of King Death."

5   Konstam, *History of Pirates*, 11.

6   Snelders, 94.

7   Masefield, 111.

8   Earle, *Pirate Wars*, 146.

9   A. Hyatt Verrill, back cover of Philip Gosse, *The History of Piracy* and *The Pirates' Who's Who*, Rio Grande Press reprints.

10 Konstam, *Buccaneers,* 17.

11 Rogoziński, *A Brief History of the Caribbean*, 94.

12 Knight, 102.

13 Ibid., 103.

14 Earle, *Pirate Wars*, 137.

15 Galvin, 119.

16 Williams, *Captains Outrageous*, 125–26.

17 Anonymous, "Pirate Utopias: Under the Banner of King Death."

18 Rediker, *Villains of All Nations*, 8.

19 Ibid., 164.

20 David Cordingly, introduction to *The History of Pirates* by Angus Konstam (New York: The Lyons Press, 1999), 9.

21   Marley, *Pirates*, 98.

22   Boston News-Letter, 22nd of August 1720, quoted from Jameson, *Privateering and Piracy in the Colonial Period*, 318.

23   Johnson, 182.

24   Rediker, *Villains of All Nations*, 7.

25   Linebaugh and Rediker, 164.

26   Robert L. Bledsoe and Boleslaw A. Boczek, *The International Law Dictionary* (Santa Barbara, CA: ABC-Clio, 1987), 231.

27   Williams, *Captains Outrageous*, 162.

28   *Mutineer*, 1699, quoted in Linebaugh and Rediker, 165.

3.3. Satanists and Sabbatarians: Piracy and Religion

1   Konstam, *Buccaneers*, 54.

2   Turley, 35.

3   Ibid., 35.

4   Snelders, 11.

5   Howard Pyle, *Howard Pyle's Book of Pirates: Fiction, Fact and Fancy Concerning the Buccaneers and Marooners of the Spanish Main: From the Writing and Pictures of Howard Pyle*, compiled by Merle Johnson (New York and London: Harper & Brothers Publishers, 1921), xvi.

6   AlexanderWinston, *No Purchase, No Pay: Morgan Kidd and Woodes Rogers in the Great Age of Privateers and Pirates 1665–1715* (London: Eyre & Spottiswoode, 1970), 22.

7   See, for example, Snelders, 138, 141; Sherry, 137; and Johnson, 289.

8   Marx, "The Golden Age of Piracy," 103.

9   Turley, 35–36.

10   Gosse, *The Pirates' Who's Who*, 220.

11   See Earle, *Pirate Wars*, 92.

12   See Besson, 190.

13   See Haring, 74–75.

14   Masefield, *On the Spanish Main*, 119.

15   Ringrose, *The Dangerous Voyage and Bold Assaults of Captain Bartholomew Sharp and Others*.

16   Gosse, *The Pirates' Who's Who*, 312.

17   Johnson, 184, 274, 425.

18   Ibid., 184.

19   Gosse, *The Pirates' Who's Who*, 261.

20   Johnson, 199.

21   Ibid., 439.

22   Ibid., 555.

23   Earle, *Pirate Wars*, 115.

24   Gosse, *The Pirates' Who's Who*, 229.

25   Ibid., 149.

26   Cordingly, *Life Among the Pirates*, 272.

27   Ibid., 277.

28 Johnson, 489.
29 Ibid., 324.
30 Rediker, *Villains of All Nations*, 152.
31 Johnson, 57–58.
32 Rediker, *Villains of All Nations*, 152.
33 Ibid., 153.
34 Ibid., 166.
35 Snelders, 175.
36 Rediker, *Villains of All Nations*, 151–52.
37 Johnson, 341.
38 Besson, 12.

3.4. A Colorful Atlantic? Piracy and Race

1   Paul Gilroy, *The Black Atlantic: Modernity and Double Consciousness* (New York: Verso, 1993), 4, 16–17.
2   Linebaugh and Rediker, 144.
3   Ibid., 144–45.
4   See "Pirate Organization" in Chapter four.
5   See for example Exquemelin, 247, and Ringrose, 438–39, 472.
6   Exquemelin, 41.
7   Henry Gilbert, *The Book of Pirates* (London: George G. Harrap & Co., 1916), 225–26.
8   Marley, *Pirates*, 21.
9   Besson, 184.
10 See Johnson, 500, 535, 544, 556.
11 Ibid., 437.
12 Ritchie, 84.
13 Botting, 74. For a detailed description of the relationship between Baldridge and Philipse see Ritchie, 113–16.
14 Johnson, 526.
15 Earle, *Pirate Wars*, 115.
16 See Johnson, 100.
17 Ibid., 196–97.
18 Ibid., 204.
19 Linebaugh and Rediker, 171.
20 Rediker, *Villains of All Nations*, 143.
21 Linebaugh and Rediker, 172.
22 Pérotin-Dumon, "French, English and Dutch in the Lesser Antilles: from privateering to planting, c. 1550–c. 1650," 120.
23 Gosse, *The Pirates' Who's Who*, 50.
24 Ibid., 58.
25 Ibid., 76.
26 See Exquemelin, 249–50.
27 Dampier, 112–14.

28   Manuel Schonhorn, Commentary and Notes to Daniel Defoe, *A General History of the Pyrates*, ed. Manuel Schonhorn (London: J.M. Dent & Sons, 1972), 681.

29   Lionel Wafer, *A New Voyage & Description of the Isthmus of America* (London: James Knapton, 1699; Oxford: The Haklyt Society, 1934).

30   Dampier, 62.

31   Ibid., 156.

32   Exquemelin, 240.

33   Ibid., 113.

34   Ibid., 36.

35   See, for example, the chapter "Military Leadership in the Age of the Buccaneers, 1667–1698" in Ignacio Gallup-Diaz, *The Door of the Seas and Key to the Universe: Indian Politics and Imperial Rivalry in the Darién* (New York: Columbia University Press, 2001).

36   See Ringrose, 277–78.

37   Stout, 4: 263.

38   Kirchhoff, 227.

39   Johnson, 88.

40   Sherry, 335.

41   Exquemelin, 250.

42   Dampier, 39.

43   See Earle, 171, for a summary, and Dampier, 39–42 for more detail.

44   Earle, *Pirate Wars*, 171.

45   Linebaugh and Rediker, 165. See also the illuminative chart listing black pirates in Kenneth Kinkor, "Black Men under the Black Flag," in *Bandits at Sea: A Pirates Reader*, ed. C.R. Pennell (New York: New York University Press, 2001), 201.

46   Johnson, 55.

47   Earle, *Pirate Wars*, 198.

48   Rediker, "Hydrarchy and Libertalia," 34.

49   Kinkor, 200.

50   Cordingly, *Life Among the Pirates*, 27–28.

51   Hugh F. Rankin, *The Golden Age of Piracy* (New York: Holt, Rinehart and Winston, 1969), 82. The author's emphasis.

52   Kinkor, 202.

53   Ibid., 201.

54   Sherry, 212.

55   Ibid., 212.

56   Linebaugh and Rediker, 167.

57   See also the concluding chapter on "The Golden Age Pirates' Political Legacy."

3.5. Anne Bonny, Mary Read, and a Co-opted Myth: Piracy and Gender

1   Fuller and Leslie-Melville, 72.

2   Ibid., 68.

3   Ibid., 72.

4   Klausmann, et al., 170.

5   Johnson, 141.

6   Hobsbawm, *Bandits*, 68. Hobsbawm makes this statement in connection with women who lived disguised as men among the haiduks, a bandit community of the Balkans; see also "Pirates as Social Bandits."

7   Rediker, "Liberty beneath the Jolly Roger: The Lives of Anne Bonny and Mary Read," in *Bandits at Sea: A Pirates Reader,* ed. C.R. Pennell (New York: New York University Press, 2001), 308.

8   Ibid.

9   Ibid., 300.

10   John C. Appleby, "Women and Piracy in Ireland: From Gráinne O'Malley to Anne Bonny," in *Bandits at Sea: A Pirates Reader,* ed. C.R. Pennell (New York: New York University Press, 2001), 294–95.

11   Rediker, *Villains of All Nations,* 118.

12   Appleby, 285.

13   Klausmann, et al.; F.O. Steele, *Women Pirates: A Brief Anthology of Thirteen Notorious Female Pirates* (Lincoln, NE: iUniverse, 2007), and Jane Yolen, *Sea Queens: Women Pirates around the World* (Watertown, MA: Charlesbridge, 2008).

14   Acker, 267.

15   Appleby, 285.

16   Exquemelin, 249.

17   Johnson, 96.

18   Ibid., 255–56.

19   Ibid., 330.

20   Ibid., 504.

21   Cordingly, *Life Among the Pirates,* 113.

22   Klausmann et al., 170.

23   Cordingly, *Life Among the Pirates,* 281–82.

24   Acker, 272.

3.6. On Sodomites and Prostitutes: Piracy and Sexuality

1   Exquemelin, 39–40.

2   Marx, "The Brethren of the Coast," 39.

3   Apestegui, 159.

4   Konstam, *Buccaneers,* 15.

5   B.R. Burg, *Sodomy and the Pirate Tradition: English Sea Rovers in the Seventeenth-Century Caribbean,* 2nd ed. (New York: New York University Press, 1995), xl.

6   Ibid., xxxix.

7   Ibid., 41.

8   Cordingly, *Life Among the Pirates,* 123.

9   Earle, *Pirate Wars,* 5.

10   Ritchie, 270.

11   Turley, 2.

12   Kemp and Lloyd, 3.

13   Charles Leslie, *A New History of Jamaica, from the Earliest Accounts, to the Taking of Porto Bella by Vice-Admiral Vernon* (London: J. Hodges, 1740), 100, quoted in Turley, 29.

14　Apestegui, 153.

15　Johnson, 50.

16　Ibid., 88.

17　Ibid., 514.

18　Ibid., 545.

19　Ritchie, 123.

20　Anonymous, "Pirate Utopias: Under the Banner of King Death."

21　See Ritchie, 124.

22　Ibid.

23　Anonymous, "Pirate Utopias: Under the Banner of King Death."

24　Burg, xlv.

25　Ibid., 173.

26　Michel Foucault, *The Will to Knowledge: The History of Sexuality,* trans. Robert Hurley (London: Penguin Books, 1990), 1:43.

27　Ibid., 1:157.

3.7. Escaping Discipline and "Biopolitics": The Pirate Body

1　Ibid., 1:126.

2　Michel Foucault, *Discipline and Punish: The Birth of the Prison,* trans. Alan Sheridan. (Harmondsworth, Middlesex: Penguin Books, 1979), 143. Foucault describes this process in more detail in Chapter two, "The Great Confinement," of *Madness and Civilization: A History of Insanity in the Age of Reason,* trans. R. Howard (New York: Pantheon Books, 1965), 38–64.

3　Foucault, *History of Sexuality,* 1:139.

4　Ibid.

5　Foucault, *"Society Must Be Defended": Lectures at the College de France, 1975–76,* ed. Mauro Bertani, trans. David Macey (London: Penguin Books, 2004), 242–43.

6　Rediker, *Between the Devil and the Deep Blue Sea,* 206.

7　Ibid. This is also confirmed in Earle's *Sailors.* Earle speaks of an "increase in both strictness and the severity of punishment over time," on both navy and merchant ships, from 1670 to 1740; see "Discipline and Punishment," in *Sailors,* 145–63.

8　Rediker, *Between the Devil and the Deep Blue Sea,* 212.

9　Ibid., 224.

10　Giorgi Agamben, *Homo Sacer: Sovereign Power and Bare Life,* trans. Daniel Heller-Roazen (Stanford, CA: Stanford University Press, 1998), 120.

11　Agamben, 123.

12　Cordingly, *Life Among the Pirates,* 113.

13　Christopher Hill, *Liberty Against the Law: Some Seventeenth-Century Controversies* (London: Penguin Press, 1996), 118.

14　Richard Sennett, *Flesh and Stone: The Body and the City in Western Civilization* (London: Faber and Faber, 1994), 15.

3.8. Eye Patches, Hook Hands, and Wooden Legs: Piracy and Disability

1 This, of course, is only true for certain physical disabilities, most notably amputations. I am not able to explore the extremely complex nature of disability in its different dimensions and discursive significances here but have to employ strategic generalizations. For detailed discussions see volumes like Lennard J. Davis, ed., *The Disability Studies Reader*, 5th ed. (London: Routledge, 2016), or Dianne Pothier, and Richard Devlin, eds., *Critical Disability Theory: Essays in Philosophy, Politics, Policy, and Law* (Vancouver: UBC Press, 2006).

2 Johnson, 92.

3 Trial report of William Phillips and others, quoted in Jameson, 334.

4 Earle, *Pirate Wars*, 200.

5 Ibid., 201.

6 Tew's crew; Johnson, 400.

7 David Gerber, ed., *Disabled Veterans in History* (Ann Arbor: University of Michigan Press, 2000), 3.

8 Ibid., 12.

9 Johnson, 274.

10 Konstam, *History of Pirates,* 187.

11 Rediker, *Villains of All Nations*, 73.

12 Robert McRuer, *Crip Theory: Cultural Signs of Queerness and Disability* (New York & London: New York University Press, 2006), 2.

13 Ibid., xi.

14 Catherine J. Kudlick, "Disability History: Why We Need Another 'Other,'" *American Historical Review* 108, no. 3 (2003): 766.

15 Rosemarie Garland Thomson, *Extraordinary Bodies: Figuring Physical Disability in American Culture and Literature* (New York: Columbia University Press, 1997), 45.

16 Ibid., 44.

17 Ibid., 46.

4. "Ni dieu, ni maître": golden age piracy and politics

4.1. From "Brethren of the Coast" to a "Commonwealth of Outlaws": Pirate Organization

1 Knight, 90.

2 Cordingly, *Life Among the Pirates*, 117.

3 Peter Earle, *The Sack of Panama* (London: Jill Norman & Hobhouse, 1981), 66.

4 Fuller and Leslie-Melville, 73.

5 Williams, *Captains Outrageous*, 150.

6 For example, Larry Law, *A True Historie & Account of the Pyrate Captain Misson, His Crew & Their Colony of Libertatia* [sic] *Founded on Peoples Rights & Liberty on the Island of Madagascar* (London: Spectacular Times, 1980), 5.

7 Marx, "The Brethren of the Coast," 41.

8 Exquemelin, 59–60.

9   Snelders, 83.

10   Ibid., 80.

11   Johnson, 307.

12   Ibid., 182.

13   Ibid., 184.

14   Ibid., 274–75.

15   Ibid., 307–8.

16   Ibid., 182–84.

17   Ritchie, 25–26.

18   Johnson, 400.

19   Quoted in Jameson, 342.

20   Joel Baer, *Pirates* (Gloucestershire: Stroud, 2007), 208.

21   Rediker, *Villains of All Nations*, 69.

22   Ibid., 164–65.

23   Sherry, 94.

24   Snelders, 198.

25   Earle, *Pirate Wars*, 179.

26   Rediker, *Villains of All Nations*, 94.

27   Sherry, 20.

28   Grey, 19.

29   Snelders, 172.

30   See Rediker, *Villains of All Nations*, 29–30. For the estimate on the number of ships see Earle, *Pirate Wars*, 162.

31   Rediker, *Villains of All Nations*, 80.

32   Ibid., 81.

33   Johnson, 409.

34   Sherry, 94–95.

35   Earle, *Pirate Wars*, 178.

36   Johnson, 439.

37   Fuller and Leslie-Melville, 76–77.

38   Exquemelin, 72.

39   Ringrose, 502.

40   Rediker, *Villains of All Nations*, 82.

41   Ibid., 81.

42   Ibid., 155.

43   Rediker, *Between the Devil and the Deep Blue Sea*, 287.

44   Ibid., 243.

45   Ritchie, 124.

46   Rediker, *Between the Devil and the Deep Blue Sea*, 261.

47   Ibid., 248.

48   Peter Lamborn Wilson, preface to Stephen Snelders, *The Devil's Anarchy: The Sea Robberies of the Most Famous Pirate Claes G. Compaen & The Very Remarkable Travels of Jan Erasmus Reyning, Buccaneer* (New York: Autonomedia, 2005), ix.

49   Snelders, 146.

50   Sherry, 297.

51   Land, 180.

52   The strong stratification and hierarchy of these groups constitutes of course a considerable difference to the buccaneer and pirate communities. Many of the problems associated with the value of "brotherhood," though, seem to remain the same.

53   Rediker, *Villains of All Nations*, 84.

54   Cordingly and Falconer, 99.

55   Rediker, "Liberty beneath the Jolly Roger," 306.

56   Ibid., 307.

57   Sherry, 330.

58   Snelders, 109.

59   Rediker, *Villains of All Nations*, 101.

60   Treinen, 33–34.

61   Ibid., 34.

62   Johnson, 544.

63   Anonymous, "Pirate Utopias: Under the Banner of King Death."

4.2. Flying the Black Flag: The Jolly Roger

1   Marley, *Pirates*, 98.

2   Ibid.

3   Konstam, *History of Pirates*, 98.

4   See, for example, Rediker, *Villains of All Nations*, 165–68.

5   A useful overview can be found in Cordingly and Falconer, 78–79.

6   Rediker, *Villains of All Nations*, 165.

7   Cordingly and Falconer, 78–79; Cordingly, *Life Among the Pirates*, 139ff; Rediker, *Villains of All Nations*, 164–69.

8   Rediker, *Villains of All Nations*, 164. Rediker's specification of the pirate outlaws as "proletarian" has been omitted here as I want to save the discussion on piracy and class, including Rediker's partiality towards perceiving the golden age pirates as proletarians, for "Revolutionary, Radical, and Proletarian Pirates?"

9   Rediker, *Villains of All Nations*, 98. See also the previous chapter.

10   Land, 178. This analysis stands in stark contrast to that of Frank Sherry: "If the Jolly Roger was the symbol of a loose pirate confederacy, it was also an indication of the impulse toward unity and authentic statehood among the pirates of Madagascar. Still another indication of this impulse was their propensity to form an attachment for the land itself and to settle there as permanent residents" (98). This is probably the prime example of Sherry overrating the pirate community in Madagascar, misjudging its intentions, and projecting political ambitions into the golden age that were not there.

4.3. Is This Anarchy? Matters of Definition I

1   Snelders, 94.

2   Gill, 87.

3   David Starkey, "Pirates and Markets," in *Bandits at Sea,* ed. C.R. Pennell (New York: New York University Press, 2001), 111.
4   Turley, 39.
5   Botting, 47.
6   Wilson, *Pirate Utopias*, 30.
7   Sherry, 130.
8   Rediker, *Villains of All Nations*, 122.
9   Anonymous, "Pirate Utopias: Under the Banner of King Death."
10 Klausmann et al., *Women Pirates*, 169.
11 Leeson.
12 Land, 180–81.

4.4. The War Machine: Reading Piracy with Deleuze and Guattari

1   Foucault, *"Society Must Be Defended,"* 23.
2   Ibid., 50–51.
3   Ibid., 51.
4   Ibid., 59–60.
5   Linebaugh and Rediker, 173.
6   Preface to Charles Ellms, ed., *The Pirates Own Book, or Authentic Narratives of the Lives, Exploits, and Executions of the Most Celebrated Sea Robbers* (Salem, MA: Marine Research Society, 1924), iii.
7   Gosse, *The History of Piracy*, 139.
8   Johnson, 285.
9   Sherry, 297.
10 Rediker, *Villains of All Nations*, 198.
11 Deleuze and Guattari, *Nomadology*, 67.
12 Ibid., 1.
13 Ibid., 120.
14 Ibid., 113.
15 Ibid.
16 Ibid., 120.
17 Ibid., 60.
18 See "Pirates and Violence" in this chapter.
19 Snelders, 108.
20 Konstam, *History of Pirates*, 117.
21 Rediker, *Villains of All Nations*, 79.
22 Deleuze and Guattari, *Nomadology*, 11.
23 Winston, 231.
24 Thomson, 54.
25 Johnson, 37–38.
26 Earle, *Pirate Wars*, 159; Rediker, *Villains of All Nations*, 19.
27 Gosse, *The History of Piracy*, 177.

4.5. Tactics: Pirates and Guerrilla Warfare

1   Snelders, 167.

2   Mao Tse-tung, "On Guerrilla Warfare," trans. Samuel B. Griffith, in *Guerrilla Warfare*, eds. Mao Tse-tung and Che Guevara (London: Cassell & Company, 1962), 31.

3   Carlos Marighella, "Problems and Principles of Strategy," in *Urban Guerrilla Warfare in Latin America*, trans. and eds. James Kohl and John Litt (Cambridge, MA: MIT Press, 1974), 86.

4   Mao, *On Guerrilla Warfare*, 33.

5   Che Guevara, "What Is a Guerrilla?" in *Guerrilla Warfare & Marxism*, ed. William J. Pomeroy, (New York: International Publishers, 1970), 288–89.

6   Che Guevara, "Guerrilla Warfare," in *Guerrilla Warfare*, eds. Mao Tse-tung and Che Guevara (London: Cassell & Company, 1962), 113.

7   Mao, "On Guerrilla Warfare," 55.

8   Guevara, "Guerrilla Warfare," 131.

9   Marighella, "Minimanual of the Urban Guerrilla," in *Urban Guerrilla Warfare in Latin America*, eds. James Kohl and John Litt (Cambridge, MA: MIT Press, 1974), 101–2.

10 Marighella, "Minimanual," 93–94. The only thing omitted in this list was "training as a frogman," something that was hard to do on 17th-century Hispaniola.

11 Marighella, "Minimanual," 97.

12 Marley, *Pirates*, 62.

13 Snelders, 130.

14 Marighella, "Minimanual," 95.

15 Mao, "On Guerrilla Warfare," 59–60.

16 Snelders, 67.

17 Mao, "On Guerrilla Warfare," 60.

18 Guevara, "Guerrilla Warfare," 115.

19 Kemp and Lloyd, 5.

20 Marighella, "Minimanual," 100.

21 Gosse, *Pirates' Who's Who*, 52.

22 James Connolly, "Street Fighting," in *Guerrilla Warfare & Marxism*, ed. William J. Pomeroy (New York: International Publishers, 1970), 136.

23 Galvin, 164.

24 Régis Debray, "Revolution in the Revolution?" in *Guerrilla Warfare & Marxism*, ed. William J. Pomeroy (New York: International Publishers, 1970), 299.

25 Mao, "On Guerrilla Warfare," 70–71.

26 Cordingly and Falconer, 114.

27 Botting, 55.

28 Marighella, "Minimanual," 102.

29 Mao, "On Guerrilla Warfare," 70.

30 Guevara, "Guerrilla Warfare," 118.

31 Ibid., 114.

32 Konstam, *Buccaneers*, 10.

33 Botting, 55.

34 Cordingly and Falconer, 70.
35 Marighella, "Minimanual," 102.
36 Mao, "On Guerrilla Warfare," 74.
37 Debray, 300.
38 Cordingly, *Life Among the Pirates*, 242.
39 Galvin, 68.
40 Marighella, "Minimanual," 102.
41 Ibid., 103.
42 Guevara, "Guerrilla Warfare," 113.
43 Guevara, "What Is a Guerrilla?" 290.
44 Earle, *Pirate Wars*, 184.
45 Ibid.
46 Marighella, "Problems and Principles of Strategy," 85.
47 Marighella, "Minimanual," 97.
48 Mao, "On Guerrilla Warfare," 39.
49 Guevara, "Guerrilla Warfare," 117.
50 Guevara, "What Is a Guerrilla?" 290.
51 Snelders, 198.
52 Ritchie, 19.
53 Cordingly, *Life Among the Pirates*, 110.
54 Marighella, "Questions of Organization," in *Urban Guerrilla Warfare in Latin America*, trans. and eds. James Kohl and John Litt (Cambridge, MA: MIT Press, 1974), 78.
55 Marighella, "Minimanual," 99.
56 Mao, "On Guerrilla Warfare," 65.
57 Ibid., 66.
58 Ibid., 66.
59 Guevara, "Guerrilla Warfare,"130–31.
60 Cordingly, *Life Among the Pirates*, 117.
61 Rediker, *Villains of All Nations*, 69.
62 Ibid., 81.
63 Sherry, 128.
64 Snelders, 187.
65 Ritchie, 25–26.
66 Marighella, "Questions of Organization," 73.
67 Ibid., 79.
68 Marighella, "Minimanual," 105.
69 Mao, "On Guerrilla Warfare," 70.
70 Ibid., 75.
71 Guevara, "Guerrilla Warfare," 118.
72 Ibid., 129.
73 Ibid., 132.
74 V.I. Lenin, "Guerrilla Warfare," in *Guerrilla Warfare & Marxism*, ed. William J. Pomeroy (New York: International Publishers, 1970), 87.

75   Anonymous, "Pirate Utopias: Under the Banner of King Death."

4.6. Revolutionary, Radical, and Proletarian Pirates? Matters of Definition II

1   Rediker, *Villains of All Nations*, 101.
2   Linebaugh and Rediker, 172–73.
3   Rediker, *Villains of All Nations*, 101.
4   Turley, 30.
5   Jameson, 304.
6   Johnson, 252.
7   Ibid., 435.
8   Ibid., 135–36.
9   See "Pirate Ethics" in this chapter.
10   Boston News-Letter, 22nd of August 1720, quoted from Jameson, Piracy and
      Privateering in the Colonial Period, 315.
11   Hill, "Radical Pirates?" 180.
12   Ibid., 174.
13   Ibid., 173–74.
14   Christopher Hill, *The World Turned Upside Down: Radical Ideas During the English
      Revolution* (New York: The Viking Press, 1973), 339.
15   J.C. Davis, *Fear, Myth and History: The Ranters and the Historians* (Cambridge:
      Cambridge University Press, 1986), 75.
16   Hill, "Radical Pirates?" 178.
17   See, for example, The Online Etymology Dictionary (http://www.etymonline.com).
18   For example, John Pro, in Cordingly, *Life Among the Pirates*, 25–26.
19   Gosse, *The History of Piracy*, 238–43.
20   William C. Braithwaite, *The Beginnings of Quakerism* (London: Macmillan & Co.,
      1912), 402.
21   Johnson, 179–80.
22   Ian Gentles, *The New Model Army in England, Ireland and Scotland 1645–1653*
      (Oxford: Blackwell, 1992), 118.
23   Oliver Cromwell, "Speech at the Opening of Parliament 1656," in *The Black
      Legend: Anti-Spanish Attitudes in the Old World and the New,* ed. Charles Gibson
      (New York: Alfred A. Knopf, 1971), 54–62.
24   See Rogoziński, *A Brief History*, 88.
25   J.S. Bromley's essay "Outlaws at Sea, 1660–1720: Liberty, Equality and Fraternity
      among the Caribbean Freebooters" in *History from Below: Studies in Popular Protest
      and Popular Ideology in Honour of George Rudé,* ed. Frederick Krantz (Montreal:
      Concordia University, 1985) includes arguments similar to Hill's, only with respect to
      the French buccaneers. Bromley argues that the French *engagés*—basically indentured
      laborers—included many deported French radicals. Since a fair number of *engagés*
      ended joining the buccaneers, a corresponding influence would seem likely. As in
      Hill's case, however, empirical evidence is scarce and a lot seems left to speculation.
26   At this point, some troubling implications of Hill's understanding of the pirates'
      freedom ought to not be overlooked either: "Pirate freedom extended to sexual

relations. Women were not unknown on board, and wife-sharing was reported. One crew traded a vessel to a slaver in exchange for sixty African women. The ship was renamed *The Bachelor's Delight*. ... Marlene Brant points out that a favourite metaphor for harlot was ship" (*Liberty Against the Law*, 120). Hill takes a lot of liberty here as far as the origins of *The Bachelor's Delight* are concerned.

27 Hill, *Liberty Against the Law*, 118.
28 Hill, "Radical Pirates?" 174.
29 Ibid., 173.
30 Sherry, 327.
31 Johnson, 591.
32 Gosse, *The Pirates' Who's Who*, 228.
33 Angus Konstam, *Pirates: Predators of the Sea* (New York: Skyhorse Publishing, 2007), 152–53.
34 Marley, *Pirates*, 133.
35 Earle, *Pirate Wars*, 123.
36 Ibid., 170.
37 See also Colin Woodard, *The Republic of Pirates* (Orlando: Harcourt, 2007), 3–4.
38 Rediker, *Villains of All Nations*, 8.
39 Rediker, "Hydrarchy and Libertalia," 29.
40 Rediker, *Villains of All Nations*, 176.
41 Linebaugh and Rediker, 163.
42 Anonymous, "Pirate Utopias: Under the Banner of King Death."
43 Erik Olin Wright, *Classes* (London: Verso, 1985), 6.
44 See also Turley: "The pirates, outside the conventions of English society, do not belong to any class" (85).
45 Thomson, 48.
46 Anonymous, "Pirate Utopias: Under the Banner of King Death."
47 Turley, 172.
48 Clastres, 218.

4.7. Pirates as Social Bandits: Homage to Eric Hobsbawm

1 Wilson, *Pirate Utopias*, 22.
2 Kinkor, 195, 204; Hill, "Radical Pirates?" 179–80; Haude, 595; Wilson, preface to Snelders, *The Devil's Anarchy*, ix; Bromley, 314.
3 Kinkor, 204.
4 Rediker, *Between the Devil and the Deep Blue Sea*, 269.
5 Hobsbawm, *Bandits*, 13.
6 Lucie-Smith, 8.
7 Gosse, *The History of Piracy*, 299.
8 Earle, Pirate Wars, 212.
9 Gosse, *The History of Piracy*, 213.
10 Wilson, preface to Snelders, *The Devil's Anarchy*, ix.
11 Hobsbawm, *Bandits*, 13.
12 Earle, *Pirate Wars*, 185.

13 John Franklin Jameson, *Privateering and Pirating in the Colonial: Illustrative Documents* (New York: Macmillan, 1923), viii.

14 Hobsbawm, *Bandits*, 16.

15 Ibid., 14.

16 Ibid., 17.

17 Ibid., 72.

18 Ibid., 73.

19 Ibid., 68.

20 Ibid.

21 Ibid., 24.

22 Ibid., 71.

23 Ibid., 27.

24 Ibid.

25 Ibid., 28–29. The "peasant" references have been omitted in this quote as they do not seem relevant to the argument. The question of how golden age pirates fit into this analysis despite not being peasants will be discussed below.

26 Hobsbawm, *Bandits*, 45–46.

27 Ibid., 15.

28 Jameson, 304.

29 Rediker, *Villains of All Nations*, 38, 173.

30 Hobsbawm, *Bandits*, 46.

31 Ibid., 35.

32 Lucie-Smith, 9.

33 Hobsbawm, *Bandits*, 94.

34 Ibid., 67.

35 Ibid., 61.

36 Ibid., 67.

37 Ibid., 66.

38 Ibid.

39 Ibid., 62. Again, the peasant attribute has been omitted.

40 Hobsbawm, *Bandits*, 50.

41 Rediker, *Villains of All Nations*, 5–6.

42 Hill, "Radical Pirates?" 165.

43 Hobsbawm, *Bandits*, 56.

44 Ibid., 55.

45 Ibid., 109.

46 Ibid., 15.

47 Ibid.

48 Ibid., 31. Hill has also pointed at the fact that the following analysis of the "criminal underworld" is more applicable to golden age piracy than Hobsbawm's concept of the peasant bandit ("Radical Pirates?" 180).

49 Hobsbawm, *Bandits*, 32.

50 Eric Hobsbawm, *Primitive Rebels: Studies in Archaic Forms of Social Movement in the 19th and 20th Centuries,* 3rd ed. (Manchester: Manchester University Press, 1971), 5.

51　Ibid., 24

52　Hobsbawm, *Bandits*, 62

53　Hobsbawm, *Primitive Rebels*, 13.

54　See Hobsbawm, *Bandits*, 91.

55　Ibid., 48.

56　Ibid., 20.

57　Ibid., 19–20.

58　Ibid., 21.

59　Hobsbawm, *Primitive Rebels*, 24.

60　Ibid., 22–23.

61　Hobsbawm, *Bandits*, 76.

62　Hobsbawm, *Primitive Rebels*, 28.

63　Hobsbawm, *Bandits*, 84.

64　Ibid., 22.

65　Hobsbawm, *Primitive Rebels*, 28.

4.8. Libertalia: Another Reading

1　Manuel Schonhorn's "Commentary and Notes" to his 1972 edition of *A General History of the Pyrates* proved crucial for this debate.

2　Wilson, *Pirate Utopias*, 196–98. Hill writes similarly: "*The History of the Pyrates*, sometimes attributed to Defoe, is not necessarily reliable as evidence of what pirates actually did or said. But it is evidence of what public opinion was prepared to believe" (*Liberty Against the Law*, 115).

3　Land, 183.

4　Turley, 80.

5　Rediker, "Hydrarchy and Libertalia," 31.

6　Land, 183.

7　Rediker, "Hydrarchy and Libertalia," 41–42.

8　Law, 8.

9　Snelders, 102.

10　Johnson, 347.

11　Ibid., 349.

12　Ibid., 350.

13　Ibid., 349.

14　Ibid., 358.

15　Ibid., 348.

16　Ibid., 358–59.

17　Ibid., 350. This did not keep him from accepting special gifts from his crew (ibid.).

18　Ibid., 351.

19　Ibid., 403.

20　Ibid.

21　Ibid., 366.

22　Ibid., 351.

23　Ibid., 409–10.

24 Rediker, "Hydrarchy and Libertalia," 36.
25 Rediker, "Libertalia: The Pirate's Utopia," in *Pirates: An Illustrated History of Privateers, Buccaneers, and Pirates from the Sixteenth Century to the Present,* ed. David Cordingly (London: Salamander, 1996), 125.
26 Johnson, 410.
27 Ibid., 411.
28 Ibid.
29 Ibid., 371.
30 Ibid., 411.
31 Wilson, *Pirate Utopias,* 197.
32 Snelders, 190.
33 Johnson, 411.
34 Ibid., 412.
35 Law, in his radical version of the Libertalia story, does not abruptly end the account in the same manner, but offers a very abbreviated and selective ending.
36 Johnson, 412.
37 Johnson, 413–14.
38 See also Lucie-Smith, 24.

4.9. Safe Havens, Onshore Settlements, Pirate Utopias: Pirates on Land

1   Linebaugh and Rediker, 167–68. For a useful general overview, see also the chapter "Pirate Haunts and Strongholds," in Galvin, *Patterns of Pillage.*
2   Snelders, 151.
3   Ibid., 172.
4   Thomson, 46.
5   Galvin, 109.
6   Cordingly and Falconer, 36.
7   Sherry, 203.
8   Snelders, 69–70.
9   Konstam, *Buccaneers,* 14.
10 Gosse, *The Pirates' Who's Who,* 143.
11 Ibid., 19.
12 Masefield, 117.
13 Fuller and Leslie-Melville, 80.
14 Besson, 177.
15 Konstam, *Buccaneers,* 53.
16 Ibid.
17 Rogoziński, *Brief History,* 94.
18 Lucie-Smith, 158, 160.
19 Cordingly and Falconer, 38.
20 Konstam, *Buccaneers,* 52.
21 Earle, *Pirate Wars,* 91.
22 Burg, 94.
23 Fuller and Leslie-Melville, 84.

24 Ned Ward, author of *The London Spy* (1698), quoted in Fuller and Leslie-Melville, 85.
25 Williams, *Captains Outrageous*, 126.
26 Dampier, 155.
27 Cordingly, *Life Among the Pirates*, 176.
28 Linebaugh and Rediker, 268.
29 O. Nigel Bolland, *The Formation of a Colonial Society: Belize, from Conquest to Crown Colony* (Baltimore and London: Johns Hopkins University Press, 1977), 21.
30 Fuller and Leslie-Melville, 104.
31 Cordingly, *Life Among the Pirates*, 178.
32 Ibid., 239.
33 Sherry, 208.
34 Woodard, 131.
35 Snelders, 172.
36 Williams, *Captains Outrageous*, 150.
37 Marley, *Pirates*, 130.
38 Botting, 128.
39 Marx, "The Golden Age of Piracy," 109.
40 Sherry, 207–8.
41 Lucie-Smith, 214.
42 Marx, "The Golden Age of Piracy," 109.
43 Williams, *Captains Outrageous*, 153.
44 Mitchell, 1976, 84, in Galvin, 108.
45 Galvin, 107.
46 Marley, *Pirates*, 117.
47 Cordingly and Falconer, 80.
48 Earle, *Pirate Wars*, 122.
49 Cordingly and Falconer, 80.
50 1704 Parliamentary Proposal, quoted in Botting, 90.
51 Earle, *Pirate Wars*, 129.
52 Ritchie, 112–13.
53 Sherry, 122.
54 Ibid., 96.
55 Ibid., 94.
56 Johnson, 543.
57 Ibid., 32–34.
58 Ritchie, 116.
59 Earle, *Pirate Wars*, 130.
60 Cordingly and Falconer, 83.
61 Marley, *Pirates*, 140.
62 Rediker, *Villains of All Nations*, 95.
63 Wilson, preface to Snelders, *The Devil's Anarchy*, ix.
64 Treinen, 32.
65 Hill, *Liberty Against the Law*, 120.

4.10. "Piratical Imperialism," Hypocrisy, and the Merchants' Wrath: Piracy and Capitalism

1   Williams, *Captains Outrageous*, x. A very useful general overview of the relations between the state, commerce, and piracy can also be found in Pérotin-Dumon, "The Pirate and the Emperor: Power and the Law on the Seas, 1450–1850."
2   Knight, 104.
3   Earle, *Pirate Wars*, xi.
4   Land, 172.
5   Marx, "The Brethren of the Coast," 37.
6   Knight, 102.
7   Lucie-Smith, 179.
8   Jameson, *Privateering and Piracy in the Colonial Period*, viii.
9   Thomson, 50.
10 Konstam, *History of Pirates*, 138.
11 Earle, *Pirate Wars*, 135.
12 Ibid., 147.
13 Ritchie, 19.
14 Marley, *Pirates*, 148.
15 Knight, 104.
16 Snelders, 155.
17 Land, 186.
18 Hobsbawm, *Bandits*, 82.
19 Galvin, 186.
20 Marley, *Pirates*, 130.
21 Johnson, 1.
22 Botting, 194.
23 Rediker, *Villains of All Nations*, 15.
24 Rediker, *Between the Devil and the Deep Blue Sea*, 254.
25 Marley, *Pirates*, 140.
26 Johnson, 231.
27 Boston News-Letter, 22nd of August 1720, quoted in Jameson, 314.
28 Earle, *Pirate Wars*, 178–79.
29 Hobsbawm, *Bandits*, 56.
30 Linebaugh and Rediker, 172–73.
31 Earle, *Pirate Wars*, 146–47.
32 Anonymous, "Pirate Utopias: Under the Banner of King Death."
33 Deleuze and Guattari, *Nomadology*, 117.
34 Rediker, *Villains of All Nations*, 142.
35 Ibid., 144.
36 Galvin, 66–67.
37 See "A Little History" in Chapter 2.
38 Hill, "Radical Pirates?" 174.
39 Rediker, *Villains of All Nations*, 145.
40 Boston News-Letter Extra, June 30, 1704, quoted in Jameson, 283.

41   Ibid., 284.
42   Marley, *Pirates*, 143.
43   Wilson, preface to Snelders, *The Devil's Anarchy*, xi.
44   Cordingly and Falconer, 96.

4.11. Victims of Circumstance or Bloodthirsty Sadists? Piracy and Violence

1   Friedrich Nietzsche, *Zur Genealogie der Moral*, in *Kritische Gesamtausgabe*, Band 5 (Deutscher Taschenbuch Verlag; Berlin: Walter de Gruyter, 1980), 295.
2   Turley, 13.
3   Cordingly, *Life Among the Pirates*, 54.
4   Johnson, 57.
5   Ibid., 299.
6   Gosse, *The Pirates' Who's Who*, 234.
7   Masefield, 126.
8   Burg, 162.
9   Konstam, *History of Pirates*, 83.
10 Snelders, 80.
11 Cordingly, *Life Among the Pirates*, 153.
12 Botting, 55.
13 Ibid.
14 Rediker, *Villains of All Nations*, 176.
15 Ibid., 89.
16 Snelders, 205.
17 Ibid., 111.
18 Burg, 164.
19 Cordingly and Falconer, 41.
20 Snelders, 110.
21 Robert I. Burns, *Muslims, Christians and Jews in the Crusader Kingdom of Valencia: Societies in Symbiosis* (Cambridge: Cambridge University Press, 1984), quoted in Thomson, *Mercenaries*, 45.
22 Cordingly, *Life Among the Pirates*, 159.
23 Knight, 100.
24 Sherry, 136.
25 Snelders, 205.
26 Rediker, 170.
27 Sherry, 350.
28 Anonymous, "Pirate Utopias: Under the Banner of King Death."
29 Hobsbawm, *Bandits*, 58.
30 Rediker, *Villains of All Nations*, 14.

4.12. Vengeance as Justice: Pirate Ethics

1   Haude, 610.
2   Rediker, *Between the Devil and the Deep Blue Sea*, 287.
3   Sherry, 135.

4   Land, 177.
5   Ritchie, 234.
6   Rediker, *Villains of All Nations*, 90–91.
7   Marley, *Pirates*, 136–37.
8   Johnson, 304. Author's emphasis.
9   Earle, *Pirate Wars*, 176.
10   Ibid., 175.
11   Rediker, *Villains of All Nations*, 88.
12   Ibid.
13   Johnson, 193.
14   Service, 48.
15   Johnson, 252.
16   Snelders, 203.

4.13. Dionysus in the West Indies: A Nietzschean Look at Golden Age Piracy

1   Friedrich Nietzsche, *Die Geburt der Tragödie*, in *Kritische Gesamtausgabe*, Band 1
      (Deutscher Taschenbuch Verlag; Berlin: Walter de Gruyter, 1980), 79.
2   Ibid., 128.
3   Nietzsche, *Zur Genealogie der Moral*, 137.
4   Friedrich Nietzsche, *Jenseits von Gut und Böse*, in *Kritische Gesamtausgabe*, Band 5
      (Deutscher Taschenbuch Verlag; Berlin: Walter de Gruyter, 1980), 238.
5   Nietzsche, *Zur Genealogie der Moral*, 13.
6   Nietzsche, *Jenseits von Gut und Böse*, 122.
7   Nietzsche, *Zur Genealogie der Moral*, 266.
8   Gilles Deleuze, *Nietzsche and Philosophy*, trans. Hugh Tomlinson (London:
      Athlone Press, 1983), 18.
9   Nietzsche, *Die Geburt der Tragödie*, 28.
10   Ibid., 105.
11   Deleuze, 185–86.
12   Ibid., 16.
13   Gosse, *The Pirates' Who's Who*, 169.
14   Earle, *Pirate Wars*, 168–69.
15   Johnson, 563.
16   Snelders, 98.
17   Rediker, *Villains of All Nations*, 59.
18   Friedrich Nietzsche, *Die fröhliche Wissenschaft*, in *Kritische Gesamtausgabe*, Band 3
      (Deutscher Taschenbuch Verlag; Berlin: Walter de Gruyter, 1980), 574.
19   Ibid., 530.
20   Wilson, Preface to Snelders, *The Devil's Anarchy*, ix–x.
21   Snelders, 187.
22   Sherry, 123.
23   Land, 177. It is not surprising that the perspectives of non-radical historians differ.
      David Cordingly writes unceremoniously: "It was the lure of plunder and riches

which was the principal attraction of piracy, just as it has been for every bandit, brigand, and thief throughout history" (*Life Among the Pirates*, 225).

24 Rediker, *Villains of All Nations*, 173.

25 Friedrich Nietzsche, *Morgenröthe*, in *Kritische Gesamtausgabe*, Band 3 (Deutscher Taschenbuch Verlag; Berlin: Walter de Gruyter, 1980), 32.

26 Friedrich Nietzsche, *Der Antichrist*. in *Kritische Gesamtausgabe*, Band 6 (Deutscher Taschenbuch Verlag; Berlin: Walter de Gruyter, 1980).

27 See Nietzsche's 1889 book of the same name.

28 Rediker, *Between the Devil and the Deep Blue Sea*, 286.

29 Rediker, *Villains of All Nations*, 69.

30 Nietzsche, *Jenseits von Gut und Böse*, 47–48.

31 Wilson, *Pirate Utopias*, 52.

32 Rediker, *Between the Devil and the Deep Blue Sea*, 248.

33 Marley, *Pirates*, 139.

34 Rediker, *Villains of All Nations*, 128.

35 Snelders, 48.

36 Ibid., 192.

37 Johnson, 482.

38 Ritchie, 85.

39 Snelders, 155.

40 Besson, 11.

41 See Friedrich Nietzsche, *Also sprach Zarathustra*, in *Kritische Gesamtausgabe*. Band 4 (Deutscher Taschenbuch Verlag; Berlin: Walter de Gruyter, 1980), or *Zur Genealogie der Moral*.

42 Nietzsche, *Die Geburt der Tragödie*, 80.

43 Ibid., 36.

44 Ibid., 128.

45 Deleuze, *Nietzsche and Philosophy*, 176.

46 Snelders, 190.

47 Anonymous, "Pirate Utopias: Under the Banner of King Death."

48 Rediker, *Villains of All Nations*, 72.

49 Ibid., 71.

50 Sherry, 129–30. About music on pirate ships, see also Cordingly, *Life Among the Pirates*, 115–16.

51 Snelders, 180.

52 Nietzsche, *Jenseits von Gut und Böse*, 133.

53 Nietzsche, *Morgenröthe*, 629.

54 See Jean-François Lyotard, *Libidinal Economy*, trans. Iain Hamilton Grant (Bloomington: Indiana University Press, 1993).

55 Snelders, 108.

56 Ibid.

57 Friedrich Nietzsche, *Nachgelassene Fragmente*, in *Kritische Gesamtausgabe*, Band 10 (Deutscher Taschenbuch Verlag; Berlin: Walter de Gruyter, 1980), 568.

58 Besson, 22. The obsession with gambling is also confirmed by other sources: see, for example, Cordingly, *Life Among the Pirates*, 114–15; Besson, 14; Wafer, 127.

59 Botting, 29.

60 Rediker, *Between the Devil and the Deep Blue Sea*, 266.

61 Besson, x.

62 Nietzsche, *Die Geburt der Tragödie*, 99.

63 Nietzsche, *Die fröhliche Wissenschaft*, 519.

64 Deleuze, 16.

65 Nietzsche, *Zur Genealogie der Moral*, 277.

66 Nietzsche, *Also sprach Zarathustra*, 93.

67 Rediker, *Villains of All Nations*, 163.

68 Gosse, *The Pirates' Who's Who*, 157.

69 David Cordingly, introduction to Konstam, *The History of Pirates*, 9.

70 Rediker, *Between the Devil and the Deep Blue Sea*, 230.

71 Rediker, *Villains of All Nations*, 147.

72 Johnson, 212.

73 Konstam, *History of Pirates*, 101.

74 Rediker, *Villains of All Nations*, 169.

75 Johnson, 135f.

76 *Boston News-Letter*, August 22, 1720, quoted from Jameson, 315.

77 Rediker, *Villains of All Nations*, 149.

78 William Snelgrave, *A New Account of Some Parts of Guinea and the Slave Trade* 2nd ed. (London: C. Ward and A. Chandler, 1735; London: Frank Cass, 1970), 167.

79 Johnson, 214.

80 Nietzsche, *Jenseits von Gut und Böse*, 205–6.

81 Deleuze, 174–75.

82 Nietzsche, *Zur Genealogie der Moral*, 311.

83 Nietzsche, *Jenseits von Gut und Böse*, 125.

84 Nietzsche, *Die Geburt der Tragödie*, 26.

85 Snelders, 197.

86 Rediker, *Villains of All Nations*, 71.

87 Sherry, 132.

88 Exquemelin, 40.

89 Johnson, 192–93.

90 Ibid., 542.

91 Nietzsche, *Morgenröthe*, 54–55.

92 Nietzsche, *Die Geburt der Tragödie*, 24. Of course the drinking of the pirates must not be romanticized. Marx notes that "alcoholism was an occupational hazard and led to many untimely deaths" ("The Golden Age of Piracy," 109), which is confirmed by Konstam who writes that "many [pirates] died from alcohol abuse" (*History of Pirates*, 184). Johnson's *General History* includes at least one episode in which two pirates who have been sentenced to death blame their pirating ways on their drinking (315–16). For a summary of pirate crews' problems with alcohol see also Burg, 155–56. In this light it also seems not random that the most successful

of the golden age pirate captains, Bartholomew Roberts, has been described as a teetotaler. Every reputedly did not drink either (Sherry, 69), and the famous, yet most probably fictional, pirate captain Misson explicitly speaks out against alcohol (Johnson, 359–60).

93 Nietzsche, *Zur Genealogie der Moral*, 117.

5. CONCLUSION: THE GOLDEN AGE PIRATES' POLITICAL LEGACY

1   Anonymous, "Pirate Utopias: Under the Banner of King Death."
2   See Ramor Ryan, *Clandestines: The Pirate Journals of an Irish Exile* (Oakland: AK Press, 2006).
3   See http://www.crimethinc.com.
4   See Capt'n Mayhem, *Long Live Mutiny! A Pirate Handbook* (Baltimore: Firestarter Press, n.d.)
5   A simple Google Image search will bring up relevant results.
6   See http://www.piratesforpeace.com.
7   See http://www.constituentimagination.net.
8   Introduction to *No Quarter: An Anarchist Zine about Pirates* (n.p., n.d.), 2.
9   Williams, *Captains Outrageous*, 153.
10 Land, 190.
11 Kinkor, 204–5.
12 Rediker, *Between the Devil and the Deep Blue Sea*, 285.
13 Guevara, "What is a Guerrilla?" 288–89.
14 Mao, *On Guerrilla Warfare*, 77. The specification of "peasant" revolt has been omitted as the argument seems to extend systematically to the situation of the golden age pirates.
15 Lucie-Smith, 210–11.
16 Johnson, 535.
17 Ibid., 514.
18 Rediker, "Liberty beneath the Jolly Roger: The Lives of Anne Bonny and Mary Read," 316.
19 Hobsbawm, *Bandits*, 67.
20 Land, 190.
21 Ibid.
22 Hobsbawm, *Bandits*, 93.
23 Rediker, *Villains of All Nations*, 175.
24 Sherry, 365.
25 Gill, 42.
26 Hobsbawm, *Bandits*, 21.
27 Ibid.
28 Ibid., 22.
29 Snelders, 204–5.
30 Hobsbawm, *Bandits*, 76.
31 Snelders, 80.

32   Linebaugh and Rediker, 162.

33 Hobsbawm, *Bandits*, 77.

34 Thomson, 46.

35   Rediker, *Villains of All Nations*, 176.

36   Snelders, 3.

37   Land, 171.

38   Ibid.

39   Linebaugh and Rediker, 173.

40   Land, 190.

41   Hakim Bey, *T.A.Z.: The Temporary Autonomous Zone, Ontological Anarchy, Poetic Terrorism* (New York: Autonomedia, 1991).

42   Rediker, *Villains of All Nations*, 175.

43   Ibid.

44   Land, 188.

45   Gosse, *The Pirates' Who's Who*, 19.

46   Land, 185.

47   See http://www.piratbyran.org and http://www.thepiratebay.org.

48   See http://www.freegan.info.

49   See http://www.crimethinc.com.

50   Ron Sakolsky, "Rhizomatic Radio and the Great Stampede," in *Seizing the Airwaves: A Free Radio Handbook,* eds. Stephen Dunifer and Ron Sakolsky (Edinburgh: AK Press, 1998), 9.

51   Land, 190.

52   Linebaugh and Rediker, 173.

6. NOTES ON PIRATE LITERATURE

1   Burg, 196–97.

BIBLIOGRAPHY

Acker, Kathy. *Pussy, King of the Pirates.* New York: Grove Press, 1996.

Agamben, Giorgi. *Homo Sacer: Sovereign Power and Bare Life.* Translated by Daniel Heller-Roazen. Stanford, CA: Stanford University Press, 1998. Originally published as *Homo sacer: Il potere sovrado e la nuda vita.* Torino: Einaudi, 1995.

Ali, Tariq. *Pirates of the Caribbean.* London: Verso, 2006.

Anderson, John L. "Piracy and World History: An Economic Perspective on Maritime Predation." In *Bandits at Sea,* edited by C.R. Pennell, 82–106. New York: New York University Press, 2001.

Anonymous. *Evasion.* Atlanta: CrimethInc., 2001.

Anonymous. "Pirate Utopias: Under the Banner of King Death," *Do or Die,* no. 8, 1999. Quoted from www.eco-action.org/dod/no8/pirate.html.

Apestegui, Cruz. *Pirates in the Caribbean: Buccaneers, Privateers, Freebooters and Filibusters 1493–1720.* Translated by Richard Lewis Rees. London: Conway Maritime Press, 2002. Originally published as *Piratas en el Caribe: Corsarios, filibusteros y bucaneros, 1493–1700.* Barcelona: Lunwerg, 2000.

Appleby, John C. "Women and Piracy in Ireland: From Gráinne O'Malley to Anne Bonny." In *Bandits at Sea,* edited by C.R. Pennell, 283–98. New York: New York University Press, 2001.

Baer, Joel. *Pirates.* Stroud: Gloucestershire 2007.

Bark, Trevor. "Victory of the Wreckers." *Mayday: Magazine for Anarchist/Libertarian Ideas and Action* no. 1 (Winter 2007–2008): 16–18.

Barnes, Colin, Geof Mercer, and Tom Shakespeare. *Exploring Disability: A Sociological Introduction,* second edition. Cambridge, UK: Polity Press, 2002.

Basso, Ellen B. "The Status of Carib Ethnology." In *Carib-Speaking Indians: Culture, Society and Language. Anthropological Papers of the University of Arizona* no. 28, edited by Ellen B. Basso, 9–22. Tucson: University of Arizona Press, 1977.

Besson, Maurice, ed. *The Scourge of the Indies: Buccaneers, Corsairs and Filibusters.* Translated by Everard Thornton from original texts and contemporary engravings. London: George Routledge & Sons, 1929.

Bey, Hakim, *T.A.Z.: The Temporary Autonomous Zone, Ontological Anarchy, Poetic Terrorism.* New York: Autonomedia, 1991.

Bledsoe, Robert L., and Boleslaw A. Boczek. *The International Law Dictionary.* Santa Barbara, CA: ABC-Clio, 1987.

Bolland, O. Nigel. *The Formation of a Colonial Society: Belize, from Conquest to Crown Colony.* Baltimore: Johns Hopkins University Press, 1977.

Botting, Douglas. *The Pirates.* Amsterdam: Time-Life Books, 1979.

Braithwaite, William C. *The Beginnings of Quakerism.* London: Macmillan & Co.,1912.

Bridenbaugh, Carl and Roberta Bridenbaugh. *No Peace Beyond the Line: The English in the Caribbean 1624–1690.* New York: Oxford University Press, 1972.

Bromley, J.S. "Outlaws at Sea, 1660–1720: Liberty, Equality and Fraternity among the Caribbean Freebooters." In *History from Below: Studies in Popular Protest and Popular Ideology in Honour of George Rudé,* edited by Frederick Krantz, 301–20. Montréal: Concordia University,1985.

Burg, B.R. *Sodomy and the Pirate Tradition: English Sea Rovers in the Seventeenth-Century Caribbean.* 2nd ed. with a new introduction by the author. New York: New York University Press, 1983 & 1995.

Burroughs, William S. *Ghost of Chance.* New York: Serpent's Tail, 1995.

Capt'n Mayhem. *Long Live Mutiny! A Pirate Handbook.* Baltimore: Firestarter Press, n.d.

Chomsky, Noam. *Pirates and Emperors, Old and New: International Terrorism in the Real World.* London: Pluto Press, 2002.

Clastres, Pierre. *Society Against the State.* Translated by Robert Hurley in collaboration with Abe Stein. New York: Zone Books, 1987. Originally published as *La société contre l'état.* Paris: Minuit, 1974.

Connolly, James. "Street Fighting." In *Guerrilla Warfare & Marxism,* 2nd ed., edited by William J. Pomeroy, 136–39. New York: International Publishers, 1970. Article first published in 1915.

Cordingly, David. Introduction to *The History of Pirates,* by Angus Konstam, 7–9. New York: The Lyons Press, 1999.

———. Introduction to *Pirates: An Illustrated History of Privateers, Buccaneers, and Pirates from the Sixteenth Century to the Present,* edited by David Cordingly, 6–15. London: Salamander 1996.

———. *Life Among the Pirates: The Romance and the Reality.* London: Little, Brown and Company, 1995.

Cordingly, David, ed. *Pirates: An Illustrated History of Privateers, Buccaneers, and Pirates from the Sixteenth Century to the Present.* London: Salamander, 1996.

Cordingly, David and John Falconer. *Pirates: Fact & Fiction*. London: Collins & Brown, 1992.

Cromwell, Oliver. "Speech at the Opening of Parliament 1656." In *The Black Legend: Anti-Spanish Attitudes in the Old World and the New*, edited by Charles Gibson, 54–62. New York: Alfred A. Knopf, 1971.

Dampier, William. *Dampier's Voyages. Vol. I & II*. Edited by John Masefield. London: E. Grant Richards, 1906. Original texts published between 1697 and 1729.

Davis, J.C. *Fear, Myth and History: The Ranters and the Historians*. Cambridge et al: Cambridge University Press, 1986.

Davis, Lennard J., ed. *The Disabilities Studies Reader*. London: Routledge, 2006.

Debray, Régis. "Revolution in the Revolution?" In *Guerrilla Warfare & Marxism*, edited by William J. Pomeroy, 298–304. New York: International Publishers, 1970. Article first published in 1967.

de Lussan, Ravenau. *Memoirs: His Journey to the Southern Sea with the Filibusters of America: 1685 to 1686*. In *The Scourge of the Indies: Buccaneers, Corsairs and Filibusters*, edited by Maurice Besson. London: George Routledge & Sons, 1929.

Deleuze, Gilles. *Nietzsche and Philosophy*. Translated by Hugh Tomlinson. London: The Athlone Press 1983. Originally published as *Nietzsche et la philosophie*. Paris: Presses universitaires de France, 1962.

Deleuze, Gilles and Félix Guattari. *A Thousand Plateaus*. Translated by Brian Massumi. London: Continuum, 2004. Originally published as *Mille Plateaux: Capitalisme et schizophrénie 2*. Paris: Minuit, 1980.

———. *Nomadology: The War Machine*. Translated by Brian Massumi. New York: Semiotext(e), 1986. Originally published as Chapter Twelve of *Mille Plateaux: Capitalisme et schizophrénie 2*. Paris: Minuit, 1980.

DeMello, Margo. *Bodies of Inscription: A Cultural History of the Modern Tattoo Community*. Durham, NC: Duke University Press, 2000.

Earle, Peter. *Sailors: English Merchant Seamen 1650–1775*. London: Methuen, 1998.

———. *The Pirate Wars*. London: Methuen, 2003.

———. *The Sack of Panama*. London: Jill Norman & Hobhouse, 1981.

Ellms, Charles, ed. *The Pirates Own Book, or Authentic Narratives of the Lives, Exploits, and Executions of the Most Celebrated Sea Robbers*. Boston: Samuel N. Dickinson, 1837. Reprinted Salem, MA: Marine Research Society, 1924. All references to the 1924 edition.

Emmer, P.C., ed. *General History of the Caribbean*. Vol. 2, *New Societies: The Caribbean in the Long Sixteenth Century*. London and Basingstoke: UNESCO Publishing, 1999.

Engels, Friedrich. *Der Ursprung der Familie, des Privateigentums und des Staats*. In *Werke*, Band 21, by Karl Marx and Friedrich Engels, 5th ed.

Hottingen-Zürich: Schweizerische Genossenschaftsdruckerei, 1884; Berlin: Dietz, 1975.

Exquemelin [Esquemeling], John. *The Buccaneers of America*. London: Swan Sonnenschein & Co. / New York: Charles Scribner's Sons, 1893. Originally published as *De Americaensche Zee-Roovers*. Amsterdam: Jan ten Hoorn, 1678.

Fleming, Juliet. "The Renaissance Tattoo." In *Written on the Body: The Tattoo in European and American History*, edited by Jane Caplan, 61–82. London: Reaktion, 2000.

Foucault, Michel. *Discipline and Punish: The Birth of the Prison*. Translated by Alan Sheridan. Harmondsworth, Middlesex: Penguin Books, 1979. Originally published as *Surveiller et punir: Naissance de la prison*. Paris: Gallimard, 1975.

———. *Madness and Civilization: A History of Insanity in the Age of Reason*. Translated by R. Howard. New York: Pantheon Books, 1965. Originally published as *Histoire de la folie à l'âge classique*, Paris: UGE, 1964.

———. "Nietzsche, Genealogy, History." In *Language, Counter-Memory, Practice: Selected Essays and Interviews*, Michel Foucault, edited by Donald F. Bouchard, translated Donald F. Bouchaurd and Sherry Simon. Ithaca: Cornell University Press, 1977. Article originally published in 1971.

———. *"Society Must Be Defended": Lectures at the Collège de France, 1975–76*. Edited by Mauro Bertani, translated by David Macey. London: Penguin Books, 2004.

———. *The Will to Knowledge: The History of Sexuality*. Vol. 1. Translated by Robert Hurley. London et al.: Penguin Books, 1990. Originally published as *La volonté de savoir Histoire de la sexualité*, Paris: Gallimard, 1976.

Fuller, Basil and Ronald Leslie-Melville. *Pirate Harbours and Their Secrets*. London: Stanley Paul & Co., 1935.

Furbank, P.N. and W.R. Owens. *The Canonisation of Daniel Defoe*. New Haven, CT: Yale University Press, 1988.

Gallup-Diaz, Ignacio. *The Door of the Seas and Key to the Universe: Indian Politics and Imperial Rivalry in the Darién*. New York: Columbia University Press, 2001.

Galvin, Peter R. *Patterns of Pillage: A Geography of Caribbean-based Piracy in Spanish America, 1536–1718*. New York: Peter Lang, 1999.

Gellner, Ernest. Introduction to *Nomads and The Outside World*, by A.M. Khazanov, ix–xxv. Cambridge et al.: Cambridge University Press, 1984.

Gentles, Ian. *The New Model Army in England, Ireland and Scotland, 1645–1653*. Oxford: Blackwell,1992.

Gerber, David A., ed. *Disabled Veterans in History*. Ann Arbor: University of Michigan Press, 2000.

Gibson, Charles, ed. *The Black Legend: Anti-Spanish Attitudes in the Old World and the New.* New York: Alfred A. Knopf, 1971.

Gilbert, Henry. *The Book of the Pirates.* London: George G. Harrap & Co., 1916.

Gill, Anton. *The Devil's Mariner: A Life of William Dampier, Pirate and Explorer, 1651–1715.* London: Michael Joseph, 1997.

Gilroy, Paul. *The Black Atlantic: Modernity and Double Consciousness.* London: Verso, 1993.

Gosse, Philip. *The History of Piracy.* New York: Tudor Publishing Company, 1932. Reprinted Glorieta, NM: The Rio Grande Press, 1990. All references to the 1990 edition.

———. *The Pirates' Who's Who: Giving Particulars of the Lives & Deaths of the Pirates & Buccaneers.* London: Dulau and Company, 1924. Reprinted Glorieta, NM: The Rio Grande Press, n.d. All references to the n.d. edition.

Graeber, David, *Fragments of an Anarchist Anthropology.* Chicago: Prickly Paradigm Press, 2004.

Granberry, Julian. *The Americas That Might Have Been: Native American Social Systems through Time.* Tuscaloosa, AL: The University of Alabama Press, 2005.

Grey, Charles. *Pirates of the Eastern Seas (1618–1723): A Lurid Page of History.* London: Sampson Low, Marston & Co., 1933.

Guevara, Che. "Guerrilla Warfare." In *Guerrilla Warfare,* by Mao Tse-tung and Che Guevara, 111–56, London: Cassell 1962. Originally published as *La guerra de guerrillas.* Havana: MINFAR, 1960.

———. "What Is a Guerrilla?" In *Guerrilla Warfare & Marxism,* edited by William J. Pomeroy, 288–90. New York: International Publishers, 1970. Article first published in 1967.

Haring, C.H. *The Buccaneers in the West Indies in the XVII Century.* London: Methuen & Co., 1910.

Haude, Rüdiger: "Frei-Beuter: Charakter und Herkunft piratischer Demokratie im frühen 18. Jahrhundert." *Zeitschrift für Geschichtswissenschaft* no. 7/8 (2008), 593–616.

Hill, Christopher. *Liberty Against the Law: Some Seventeenth-Century Controversies.* London: Allen Lane, 1996.

———. "Radical Pirates?" In *Collected Essays.* Vol. 3, *People and Ideas in 17th Century England.* Brighton: The Harvester Press 1986, 161–87.

———. *The World Turned Upside Down: Radical Ideas During the English Revolution.* New York: The Viking Press, 1973.

Hobsbawm, Eric. *Bandits.* London: Weidenfeld and Nicolson, 1969.

———. *Primitive Rebels: Studies in Archaic Forms of Social Movement in the 19th and 20th Centuries.* 3rd ed. with a new preface and minor amendments. Manchester: Manchester University Press, 1959 & 1971.

Jameson, John Franklin. *Privateering and Piracy in the Colonial Period: Illustrative Documents*. New York: Macmillan, 1923.

Jenks, Chris. *Subculture: The Fragmentation of the Social*. London: Sage, 2005.

Johnson, Charles. *A General History of the Robberies and Murders of the Most Notorious Pirates*. Edited by Arthur L. Hayward. George Routledge & Sons, 1926. Based on the fourth and complete edition, London: T. Woodward, 1726.

Kemp, P.K. and Christopher Lloyd. *Brethren of the Coast: Buccaneers of the South Seas*. New York: St. Martin's Press, 1961.

Khazanov, A.M. *Nomads and the Outside World*. Translated by Julia Crookenden. Cambridge et al.: Cambridge University Press, 1984. Originally published in Russian in 1983.

Kinkor, Kenneth J. "Black Men under the Black Flag." In *Bandits at Sea*, edited by C.R. Pennell, 195–210. New York: New York University Press, 2001.

Kirchhoff, Paul. "The Caribbean Lowland Tribes: The Mosquito, Sumo, Paya, and Jicaque." In *Handbook of South American Indians*. Vol. 4: *The Circum-Caribbean Tribes*, edited by Julian H. Steward, 219–29. Washington: United States Government Printing Office, 1948.

Klausmann, Ulrike, Marion Meinzerin and Gabriel Kuhn, *Women Pirates and the Politics of the Jolly Roger*. Translated by Nicholas Levis. Montreal: Black Rose, 1997.

Knight, Franklin W. *The Caribbean: The Genesis of a Fragmented Nationalism*. 2nd ed. New York: Oxford University Press, 1978 & 1990.

Kohl, James and John Litt, eds. *Urban Guerrilla Warfare in Latin America*. Cambridge, MA: MIT Press, 1974.

Konstam, Angus. *Buccaneers*. Oxford: Osprey, 2000.

———. *Pirates: Predators of the Seas*. With Roger Michael Kean. New York: Skyhorse Publishing, 2007.

———. *Scourge of the Seas: Buccaneers, Pirates and Privateers*. Oxford: Osprey, 2007.

———. *The History of Pirates*. New York: The Lyons Press, 1999.

Kudlick, Catherine J. "Disability History: Why We Need Another 'Other.'" *American Historical Review*, vol. 108, no. 3 (June 2003): 763–93.

Labat, Jean-Baptiste. *The Memoirs of Père Labat 1693–1705*. Translated by John Eaden. London: Frank Cass, 1970.

Land, Chris. "Flying the Black Flag: Revolt, Revolution and the Social Organization of Piracy in the 'Golden Age.'" *Management & Organizational History* 2, no. 2 (2007): 169–92.

Law, Larry. *A True Historie & Account of the Pyrate Captain Misson, His Crew & Their Colony of Libertatia* [sic] *Founded on Peoples Rights & Liberty on the Island of Madagascar*. London: Spectacular Times, 1980.

Leeson, Peter T. "An-*arrgh*-chy: The Law and Economics of Pirate Organization."
    Journal of Political Economy 115, no. 6 (2007): 1049–94.

Lenin, V.I. "Guerrilla Warfare." In *Guerrilla Warfare & Marxism*, edited by William
    J. Pomeroy, 84–94, New York: International Publishers 1970. Article first
    published in 1906.

Linebaugh, Peter and Marcus Rediker. *The Many-Headed Hydra: Sailors, Slaves,
    Commoners, and the Hidden History of the Revolutionary Atlantic*. Boston:
    Beacon Press, 2000.

López Nadal, Gonçal. "Corsairing as a Commercial System: The Edges of
    Legitimate Trade." In *Bandits at Sea*, edited by C.R. Pennell, 125–38. New
    York: New York University Press, 2001.

Lothrop, Samuel K. "The Archeology of Panamá." In *Handbook of South American
    Indians*. Vol. 4: *The Circum-Caribbean Tribes*, edited by Julian H. Steward,
    143–67. Washington: United States Government Printing Office, 1948.

Lucie-Smith, Edward. *Outcasts of the Sea: Pirates and Piracy*. New York: Paddington
    Press, 1978.

Lunsford, Virginia W. *Piracy and Privateering in the Golden Age Netherlands*. New
    York & Basingstoke: Palgrave Macmillan, 2005.

Lyotard, Jean-François. *Libidinal Economy*. Translated by Iain Hamilton Grant.
    Bloomington: Indiana University Press, 1993. Originally published as
    Economie Libidinale. Paris: Minuit, 1974.

MacPhee, Josh, ed. *Stencil Pirates*, New York: Soft Skull Press, 2004.

Mao Tse-tung, *On Guerrilla Warfare*. Translated by Samuel B. Griffith. In *Guerrilla
    Warfare*, by Mao Tse-tung and Che Guevara, 31–81, London: Cassell, 1962.
    Originally published in Chinese in 1937.

Marighella, Carlos. *Minimanual of the Urban Guerrilla*. In *Urban Guerrilla Warfare
    in Latin America*, edited by James Kohl and John Litt, 87–135. Cambridge,
    MA: MIT Press, 1974. Originally self-published as *Mini-Manual do
    guerrilheiro urbano*, 1969.

———. "Problems and Principles of Strategy." Translated by James Kohl and
    John Litt. In Kohl and Litt, *Urban Guerrilla Warfare in Latin America*, 81–86.
    Article originally published in 1971.

———. "Questions of Organization." Translated by James Kohl and John Litt.
    In Kohl and Litt, *Urban Guerrilla Warfare in Latin America*, 73–80. Article
    originally published in 1971.

Marley, David F. *Pirates: Adventurers of the High Seas*. London: Arms and Armour
    Press, 1997.

———. "The Lure of Spanish Gold." In *Pirates: An Illustrated History of Privateers,
    Buccaneers, and Pirates from the Sixteenth Century to the Present*, edited by
    David Cordingly, 16–35. London: Salamander, 1996.

Martin-Fragachan, Gustavo. "Intellectual, artistic and ideological aspects of cultures in the New World." In *General History of the Caribbean*. Vol. 2, *New Societies: The Caribbean in the Long Sixteenth Century*, edited by P.C. Emmer, 247–307. London and Basingstoke: UNESCO Publishing, 1999.

Marx, Jenifer G. "The Brethren of the Coast." In *Pirates: An Illustrated History of Privateers, Buccaneers, and Pirates from the Sixteenth Century to the Present*, edited by David Cordingly, 36–57. London: Salamander, 1996.

———. "The Golden Age of Piracy." In *Pirates: An Illustrated History of Privateers, Buccaneers, and Pirates from the Sixteenth Century to the Present*, edited by David Cordingly, 100–123. London: Salamander, 1996.

———. "The Pirate Round." In *Pirates: An Illustrated History of Privateers, Buccaneers, and Pirates from the Sixteenth Century to the Present*, edited by David Cordingly, 140–63. London: Salamander, 1996.

Masefield, John. *On the Spanish Main*. London: Methuen & Co., 1906.

McRuer, Robert. *Crip Theory: Cultural Signs of Queerness and Disability*. New York: New York University Press, 2006.

Moore, John Robert. *Defoe in the Pillory and Other Studies*. Bloomington: Indiana University, 1939.

Nietzsche, Friedrich. *Also sprach Zarathustra*. In *Kritische Gesamtausgabe*, Band 4. Deutscher Taschenbuch Verlag; Berlin: Walter de Gruyter, 1980.

———. *Der Antichrist*, in *Kritische Gesamtausgabe*, Band 6. Deutscher Taschenbuch Verlag; Berlin: Walter de Gruyter, 1980.

———. *Die fröhliche Wissenschaft*. In *Kritische Gesamtausgabe*, Band 3. Deutscher Taschenbuch Verlag; Berlin: Walter de Gruyter, 1980.

———. *Die Geburt der Tragödie*. In *Kritische Gesamtausgabe*, Band 1. Deutscher Taschenbuch Verlag; Berlin: Walter de Gruyter, 1980.

———. *Jenseits von Gut und Böse*. In *Kritische Gesamtausgabe*, Band 5. Deutscher Taschenbuch Verlag; Berlin: Walter de Gruyter, 1980.

———. *Menschliches, Allzumenschliches. Ein Buch für freie Geister*, in *Kritische Gesamtausgabe*, Band 2. Deutscher Taschenbuch Verlag; Berlin: Walter de Gruyter, 1980.

———. *Morgenröthe*, in *Kritische Gesamtausgabe*, Band 3. Deutscher Taschenbuch Verlag; Berlin: Walter de Gruyter, 1980.

———. *Nachgelassene Fragmente*. In *Kritische Gesamtausgabe*, Band 10. Deutscher Taschenbuch Verlag; Berlin: Walter de Gruyter, 1980.

———. *Zur Genealogie der Moral*. In *Kritische Gesamtausgabe*, Band 5. Deutscher Taschenbuch Verlag; Berlin: Walter de Gruyter, 1980.

No Quarter: An Anarchist Zine about Pirates. n.p. n.d. [c. 2006]

Parry, J.H. and P.M. Sherlock. *A Short History of the West Indies*. London: Macmillan; New York: St. Martin's Press, 1957.

Pennell, C.R. ed., *Bandits at Sea: A Pirates Reader.* New York: New York University Press, 2001.

Pérotin-Dumon, Anne. "French, English and Dutch in the Lesser Antilles: From Privateering to Planting, c. 1550–c. 1650." In *General History of the Caribbean.* Vol. 2, *New Societies: The Caribbean in the Long Sixteenth Century,* edited by P.C. Emmer, 114–58. London and Basingstoke: UNESCO Publishing, 1999.

———. "The Pirate and the Emperor: Power and the Law on the Seas, 1450–1850." In *Bandits at Sea,* edited by C.R. Pennell, 25–54. New York: New York University Press, 2001.

Pineda, Baron L., *Shipwrecked Identities: Navigating Race on Nicaragua's Mosquito Coast.* New Brunswick, NJ: Rutgers University Press, 2006.

Pomeroy, William J., ed., *Guerrilla Warfare & Marxism.* 2nd ed. New York: International Publishers, 1968 & 1970.

Pothier, Dianne and Richard Devlin, eds., *Critical Disability Theory: Essays in Philosophy, Politics, Policy, and Law.* Vancouver: UBC Press, 2006.

Profane Existence Collective. "Anarchy, Punk, Utopia." In: Profane Existence Catalog #12, 1995, 28–29.

Pyle, Howard, *Howard Pyle's Book of Pirates: Fiction, Fact and Fancy Concerning the Buccaneers and Marooners of the Spanish Main: From the Writing and Pictures of Howard Pyle.* Compiled by Merle Johnson. New York and London: Harper & Brothers Publishers, 1921.

Rankin, Hugh F. *The Golden Age of Piracy.* New York: Holt, Rinehart and Winston, 1969.

Rediker, Marcus. *Between the Devil and the Deep Blue Sea: Merchant Seamen, Pirates, and the Anglo-American Maritime World, 1700–1750.* Cambridge: Cambridge University Press, 1987.

———. "Hydrarchy and Libertalia: The Utopian Dimensions of Atlantic Piracy in the Early Eighteenth Century." In *Pirates and Privateers: New Perspectives on the War on Trade in the Eighteenth and Nineteenth Centuries,* edited by David J. Starkey, E.S. van Eyck van Heslinga, and J.A. de Moor. Exeter: University of Exeter Press, 1997.

———. "Libertalia: The Pirate's Utopia." In *Pirates: An Illustrated History of Privateers, Buccaneers, and Pirates from the Sixteenth Century to the Present,* edited by David Cordingly, 124–39. London: Salamander, 1996.

———. "Liberty Beneath the Jolly Roger: The Lives of Anne Bonny and Mary Read." In *Bandits at Sea,* edited by C.R. Pennell, 299–320. New York: New York University Press, 2001.

———. *Villains of All Nations: Atlantic Pirates in the Golden Age.* New York: Verso, 2004.

Ringrose, Basil. "The Dangerous Voyage and Bold Assaults of Captain Bartholomew Sharp and Others, Performed in the South Sea, for the Space of Two Years, etc." In *The Buccaneers of America*, by John Exquemelin, London: Swan Sonnenschein & Co.; New York: Charles Scribner's Sons 1893. Originally published in *The Buccaneers of America*, by John Exquemelin, London: W. Crooke, 1685.

Ritchie, Robert C. *Captain Kidd and the War against the Pirates*. Cambridge, MA: Harvard University Press, 1986.

Rogoziński, Jan. *A Brief History of the Caribbean: From the Arawak and Carib to the Present*, revised edition. New York: Facts on File, 1999.

———. *Pirates! An A–Z Encyclopedia: Brigands, Buccaneers, and Privateers in Fact, Fiction, and Legend*. New York: Da Capo Press, 1996.

Rouse, Irving. "The West Indies." In *Handbook of South American Indians*. Vol. 4, *The Circum-Caribbean Tribes*, by Julian H. Steward, 495–565. Washington: United States Government Printing Office, 1948.

———. *The Tainos: Rise and Decline of the People Who Greeted Columbus*. New Haven, CT: Yale University Press, 1992.

Ryan, Ramor. *Clandestines: The Pirate Journals of an Irish Exile*. Oakland: AK Press, 2006.

Sahlins, Marshall. *Stone Age Economics*. London: Tavistock Publications, 1974.

———. *Tribesmen*. Englewood Cliffs, NJ: Prentice-Hall, 1968.

Sakolsky, Ron. "Introduction: Rhizomatic Radio and the Great Stampede." In *Seizing the Airwaves: A Free Radio Handbook*, edited by Ron Sakolsky and Stephen Dunifer, 7–14. Edinburgh & San Francisco: AK Press, 1998.

Schonhorn, Manuel. Commentary and Notes in *A General History of the Pyrates*, by Daniel Defoe, edited by Manuel Schonhorn, 663–96. London: J.M. Dent & Sons, 1972.

Sennett, Richard. *Flesh and Stone: The Body and the City in Western Civilization*. London/Boston: Faber and Faber, 1994.

Service, Elman R. *The Hunters*. 2nd ed. Englewood Cliffs, NJ: Prentice-Hall, Inc., 1966 & 1979.

Shelvocke, George. *A Voyage Round the World (by the Way of the Great South Sea)*. London: J. Senex et al., 1736.

Sherry, Frank. *Raiders & Rebels: The Golden Age of Piracy*. New York: Quill, 1986.

Snelders, Stephen. *The Devil's Anarchy: The Sea Robberies of the Most Famous Pirate Claes G. Compaen & The Very Remarkable Travels of Jan Erasmus Reyning, Buccaneer*. New York: Autonomedia, 2005.

Snelgrave, William. *A New Account of Some Parts of Guinea and the Slave Trade*. London: C. Ward and A. Chandler, 1735. Reprinted London: Frank Cass, 1970. All references to the 1970 edition.

Sopher, David E. *The Sea Nomads: A Study Based on the Literature of the Maritime Boat People of Southeast Asia*. Memoirs of the National Museum no. 5. Singapore, 1965.

Starkey, David J. "Pirates and Markets." In *Bandits at Sea*, edited by C.R. Pennell, 107–24. New York: New York University Press, 2001.

———. "The Origins and Regulation of Eighteenth-Century British Privateering." In Pennell, *Bandits at Sea*, 69–81.

Steele, F.O. *Women Pirates: A Brief Anthology of Thirteen Notorious Female Pirates*. Lincoln, NE: iUniverse, 2007.

Steward, Julian H., ed. *Handbook of South American Indians*. Vol. 4, *The Circum-Caribbean Tribes*. Washington: United States Government Printing Office, 1948.

Stout, David B. "The Chocó." In *Handbook of South American Indians*. Vol. 4, *The Circum-Caribbean Tribes*, edited by Julian H. Steward, 269–76. Washington: United States Government Printing Office, 1948.

———. "The Cuna." In *Handbook of South American Indians*. Vol. 4, *The Circum-Caribbean Tribes*, edited by Julian H. Steward, 257–68. Washington: United States Government Printing Office, 1948.

Thomson, Janice E. *Mercenaries, Pirates and Sovereigns: State-Building and Extraterritorial Violence in Early Modern Europe*. Princeton, NJ: Princeton University Press, 1994.

Thomson, Rosemarie Garland. *Extraordinary Bodies: Figuring Physical Disability in American Culture and Literature*. New York: Columbia University Press, 1997.

Treinen, Heiner. "Parasitäre Anarchie: Die karibische Piraterie im 17. Jahrhundert." *Unter dem Pflaster liegt der Strand* no. 9 (1981): 7–35.

Turley, Hans. *Rum, Sodomy and the Lash: Piracy, Sexuality & Masculine Identity*. New York: New York University Press, 1999.

van Dinter, Maarten Hesselt, *The World of Tattoos: An Illustrated History*. Amsterdam: KIT, 2005.

Wafer, Lionel. *A New Voyage & Description of the Isthmus of America*. London: James Knapton, 1699. Reprinted Oxford: The Hakluyt Society, 1934. All references to the 1934 edition.

Watts, David. "The Caribbean Environment and Early Settlement." In *General History of the Caribbean*. Vol. 2, *New societies: The Caribbean in the long sixteenth century*, edited by P.C. Emmer, 29–42. London and Basingstoke: UNESCO Publishing, 1999.

Weatherford, Jack. *Indian Givers: How the Indians of the Americas Transformed the World*. New York: Ballantine Books, 1988.

Williams, Neville. *Captains Outrageous: Seven Centuries of Piracy*. London: Barrie and Rockliff, 1961.

———. *The Sea Dogs: Privateers, Plunder & Piracy in the Elizabethan Age.* London: Weidenfeld and Nicolson, 1975.

Wilson, Peter Lamborn. *Pirate Utopias: Moorish Corsairs & European Renegadoes.* 2nd rev. ed. New York: Autonomedia, 1995 & 2003.

———. Preface to *The Devil's Anarchy: The Sea Robberies of the Most Famous Pirate Claes G. Compaen & The Very Remarkable Travels of Jan Erasmus Reyning, Buccaneer,* by Stephen Snelders. New York: Autonomedia, 2005.

Wilson, Samuel M. *Hispaniola: Caribbean Chiefdoms in the Age of Columbus.* Tuscaloosa and London: University of Alabama Press, 1990.

Winston, Alexander. *No Purchase, No Pay: Morgan, Kidd and Woodes Rogers in the Great Age of Privateers and Pirates 1665–1715.* London: Eyre & Spottiswoode, 1970.

Wood, Peter. *The Spanish Main.* Amsterdam: Time-Life Books, 1980.

Woodard, Colin. *The Republic of Pirates.* Orlando: Harcourt, 2007.

Wright, Erik Olin. *Classes.* London: Verso, 1985.

Yolen, Jane. *Sea Queens: Women Pirates around the World.* Watertown, MA: Charlesbridge, 2008.

INDEX

꽃 Gabriel Kuhn is an Austrian-born writer and translator living in Sweden. He received a PhD from the University of Innsbruck, Austria, in 1996. Among his book publications with PM Press are *Sober Living for the Revolution: Hardcore Punk, Straight Edge, and Radical Politics* (2010); *Turning Money into Rebellion: The Unlikely Story of Denmark's Revolutionary Bank Robbers* (2014); *Antifascism, Sports, Sobriety: Forging a Militant Working-Class Culture* (2017); *Soccer vs. the State: Tackling Football and Radical Politics* (2019, 2nd ed.); *X: Straight Edge and Radical Sobriety* (2019); and *Liberating Sápmi: Indigenous Resistance in Europe's Far North* (2020).

283

PM Press was founded at the end of 2007 by a small collection of folks with decades of publishing, media, and organizing experience. PM Press co-conspirators have published and distributed hundreds of books, pamphlets, CDs, and DVDs. Members of PM have founded enduring book fairs, spearheaded victorious tenant organizing campaigns, and worked closely with bookstores, academic conferences, and even rock bands to deliver political and challenging ideas to all walks of life. We're old enough to know what we're doing and young enough to know what's at stake.

We seek to create radical and stimulating fiction and non-fiction books, pamphlets, T-shirts, visual and audio materials to entertain, educate, and inspire you. We aim to distribute these through every available channel with every available technology— whether that means you are seeing anarchist classics at our bookfair stalls; reading our latest vegan cookbook at the café; downloading geeky fiction e-books; or digging new music and timely videos from our website.

PM Press is always on the lookout for talented and skilled volunteers, artists, activists, and writers to work with. If you have a great idea for a project or can contribute in some way, please get in touch.

PM Press
PO Box 23912
Oakland CA 94623
510-658-3906
www.pmpress.org

PM Press in Europe
europe@pmpress.org
www.pmpress.org.uk

FRIENDS OF PM

These are indisputably momentous times—the financial system is melting down globally and the Empire is stumbling. Now more than ever there is a vital need for radical ideas.

In the many years since its founding—and on a mere shoestring—PM Press has risen to the formidable challenge of publishing and distributing knowledge and entertainment for the struggles ahead. With hundreds of releases to date, we have published an impressive and stimulating array of literature, art, music, politics, and culture. Using every available medium, we've succeeded in connecting those hungry for ideas and information to those putting them into practice.

Friends of PM allows you to directly help impact, amplify, and revitalize the discourse and actions of radical writers, filmmakers, and artists. It provides us with a stable foundation from which we can build upon our early successes and provides a much-needed subsidy for the materials that can't necessarily pay their own way. You can help make that happen—and receive every new title automatically delivered to your door once a month—by joining as a Friend of PM Press. And, we'll throw in a free T-shirt when you sign up.

Here are your options:

- $30 a month: Get all books and pamphlets plus 50% discount on all webstore purchases
- $40 a month: Get all PM Press releases (including CDs and DVDs) plus 50% discount on all webstore purchases
- $100 a month: Superstar—Everything plus PM merchandise, free downloads, and 50% discount on all webstore purchases

For those who can't afford $30 or more a month, we have Sustainer Rates at $15, $10, and $5. Sustainers get a free PM Press T-shirt and a 50% discount on all purchases from our website.

Your Visa or Mastercard will be billed once a month, until you tell us to stop. Or until our efforts succeed in bringing the revolution around. Or the financial meltdown of Capital makes plastic redundant. Whichever comes first.

The Incomplete, True, Authentic, and Wonderful History of May Day

Peter Linebaugh

$15.95

ISBN: 978-1-62963-1-073

5 x 8 • 200 pages

"May Day is about affirmation, the love of life, and the start of spring, so it has to be about the beginning of the end of the capitalist system of exploitation, oppression, war, and overall misery, toil, and moil." So writes celebrated historian Peter Linebaugh in an essential compendium of reflections on the reviled, glorious, and voltaic occasion of May 1st.

It is a day that has made the rich and powerful cower in fear and caused Parliament to ban the Maypole—a magnificent and riotous day of rebirth, renewal, and refusal. These reflections on the Red and the Green—out of which arguably the only hope for the future lies—are populated by the likes of Native American anarcho-communist Lucy Parsons, the Dodge Revolutionary Union Movement, Karl Marx, José Martí, W.E.B. Du Bois, Rosa Luxemburg, SNCC, and countless others, both sentient and verdant. The book is a forceful reminder of the potentialities of the future, for the coming of a time when the powerful will fall, the commons restored, and a better world born anew.

"There is not a more important historian living today. Period."
—Robin D.G. Kelley, author of *Freedom Dreams: The Black Radical Imagination*

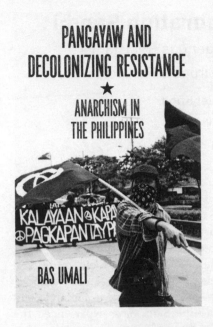

PANGAYAW AND
DECOLONIZING RESISTANCE
★
ANARCHISM IN
THE PHILIPPINES

BAS UMALI

Pangayaw and Decolonizing Resistance

Anarchism in the Philippines

Bas Umali

Edited by Gabriel Kuhn

$15.00

ISBN: 978-1-62963-7-945

5 x 8 • 128 pages

The legacy of anarchist ideas in the Philippines was first brought to the attention of a global audience by Benedict Anderson's book *Under Three Flags: Anarchism and the Anti-Colonial Imagination.* Activist-author Bas Umali proves with stunning evidence that these ideas are still alive in a country that he would like to see replaced by an "archepelagic confederation."

Pangayaw and Decolonizing Resistance: Anarchism in the Philippines is the first-ever book specifically about anarchism in the Phillipines. Pangayaw refers to indigenous ways of maritime warfare. Bas Umali expertly ties traditional forms of communal life in the archipelago that makes up the Philippine state together with modern-day expressions of antiauthoritarian politics. Umali's essays are deliciously provocative, not just for apologists of the current system, but also for radicals in the Global North who often forget that their political models do not necessarily fit the realities of postcolonial countries.

In weaving together independent research and experiences from grassroots organizing, Umali sketches a way for resistance in the Global South that does not rely on Marxist determinism and Maoist people's armies but the self-empowerment of the masses. His book addresses the crucial questions of liberation: who are the agents and what are the means?

More than a sterile case study, *Pangayaw and Decolonizing Resistance* is the start of a new paradigm and a must-read for those interested in decolonization, anarchism, and social movements of the global south.

Liberating Sápmi

Indigenous Resistance
in Europe's Far North

Gabriel Kuhn

$17.00

ISBN: 978-1-62963-7-129

5.5 x 8.5 • 220 pages

The Sámi, who have inhabited Europe's far north for thousands of years, are often referred to as the continent's "forgotten people." With Sápmi, their traditional homeland, divided between four nation-states—Norway, Sweden, Finland, and Russia—the Sámi have experienced the profound oppression and discrimination that characterize the fate of indigenous people worldwide: their lands have been confiscated, their beliefs and values attacked, their communities and families torn apart. Yet the Sámi have shown incredible resilience, defending their identity and their territories and retaining an important social and ecological voice—even if many, progressives and leftists included, refuse to listen.

Liberating Sápmi is a stunning journey through Sápmi and includes in-depth interviews with Sámi artists, activists, and scholars boldly standing up for the rights of their people. In this beautifully illustrated work, Gabriel Kuhn, author of over a dozen books and our most fascinating interpreter of global social justice movements, aims to raise awareness of the ongoing fight of the Sámi for justice and self-determination. The first accessible English-language introduction to the history of the Sámi people and the first account that focuses on their political resistance, this provocative work gives irrefutable evidence of the important role the Sámi play in the resistance of indigenous people against an economic and political system whose power to destroy all life on earth has reached a scale unprecedented in the history of humanity.

The book contains interviews with Mari Boine, Harald Gaski, Ann-Kristin Håkansson, Aslak Holmberg, Maxida Märak, Stefan Mikaelsson, May-Britt Öhman, Synnøve Persen, Øyvind Ravna, Niillas Somby, Anders Sunna, and Suvi West.